Possessors and Possessed

The publisher gratefully acknowledges the generous contribution to
this book provided by the Art Endowment Fund of the University of
California Press Associates, which is supported by a major gift from
the Ahmanson Foundation.

Possessors and Possessed

Museums, Archaeology, and the Visualization of History in the Late Ottoman Empire

WENDY M. K. SHAW

University of California Press

BERKELEY   LOS ANGELES   LONDON

University of California Press
Berkeley and Los Angeles, California

University of California Press, Ltd.
London, England

Library of Congress Cataloging-in-Publication Data

Shaw, Wendy M. K.
 Possessors and possessed : museums, archaeology, and the
visualization of history in the late Ottoman Empire /
Wendy M. K. Shaw.
  p. cm.
 Includes bibliographical references and index.
 ISBN 0-520-23335-2
 1. Museums—Turkey—History. 2. Museums—Collection
management—Turkey—History. I. Title.
AM79.T8S53 2003
069'.09561—dc21   2002013901

Manufactured in the United States of America

12   11   10   09   08   07   06   05   04   03

10 9 8 7 6 5 4 3 2 1

The paper used in this publication meets the minimum requirements of
ANSI/NISO Z39.48-1992 (R 1997) (*Permanence of Paper*). ♾

Contents

9340

Illustrations

Acknowledgments

Within a text, there is always a hidden text, from which the author arrived and toward which she is trying to go. This is the text that must be questioned as underlying the perseverance that finishing a project such as this requires. In the case of this book, one sentiment underlies my academic journey: my personal quest for discovering how to place an identity in-between.

Friends and colleagues at times have suggested that my interest in Ottoman history stems from a desire to follow in my family's footsteps. It does not. Rather, not only did a historical mode of thought pervade my education despite my every effort to avoid studying history, the political history of my early life made it imperative for me, as for many academics of mixed heritage, to discover how to exist in the world as a social being denied any single society. For to be mixed means to be always told that you really belong over there. In the academic sphere, such dual positioning becomes as tricky as it is useful. With two native languages, one always runs the risk of attempting to speak as an informed "native" and of nonetheless speaking as an outsider; or conversely, of trying to speak from outside and still holding the protective bias—or militant self-critique—of the "native." The danger here is to lose the ability to speak out of fear of simultaneous privilege and blindness.

Thus the postcolonial displacement of national experience becomes all the more personal for those caught, through migration and immigration, leaving home and returning home and never being sure which side is home. Whereas a nation, unlike an individual, does not move, the alliances that identify it do, and the ways in which it imagines its heritages produce a social sphere of nations in which it tries to become at home. And eventually that strange and unique mix becomes home, for the nation as for the person. This book is about the history of trying to create a home, and in that sense it is very personal.

More than anyone, I thank my parents, Professors Stanford Jay and Ezel Kural Shaw, for enabling me to discover my voice: through their own cultural mix, which they have never perceived as including difference; through their courageous perseverance, commitment to intellectual diversity, and devotion to freedom of expression despite the obstacles and dangers that have faced each and both of them in their careers; and through their endless excitement about discovery and thought. This book began as a dissertation in the Department of Art History at the University of California, Los Angeles (UCLA), which I appreciate immensely for its cultural and intellectual diversity. In particular, I thank my dissertation adviser, Professor Irene Bierman, for always encouraging me to ask questions, to make wild connections, and to articulate my thoughts assertively. I also thank Professor James Gelvin for his attentive reading of the early versions of this text. To the friends on whom I have relied to keep me sane as I wrote and rewrote this—Savas Arslan, Neha Choksi, Chitoh Emetarom, Ana-Mari Hamada, Mark Andreas Kayser, and Nancy Um—thanks for your affection and for figuring out our cultural salads together.

This book would not have been possible without the aid of many people in Turkey, including Dr. Alpay Pasinli, Dr. Halil Özek, and Havva Koç of the İstanbul Archaeology Museum; Prof. Dr. Nurhan Atasoy of İstanbul University; Prof. Dr. Ekmeleddin İhsanoğlu of the Research Center for Islamic History, Art, and Culture (IRCICA); and Colonel Sadık Tekeli of the İstanbul Military Museum.

I would also like to thank the Fulbright-Hayes Foundation, the American Research Institute in Turkey, the UCLA Department of Art History Dickson Fellowship, and the UCLA Dissertation Year Fellowship for providing financial support for my research and writing.

Note on Orthography

Modern Turkish is written with a modified Latin script, most letters of which are read as in English. Where appropriate, I have used Modern Standard Turkish spellings for words in Turkish and Modern Standard Turkish transliterations for words in Ottoman Turkish. The letters pronounced differently from or not part of the English alphabet are as follows:

a   a short *a*, as in *lark*

c   *j*, as in *jam*

ç   *ch*, as in *child*

e   as in the first vowel of *ever*

g   as in *get*

ğ   silent *g*, similar to an elision of vowels around the ğ

i   *ee*, as in *keep*

ı   *i* as in *girl*

j   *g*, as in French *gillette*

o   short *o*, as in *open*

ö   as in the French *oeu* of *oeuvre*

ş   *sh*, as in *show*

u   *u*, similar to the short *oo* in *foot*

ü   as in the German *über*

Introduction

Imagine a museum. A staid building, which one enters conscientiously, paying a fee at the entrance or perhaps, if it is a museum with a sizable endowment, a subtly suggested donation. A building, that is, that requires a rite of passage for entrance into an arena promising—what? Education? Culture? To transcend the boundaries of the here-and-now outside the museum doors? To enter—what? The beautiful? The valuable? The fascinating? The educational? To enter a museum is to trust that some group of institutionally invisible people—artists, artisans, historians, museum owners, purchasers, curators—will have condensed the world into an edifying format that they will be able to communicate through a primary vehicle of objects coupled with a secondary vehicle of text. A trust not far flung from the trust invested in schools or in churches. And, not surprisingly, often directly controlled or indirectly financed by the same institutional bodies—governments—entrusted to legislate and regulate other institutions of education.

Imagine a dandelion seed. When it falls far from its parent plant, is the flower that develops on new soil necessarily the same? While numerous authors have of late considered the development and functioning of the museum in the Euro-American sphere, relatively few have expanded their investigations to ask in depth how these institutions emerged in the rest of the world. Using the case of the Ottoman Empire, one of the few regions heavily influenced but never directly politically colonized by Europe, this work considers how the idea of the museum metamorphosed when it was forced to contend with different sets of political and cultural imperatives that informed the choices of possession and the rigors of display. I write with two sets of readers in mind: those familiar with Ottoman history and those familiar with museum studies. For each group, this introduction provides a brief contextual summary in which to situate this study, both as a discussion of late Ottoman history and as a discussion of the ideological implications of the museum.

A BRIEF NARRATION OF TURKISH HISTORY

In the silences between documents, not to mention the unspoken experience and identifications of the people who precede us, determining historical reality is a tricky business—trickier still in a short summary such as the one I attempt here. Through this summary, I try to clarify, for those unfamiliar with Turkish history, the multiplicities of pasts from which the Ottoman museum, as a sign of the then nascent Turkish national project, made choices in coding a historical record for visual display. In his discussion of nationalism, Anthony Smith argues that "the 'core' of ethnicity . . . resides in this quartet of 'myths, memories, values, and symbols.' " He emphasizes "the '*myth-symbol*' complex, and particularly the '*mythomoteur*' or constitutive myth of the ethnic polity [that plays a vital role in] embodying the corpus of beliefs and sentiments which the guardians of ethnicity preserve, diffuse and transmit to future generations."[1] It is the production of these myths—not in the sense of legends but in the sense of constructed narratives—within the museum during the decades of transition from Ottoman to Turkish state identity that this text addresses. Rather than conceive of a grassroots nationalism, this study examines the museum as an expression of the models of national mythmaking produced by Ottoman elites interested in constructing themselves as the guardians of ethnicity and in thereby fashioning a national identity. When the Turkish Republic was founded in 1923, these Ottoman elites were instrumental in codifying a national identity that recycled earlier models of communal identity into the constitutive historical myths of the Turkish nation (see map 1).

In 1932, nearly a decade after the foundation of the Republic of Turkey, the First Congress of Turkish History (Birinci Türk Tarih Kongresi) announced the historical threads developed by early republican historians that, when taught in schools throughout the country, would weave a communal past for the new collectivity of the Turkish nation. These threads of historical identity—the autochthonous prehistory of Thracian and Anatolian ancestors; the romantic legends of Turkic nomads riding across the central Asian plains; the glorious memories of two Turco-Islamic empires, the Seljuk and the Ottoman, that rose in the heart of Anatolia and eventu-

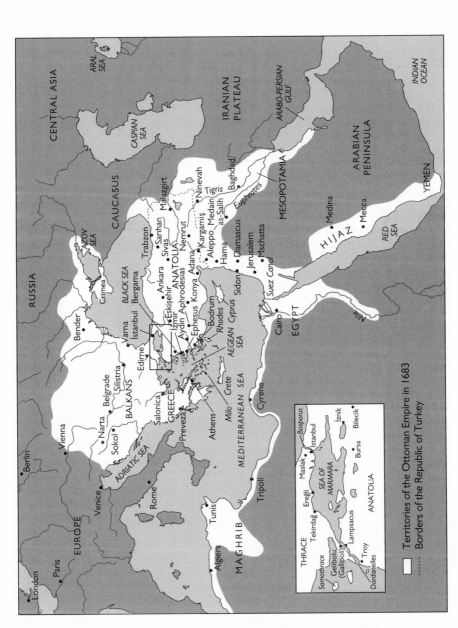

Map 1. Ancient and modern sites in and around the Ottoman Empire and the Republic of Turkey

ally subsumed the Byzantine Empire and then spread across eastern Europe and the Middle East—have become the clichés not only of Turkey's history textbooks but also of its museum collections and its political identities. These narratives, chosen to construct a national history, served to strangle the murmurs of the curtailed Ottoman quest for a different, recently elided nation that might have constituted the same communities and grown on the same territory had history taken a slightly different turn in the years preceding 1923.

The Turkish Historical Society used three primary cornerstones in constructing its narrative of Turkish history. No doubt, the same information could be recast within alternate national narratives or could include the experience of local peoples rather than focus on a history of the state. It tends instead to construct a linear narrative of territorial expansion and dynastic growth.

Above all, Turkish national identity has had to contend with a highly heterogeneous ethnic base and a history of cultural absorption, both of which are antithetical to nineteenth-century discourse on the nature of national unity. To reconcile this predilection of nationalist discourse to link each people in a binary relationship with a single territory, early Turkish historians came to assume the inheritance of all people who had ever lived in the territories of the Republic of Turkey, especially Anatolia. According to this narrative, Turkish citizens are the descendants of Hittites, Sumerians, Urartans, Phoenicians, ancient Greeks, and Romans. During the first two decades of the republic, there were popular, if by modern standards dubious, linguistic theories that linked the Sumerians with the Turks, making the Hittites and the Sumerians in particular proto-Turks and making the eventual existence of the Turkish Republic in Anatolia teleologically inevitable.[2]

The second strand of the Turkish historical narrative relies on the idea that Turks were nomadic peoples who once lived on the plains of central Asia but situates their migration in the historic rather than the prehistoric era. The earliest Turks recorded in history were the Huns (of Attila fame), whose Göktürk Empire lasted from about the sixth through the eighth century. Several other states, led by the Nine Oghuz dynasty and the Uygur dynasty, also lived in central Asia before the tenth century. This era of early Turkish history became particularly important to republican historiography in constructing a Turkish identity independent of the cosmopolitan Ottoman identity of the cities. Nationalists believed that these traditions lived not in any Ottoman tradition but in a supposedly pure heritage hidden in Turkish villages and the nomadic tribes that still populated Anatolia.[3]

In the tenth century these and other nomadic tribes, often collectively referred to as Turkomans, migrated out of central Asia and into Iran. Turkish tribes initially served as mercenary soldiers for local rulers but soon set up their own kingdoms in Iran, some of which grew into empires—most notably the Great Seljuk Empire. In the meantime, many Turkic rulers and tribespeople eventually converted to Islam. From the eighth through the twelfth century, Turkish soldiers fought under the banner of Islam during the Abbasid Caliphate, based in Baghdad. (Traditionally held by descendants of the Prophet, the caliphate was recognized until the twentieth century as holding the spiritual and often political leadership of the Islamic world.) Thus Turks, although not Arab, became intimately connected with Islamic history, in turn carefully incorporated into the Ottoman and later Turkish historiographic traditions.

Iran was bounded on the west by the Byzantine Empire. Established in A.D. 310 with the reappellation of the city of Byzantium as Constantinople by the Roman emperor Constantine, the city was designated the capital of the newly defined Eastern Roman Empire. The empire continued the Roman legacy long after the fall of the Western Roman Empire in A.D. 410. Its people continued to identify it as the Roman Empire until its fifteenth-century demise, regardless of the later European designation "Byzantine," adopted by the nineteenth century in the Ottoman Empire as well.

By the eleventh century the Seljuk Empire, located on the Iranian plateau, had become the primary defender of the Abbasid Caliphate in Baghdad and was expanding. Because of weakened eastern defenses of the Byzantine Empire, Turkoman soldiers frequently invaded and raided its Anatolian provinces. In 1071 the Seljuk sultan Alparslan set off with his soldiers planning to conquer Fatimid Egypt. On the way, he heard that the Byzantine emperor Romanus IV Diogenes (r. 1067–71) was leading his troops eastward to attack the Seljuk Empire. He turned north and met them in Malazgırt, today in eastern Turkey. When the mercenary soldiers of the nomadic Pecheneg tribe, hired in Thrace by the Byzantine emperor, discovered that they were fighting against a people who spoke the same language as they did, they deserted the emperor, leading to his capture. After agreeing to a peace treaty, Romanus was released and allowed to return home. By the time he got back, he found his wife remarried to the new emperor, Michael VII Ducas (r. 1071–78). Romanus was forced to retire to a monastery (or lose his head), so Alparslan considered the treaty null and void, and Turkoman penetration into Anatolia, or the land of Rum ("Rome," the common designation for Anatolia), continued.

Meanwhile, the Schism of 1054 that divided Christendom into Orthodox and Catholic camps had already taken place, but the possibility of a reconciliation was very much alive when the Byzantine emperor Alexius I Comnenus (r. 1081–1118) approached Pope Urban II for military help against further Seljuk expansion into his territories. The crusading movement, which was to last until the middle of the fifteenth century, was at first successful in creating a string of Crusader states along the shores of the eastern Mediterranean but of no lasting value for its original purpose of saving the shrinking Byzantine Empire.

Turkomans continued to populate Anatolia alongside the Christian communities that already lived there, creating what has been described as a symbiotic economic relationship with the settled peoples of the area. The Seljuk sultan who resided in the central Anatolian city of Konya soon lost his vassal status to the Great Seljuk Empire. This new sultanate—that of the Seljuks of Rum—reached its apogee in the early thirteenth century. Turkoman tribal leaders, called Beys, competed with this central power for local control and maintained capital cities throughout Anatolia. Nominally, all of Anatolia was part of the Byzantine Empire for some time, but the Seljuks effectively had no control over the territory.

The Seljuks of Rum ruled effectively from their capital city of Konya only for about one hundred years, but while they were there, they set up many Islamic traditions of rule that would continue throughout the Ottoman period. Religious teachers—well-known *sufi* leaders such as Mevlana Celaleddin Rumi and Hacı Bektaş—migrated from Iran to Anatolia, where their vision of Islam as unitary, eclectic, and mystical attracted many locals to the religion and aided the process of conversion. As a Muslim state, Seljuk rulers took on the construction of building complexes, called foundations or *vakıfs*, to serve the people under their rule. Such a complex would form the core of a town plan. The primary center would be a mosque. One or more schools would often be associated with the mosque, and often there would also be a large tomb of the founder of the complex located on site as well. In addition to these, a bath, a hospital, and inns would also be established as part of the complex. Making use of the roads built across Anatolia by the Romans, the Seljuks and the Beys in Anatolia also built many caravansaries for travelers, primarily merchants, to take shelter while crossing Anatolia. The foundations were funded through profit-making endowments, including the rent gathered from stores and the profits from villages and mills endowed to the *vakıf* in perpetuity.

Culturally, the empire remained very mixed, both ethnically and linguistically. The conquered peoples in Anatolia continued to speak their own languages and follow their own religious traditions. Religious activities associated with the Islamic state were conducted in Arabic, the language of the Qur'an. The elite spoke and administered their country in Persian, the language of poetry, which they had begun to use while ruling Iran. Local Anatolians continued to speak Greek, Armenian, Syriac, Kurdish, Laz, and Georgean in various regions. Among those who had migrated recently, the common people spoke Turkish, which adopted many words from the various surrounding languages, especially Persian, Arabic, and some Greek.

Just as the Seljuks of Rum were establishing a functioning system of government, the Fourth Crusade of 1204 resulted in the capture and pillage of the Byzantine capital of Constantinople by western European crusaders. The Latin Empire (1204–61), in addition to imposing the Roman Catholic (Latin) rite on the citizens and dispossessing the Orthodox Patriarchate, forced the Byzantine royal family to flee from the city, causing different branches of the dynasty to establish their own mini-kingdoms in exile. One of these was the Lascarids of Nicaea (İznik), which was closest to the capital. The Lascarids were eventually able to capture Constantinople in 1261 and reestablish a much diminished Byzantine Empire led from Constantinople.

In 1243 Anatolia was invaded by the Mongol descendants of Genghis Khan. The Seljuk Empire fell apart, and various local emirates, Beyliks, sprang up around Anatolia, all of which were nominally vassals to the Ilkhanid Mongol rulers, who established themselves in Konya. The Byzantines in northwestern Anatolia were unable to take advantage of the situation and regain their former lands.[4]

One of the small emirates was led by a Bey named Ertuğrul, who had been given lands by the Seljuk ruler because of his service as a Turkoman leader. On his death in about 1280, his son Osman became the Bey of these lands in northwestern Anatolia. Benefiting from the return of the Byzantines-in-exile of Nicaea to Constantinople, the Beylik of Osman gained a strong foothold in the vicinity of the imperial capital. The beginning of the Osmanlı, or in English, Ottoman, dynasty, dated around 1300, thus coincides with the era of Byzantine struggle for survival.

At the time that the Turkish Historical Congress wrote the country's historical narrative, the newborn republic needed the prestige of the very empire it had superseded. The Seljuk and Byzantine precedents of the Ottoman legacy became particularly attractive to Turkish historians during the 1930s, when the young republic was most eager to affiliate its heritage with the European and Turkic predecessors of the Ottoman state.[5] In addition, the Turkish government wrote a history that envisaged modern Turks as the inheritors of a mighty Ottoman Empire that had reached its peak in the sixteenth and seventeenth centuries. At that time, not only had it been the uncontested leader of the Islamic world, it had also threatened the borders of Europe with the Siege of Vienna in 1529, at a time when the Holy Roman Emperor Charles V was already quite busy trying to suppress the Reformation launched by Martin Luther. The republican narrative of Ottoman growth depended heavily on the dynastic genealogy of Ottoman historiography that had once served to legitimize the dynasty. But according to the republican version of the narrative, after the seventeenth century the empire had steadily declined, and the late Ottoman rulers were evil, selfish, and stupid, leaving the country to be saved from enslavement to European powers by brave Turks under the leadership of Mustafa Kemal Atatürk.[6]

The narrative of Ottoman history begins with Osman I (r. 1280–1324), who began to establish the empire beyond the borders of his father's kingdom by slowly eating away at Byzantine territories. In 1326 his son Orhan conquered the Byzantine city of Bursa, which became the first capital of the Ottoman Empire. He slowly lost his vassal status under the Mongol rulers of Anatolia and began to mint money in his own name and have his name said alone during the sermon (hütbe) at Friday prayers. Ottoman armies continued to win lands by building vakıfs with which to promote public welfare and convert locals and using these converts in armies against non-Muslims. The next ruler, Murat I (r. 1360–89), conquered much of Thrace, Macedonia, Bulgaria, and Serbia, building much of the Ottoman Empire in Europe. Murat I succeeded in conquering an even larger city, Thracian Edirne (Adrianople), from under the rule of the Serbs in 1364. Edirne would become the second capital of the empire. Soon before his death in 1389, Murat I also led the Battle of Kosova, a conquest that from the nineteenth century became a rallying point for Serbian nationalism.

As the empire expanded, the Ottomans developed administrative structures that would continue into the nineteenth century, when they were completely overhauled to meet the needs of the modern world. In the formative centuries, the Ottomans maintained many of the existing taxation practices, ensuring economic continuity with minimal inconvenience to local populations. In conquered territories, the main change was in the overlords who supervised the administration and collection of taxes. Two practices affected the lives of non-Muslims. One was the head-tax, cizye, collected from non-Muslims (Christians, Jews, and Zoroastrians), who as peoples with a (sacred) book were assured freedom of worship under Islam but had to pay a tax in return for their exemption from military service.

The other practice stemmed from a modified version of the Persian *penchik* tradition, whereby one-fifth of the booty gained in war was considered the share of the ruler. This tradition was applied to the subject peoples of conquered lands as a way of recruiting soldiers. Constantinople and Anatolia were exempt from this practice, which continued in the Balkans into the seventeenth century.

This *devşirme* (collecting or gathering) system functioned through Ottoman officials who periodically visited southeastern European territories and selected young boys from among those who had brothers. These boys were then brought to Constantinople, educated in the Palace School, and raised as Muslims. The brightest could rise to high administrative positions, such as grand *vezirs* or ministers, and the others joined an elite army corps known as the Janissary (from Yeniçeri, which means "Young Soldiers") corps, which would lead the cavalry (*sipahi*) forces from the provinces during campaigns. This infantry force was paid through the palace treasury and served as the personal army of the sultan. Those who rose in the system could become close friends of the sultan, marry into the imperial family, or rise as administrators. They often did not forget their home provinces and established extensive *vakıf* complexes there as well as in the capital, İstanbul. The ethnic eclecticism that this system generated contributed to the cosmopolitan nature of the Ottoman elite—which is, in fact, redundant, as the term "Ottoman" referred only to this cosmopolitan elite and not to any of the ethnic groups—Turks, Arabs, Greeks, Serbs, Bulgars, Armenians, Assyrians, Kurds, and so on—under their rule.

Aside from this system of military conscription, religious minorities enjoyed a fair amount of civic legal autonomy under Ottoman rule. Organized into quasi-national religious units known as *millets*, members of the Greek Orthodox, Armenian Orthodox, Jewish, and smaller communities enjoyed legal autonomy from the Ottoman state. Although subject to Ottoman laws when interacting with Muslims, these communities were responsible for their internal welfare and legislation as well as their religious and secular education.

Under this system, the Muslim population was but another *millet*, although privileged as the dominant community (*millet-i hakime*). The law did not recognize any ethnic or linguistic difference between Muslim Turks, Arabs, and Kurds who lived under the empire. The political elite known as Ottoman identified itself as leading this predominant community but not in terms of an ethnic identity. Until the end of the nineteenth century, the designation "Turkish" may have referred to the empire from a European perspective, but within the empire it described one of many ethnic groups among the commoners (*raya*). The Ottomans were Turks by outside observation and by later designation, but in their own eyes they constituted a cosmopolitan Muslim elite. Indeed, not only did Ottoman Turkish rely heavily on the use of the Arabic and Persian languages in a Turkish grammatical structure, until the eighteenth century Greek remained a semiofficial language in which decrees directed at Greek-speaking regions of the empire could be written.[7] İlber Ortaylı suggests that such a heterogeneous use of language was part of a Mediterranean tradition in which ruling groups expressed power not through linguistic hegemony but through linguistic eclecticism.[8] If language has since been defined as a sign of national identity, the Ottomans failed to be Turks not only through their self-image but through their modes of linguistic and cultural expression as well.

The empire continued to grow under the next Ottoman sultan, Beyazit —called lightning Beyazit because he was so fast in his conquest of European territories—until his defeat by the central Asian potentate Timurlane in 1402. After several years during which the Ottoman future looked doubtful, Mehmet I and Murat II stabilized the empire's control in Europe and extended its domain farther into Anatolia. By 1450 the Ottoman Empire had whittled away the Byzantine Empire to little more than Constantinople itself.

Early in 1453 the Ottoman army built two fortresses on the Bosporus, the strait between the Sea of Marmara and the Black Sea that divides Europe and Asia, in order to choke trade to the city and thus isolate it. In an effort to protect the city from encroaching Ottoman forces, the last emperor of the sole city left in the Byzantine Empire closed the Golden Horn with a chain. The Ottomans are said to have built ships on land on the northern shore of the Golden Horn (in the area of Galata, later including Pera) and then to have launched this fleet from giant wooden slides running down the side of the hill into the Golden Horn, thus circumventing the chain and entering the only side of the city without fortifications. By the time the Ottoman army, led by Sultan Mehmet II, invaded the city in May, most of the population had fled in fear of both famine and Islamic conquest.

As legend has it, Mehmet immediately made the conquest formal in the name of Islam by praying in the Cathedral of Hagia Sophia. Thus the church, constructed under the emperor Justinian in the sixth century A.D. and having the largest uninterrupted interior space in the world before the construction of the Pantheon of Rome, became a mosque. According to the Ottomans, with the conquest of Constantinople they had not only inherited the legacy of the Roman Empire, they had also fulfilled a Qur'anic prophecy that Muslims would someday conquer the Roman Empire. The conquest itself and the continued success of the empire thus served to legitimize the dynasty as chosen and protected by God. The city, which continued to go by the formal name Constantinople as well as by its informal Greek appellation Stanpolis (or İstanbul in Turkish pronunciation), immediately became the Ottoman capital. As Gülru Necipoğlu points out, the symbolism of Mehmet the Conqueror's transformation of the cathedral, in conjunction with his maintenance of the city's name, merged the classical imperial tradition with "the Turko-Islamic heritage of universal sovereignty and revived [it] precisely at the moment when the classical past was being rediscovered in another part of the Mediterranean world, Renaissance Italy."[9] With the development of humanism during the Renaissance, western Europe was in the process of inextricably linking itself with the ancient world, especially the pre-Christian Roman Empire and, to the extent that it had contributed to Roman culture, ancient Greece. With his interest in forging links with the Roman Empire, Mehmet the Conqueror was very much a man of his time.

The empire was faced with the transformation of a depopulated and demoralized Greek Christian city into a thriving Ottoman Muslim capital. As it imported Muslims from elsewhere in the empire to repopulate the new city, extensive architectural programs played an essential role in redefining it as an Islamic center. Although the Greek Orthodox Patriarchate remained in place, the Ottomans lost no time in transforming the most significant Christian churches of the city as a sign of the change in suzerainty. Among these, the Mosque of Hagia Sophia, today a museum and known in Turkish as Aya Sofya, remained the main ceremonial mosque of the empire until the twentieth century. Nearby, the secondary cathedral of Constantinople, the tenth-century Basilica of Hagia Irene, became a storage and distribution site for weapons used by the Ottoman army. Much as the transformation of the Church of Hagia Sophia into a mosque signified the conquest of Islam over Christianity, the transformation of the Church of Hagia Irene into the Imperial Armory (Cebhane-i Amire) signified the military nature of that conquest.

Immediately beside the Mosque of Aya Sofya and incorporating the Imperial Armory, on the former acropolis of the ancient city of Byzantium, Mehmet the Conqueror sponsored the construction of his palace. Today a museum known as the Topkapı Palace, it would serve as home to the sultans, their families, and their administrations until the nineteenth century. Located on the high point of the end of the peninsula that made up the walled city of Constantinople, the palace overlooks the Sea of Marmara on one side and the ports of the Golden Horn on the other.

The Ottoman incorporation of the Byzantine Empire was not merely cosmetic. The Ottomans saw themselves as the inheritors of the Roman Empire and began to model much of their legislation and pageantry after Byzantine traditions. Thus the Muslim-Turkic state gained a third important leg of rule and identity.

After Beyazit II (r. 1481–1512) spent his reign consolidating both the western and eastern reaches of the empire, Selim I (r. 1512–20) used his short reign to complete the conquest of Anatolia, to establish clear borders with the new Safavid rulers of Iran, and to conquer Mameluke Egypt. In doing so, the Ottoman Empire gained control over the three holy cities of Islam—Mecca, Medina, and Jerusalem—which had previously pledged their allegiance to the Mamelukes. In addition, they gained control over the Islamic Caliphate as the caliph, who had been resident in Cairo under the protection of the Mamelukes, moved for a short time to İstanbul. While the Ottoman sultans could not claim the caliphate as descendants of the Prophet, they hoped to be remembered as the "Servant and Protector of the Holy Places" and thereafter used the term "caliph" among their many official titles to emphasize their preeminence in the Islamic world.

The Ottoman Empire entered the era often identified as its political and cultural apogee—indeed, its classical age—under Sultan Süleyman the Magnificent (r. 1520–66), known in Turkish as "the Lawgiver" because of the consolidation of Islamic (*şeriat*) and Turkic legal traditions during his rule into a cohesive system valid throughout the empire. Interested in building İstanbul into a city that would reflect the glory of the mightiest Islamic empire, Süleyman supported a massive building campaign that vastly expanded the number of mosques and associated institutions—schools, baths, hotels, bazaars, and soup kitchens. The architect of this time, Sinan, perfected the traditional Ottoman style of architecture, engineering the simple mosque pattern of a half-dome on a cube to monumental proportions that surpassed even those of the Mosque of Aya Sofya. The most famous mosque built by Mimar Sinan under Sultan Süleyman was the Süleymaniye Mosque in a foundation that included the four major law schools of Sunni Islam, a huge library, a large charitable shelter (*imaret*), and Süleyman's own tomb.

Outside of the empire, Süleyman became known as "the Magnificent" because of his expansionist policies. Not only did he annex all of Arabia, extending the eastern boundaries of the empire to their maximal size, he caused great fear in Europe as his armies marched westward. The 1538 inscription on the citadel of Bender (in modern Moldova) points to his power:

I am God's slave and sultan of this world. By the grace of God I am head of Muhammad's community. God's might and Muhammad's miracles are my companions. I am Süleyman, in whose name the *hütbe* is read in Mecca and Medina. In Baghdad I am the shah; in Byzantine realms the Caesar, and in Egypt the sultan, who sends fleets to the seas of Europe, the Maghrib, and India.[10]

Although Süleyman never made it all the way west, he almost attacked Rome. He successfully conquered the island of Rhodes, a large part of Greece, Hungary, and a major part of the Austrian Empire, even laying siege to Vienna. During this time, he tried to ensure the destabilization of Europe by supporting the Protestant movements in Europe that had been growing throughout the sixteenth century. By breaking the overarching power of the Catholic Church, he hoped that the growth of Protestantism would fragment Europe and thus make it more vulnerable to invasion.

Süleyman was indeed magnificent, but the end of his reign set the first seeds for the decline of the empire. Near the end of his reign, his two favorite sons, whom he had groomed in battle and with administrative tasks to succeed him to the throne, were found guilty of betraying him and were executed. He retreated to the palace, leaving matters of state to his grand vizier and to the love of his life, his Circassian wife, Roxelana (known in Turkish as Hürrem Sultan), who was active in palace intrigue. When his remaining son, Selim, who had led a life of luxury in the harem, came to power, he had no interest in government and left the administration of the empire to his viziers. Citing this period as the beginning of the end, Ottoman historians of the early republic tell stories describing the weaknesses of the next sultans to underscore the idea that the Ottomans, once great, had lost their God-given right to rule and that the country was in a long wait for the birth of the Turkish Republic.

For example, Süleyman's son, Selim II, "the Sot" (r. 1566–74; known in Turkish as "yellow" Selim in reference to his jaundice induced by cirrhosis), is said to have been persuaded to order the conquest of Cyprus because of its reputation for vintage wine. His successor, his son Murat III (r. 1574–95), had an unusually high libido, which he satisfied with forty concubines who produced one hundred thirty sons as well as numerous daughters. As the women gained power jockeying for their sons' accession, the grand vizier Sokollu Mehmet Pasha (from Sokol in modern Bosnia) became, at times, more powerful than the sultan. In the meantime, his rivals in the government led conquests of the Caucasus and parts of western

Iran. In hindsight, the empire already may have begun some sort of decline, but its territories were still growing.

In response, Sokollu Mehmet Pasha sought stronger economic relationships with Europe. Already during the reign of Selim II, he had made an agreement with France allowing for free passage for French ships into Ottoman waters and ports and requiring vessels from other western European states to fly the French flag to enjoy similar privileges. Before long these agreements, known as capitulations, extended to the Venetians and the British. Thus Europeans who lived in İstanbul came to enjoy economic liberties within the empire. Through these capitulations, European citizens in business in the empire were subject not to the laws of the Ottoman state but to those of their own governments as represented by envoys stationed in İstanbul.

Over the next hundred years, the empire enjoyed the fruits of earlier conquests and remained quite wealthy. With the exceptions of Osman II (r. 1618–22), whose short reign prevented the realization of his hopes for the empire, and Murat IV (r. 1623–40), who reconsolidated the crumbling state, sultans continued to be weak and ministers continued to control many state functions. Murat's successor, Sultan İbrahim (r. 1640–48), was weak and had been relatively uneducated during his sequestered youth in the harem. His government was controlled by ministers who successfully conquered Crete, which had been chafing under the rule of Venice. Aside from this small victory, İbrahim is remembered for his passion for furs and silks, which covered the walls and ceilings of his palatial rooms, as well as in legends imagining him throwing pearls into a marble pool to be fetched by his naked concubines.

With poor central control throughout the century, the military began to decline. During the early years of the empire, the government administration had depended completely on a meritocratic system of advancement. In the seventeenth and eighteenth centuries, rather than bring boys from outside the system, the sons of administrators and Janissaries began to attend the court school. Even more damaging, administrators began to acquire their positions by buying their offices or through inheriting their posts rather than rising through rank or academic success. As a result, the administration became increasingly nepotistic and corrupt. Although there were occasional attempts to clean it up, by the eighteenth century government was primarily in the hands of the religious elite (*ulema*) who had bought office or of high-ranking Janissaries with little interest in military reform. The decline in the provincial cavalry system had also weakened the military, encouraging the rise of local overlords defiant of the central authority of the palace. Instead of being loyal to the person of the sultan, the Janissary corps came to engage in palace revolutions and the overthrow of sultans.

One of the most effective reformers of the seventeenth century was Mehmet Köprülü (1570–1661), who was interested in rooting out government corruption as well as in reinstating the expansionist policies that had made the government great in the first place. Following this policy, one of his successors led a second, unsuccessful siege of Vienna in 1683. When the Ottomans signed the peace treaty of Karlowitz in 1699, they lost a considerable portion of their European territories. Throughout the eighteenth century, the Ottomans continued to engage in wars with Austria and Russia.

Yet the eighteenth century also brought a new wave of cultural development to the empire. During the Tulip Era, named after an avid interest in tulips among the elite in and near the court of Sultan Ahmet III (r. 1703–30), fashions imported from the West, particularly France, became all the rage. For the first time, increased emissary traffic between Europe and the empire brought imported ideas that came to supplant those of the Turkic and Islamic traditions.

In the meantime, Europe had been busy exploring and expanding all over the world, creating trade routes that depended on the sea rather than on land. As a result, the Ottoman Empire lost many of the tax revenues it had relied on from the extensive East-West trade routes crossing its territories. Because of European expansion into the Americas and increased sea trade with Asia, the Ottoman Empire was increasingly left out of a more modern world economic order. Although many Ottomans could tell that they had lost some of their former glory, the question remained as to how to reform without threatening the delicate balances of religion, state, and tradition that had made the empire great for so many centuries.

During the first waves of reform, military, rather than cultural, changes dominated. Under Mahmut I (r. 1730–54), a French nobleman, the Comte de Bonneval, became the first European technical adviser hired by the Ottoman government. He was charged with restructuring the military by creating new corps, battalions, and uniforms. Bonneval also gave the sultan advice concerning economics and foreign affairs and opened the empire's first military engineering school. Similar efforts continued under the reign of Abdülhamid I (r. 1774–89). During this period, the Hungarian nobleman Baron François de Tott continued to establish new corps trained in the use of modern artillery and instituted a second school of military engineering. Under Selim III (r. 1789–1807), the process of reform continued. In particular, like earlier reformers, Selim III made great efforts to reduce the power of the wayward traditional military units, the Janissary corps, by supplanting them with modern professional battalions. Although reform programs continued to focus on the military, social and cultural interaction between the Ottoman elite and Europeans increased during this period.

Despite the successive waves of reform, by the 1820s the Janissary order had not only become unmanageably corrupt and inefficient; it was using archaic weaponry and was entrenched in a conservative organization. Its weak performance in the handling of the Greek War of Independence (1821–30) was the last straw that turned the Ottoman administration against it. Sultan Mahmut II (r. 1808–39) worked to gain the loyalty of the chief officers of the Janissary corps and established a new force within the corps to receive extra training in modern European tactics and artillery. He also gained favor from the religious elite and the populace by contributing to many religious buildings and causes. The mass of the Janissaries found this reform threatening. They revolted only two days after the new force had begun to drill, on June 14, 1826. The grand vizier summoned the loyal troops, who attacked, cornered, and slaughtered the rebels in their barracks at a square near the Hippodrome (the At Meydanı). Those who escaped, or others who supported the Janissaries, had to lay low until the passion against the institution had subsided.[11] The Auspicious Event (Vaka-i Hayriye), as the abolition came to be called, marked a watershed in the history of Ottoman reform. For the first time, an old institution had been completely undone to make way for new practices. Moreover, the abolition of the often wayward Janissaries reaffirmed the power of the sultan and gave him increased control over the imperial military.

At this time, Sultan Mahmut II also abolished the turban, which he saw as a sign of Ottoman backwardness. He wore Western-style clothing and expected members of his administration to do the same. The only difference between his clothing and that of a Frenchman of the same period was his hat: whereas a European would generally wear a brimmed hat, the Ottoman hat became the brimless red fez, which had formerly been the core piece of the turban (built from layers of fabric wrapped around a core similar in shape to the later fez). With the mandate of the fez for all Ottomans, particularly urban men, the sartorial distinctions that had formerly marked the members of religiously differentiated *millet*s were abolished, giving all Ottomans a similarly quasi-European—even secular—appearance.

To emphasize the transition to a more European visual order, Mahmut II began using imperial portraiture in a characteristically European manner.

Following the Hebraic tradition against idolatry, Islamic iconoclastic arts tended to avoid pictorial representation in public art. Whereas elite private arts, such as those of the book (as well as pre-Ottoman wall paintings and sculptures), often contained considerable figural imagery, public art in the Islamic world usually favored calligraphic representation as well as geometric and floral decoration. Mahmut II's extensive use of his portrait as a symbol of his authority marked a sharp break with this tradition. Not only was an oil portrait of him on horseback prominently displayed in the Selimiye Barracks in 1836, most loyal statesmen received a medallion bearing the imperial portrait. Unlike his predecessors, who had their portraits made only for private collections, Mahmut II recognized the propagandistic power of the imperial image.

As Ottomans came to look more European, Europeans living in the empire came to hold increasing economic power. By the nineteenth century the growing naval and commercial power of Europe left the Ottoman Empire almost completely isolated as European merchants used the Capitulations to compete with Ottoman businesses, draining the empire of resources. Guilds responded with increasingly restrictive regulations, using the government to take protective measures that ultimately left them technologically behind the ever-increasing growth of Europe. In addition, attempting to resist the secession of the Balkan states, the Ottoman government relied heavily on money borrowed from Europe. By the late nineteenth century many modernizing ventures—including banking, shipping, and railways—depended heavily on European financing. By the time World War I started, the empire was heavily in debt to the nations of western Europe, which were already making plans to add pieces of the empire to their colonies in the Middle East.

MUSEUMS AND THE ERA OF REFORMS

In the certainty of historical hindsight, it has become all too easy to forget that even in the latter years of the Ottoman Empire, the so-called Sick Man of Europe was hardly preparing his grave. As numerous scholars have pointed out, the teleological examination of Ottoman decline has all too often obscured the continued political might of the empire.[12] Rather, faced with the internal threat of national fragmentation as well as the external threat of European imperial aspirations of conquering its territories, the Ottoman government was eager to forge a new identity with which it would be able survive into the modern age. During its last century of power, the Ottoman government not only enacted the radical program of political reforms known as the Tanzimat, it also constructed new modes of cultural self-identification that would naturalize and nativize these reforms for an increasingly inclusive body of citizenry and an increasingly exclusive formulation of the national ideal.

As nationalism grew from a European theory of self-rule to a principle of self-determination, some nations that had developed in large part out of the traditional ethnic-national *millet* system sloughed off of the Ottoman empire and established independent nation-states, while many regions becamed subsumed into colonial empires. In 1830 France occupied Algeria; in 1881, Tunisia. In 1832 Greece won its independence with strong European backing. In 1878 Britain took Cyprus; in 1882, Egypt. In 1908 Austria-Hungary annexed Bosnia-Herzegovina, and, as a result of the Balkan Wars, by 1913 the empire had lost Serbia, Bulgaria, and what remained of Ottoman territories in Greece.[13] The empire that remained had to acquire an identity strong enough to resist the incursion of European colonial forces that had already entered it by means of the capitulations and would soon threaten the very integrity of what was left of the Ottoman state. In an ironic twist of Homi Bhabha's suggestion that "the nation fills the void left in the uprooting of communities and kin, and turns that loss into the language of metaphor,"[14] it was not the nations that left the empire that had the most difficulty forging metaphors of identity. Rather, it was the Ottoman state from which they seceded. Left without the multiple ethnicities that had for so long been part of imperial identity, the Ottoman state was left in exile from a notion of self that had previously depended on an ethnically diverse populace subject to rulers with the very different, sophisticated heterogeneity of the Ottoman elite.

As the need for the Ottoman state to reinvent itself along nationalist lines emerged over the course of the late nineteenth century, museums that could represent new communal identities began to serve as templates for developing modes of Ottoman nationalism. From their early roots in the eighteenth century through their nineteenth-century growth and twentieth-century maturity, Ottoman museums provided spaces for the concrete manifestation of new values for a state and society in rapid flux. They emerged alongside numerous European-style institutions: the university, the archives, the prison, the army, and the post office, to name a few. However, unlike these utilitarian nodes of modernization, the museum acted as a space of reflection, not only on the objects it displayed, but also on the political choices of nation building. The unique ability of a museum to recycle objects into didactic signs makes it an ideal institution through which to examine the emergent identity of the Ottoman Empire as a modern nation before it became clear that this nation would never, in fact, come to full fruition. The issues raised by the types and collections of these museums help to trace the subtle contradictions embedded in the formulation of a new national identity during the tumultuous century that preceded the Turkish War for Independence and the foundation of the Republic of Turkey.

Museums emerged during a century of radical and dynamic change that had been in progress for nearly a century but which rapidly accelerated during the late nineteenth and early twentieth century. While often disparaged as an imported and thus implicitly bastardized mode of Westernization, the rapid and radical reforms of the Tanzimat, which can be translated literally as "Orderings," mark a period of great dynamism and a newfound will to address the complex problems of an increasingly unwieldy state with outdated systems of governance. Much as the Enlightenment in Europe had established new ways in which to order objects and people alike, the reforms of the Tanzimat sought to bring order to systems that had become chaotic and dysfunctional. Thus the very use of the word "Tanzimat" suggests a deep understanding not simply of the principles that emerged from the Enlightenment, such as humanism and liberalism, but also of an underlying epistemological concern to lend order to the workings of government. Although the Ottoman Empire did not end up fully partaking in Enlightenment principles, the reforms of the Tanzimat produced new relations between the state and the populace that were expressed in a variety of new institutions, including the museum.

The Tanzimat began in 1839 as a conscious effort on the part of its initiator, the foreign minister Mustafa Reşit Pasha (1800–1858), to deliberately bring the Ottoman Empire closer to Western Civilization in the hope of fostering closer diplomatic, political, economic, and cultural ties with the increasingly powerful nations of Europe. To this end, he wrote the Imperial Edict (Hatt-i Hümayun), announced in the name of the young sultan Abdülmecid (r. 1839–61) at Gülhane, the gardens of the Topkapı Palace. It is worth noting that the edict was not prepared by the sultan himself but by a reformer who, through his extensive experience as an ambassador in England, had grown to believe that progress lay definitively in the ideals of the Enlightenment. Reinforced by a similar edict, the Edict of Reforms (İslahat Fermanı) of 1856, the Imperial Edict defined certain duties of the state toward the people within it. It recognized the rights of the individual to a just, impartial, and consistent legal system, establishing a precedent for constitutional principles of government. For the first time, the Imperial

Edict delineated branches of central government with ministries to address carefully categorized governmental functions: military, economic, interior, transportation, health, and education.[15] Moreover, showing increased concern with the individual rather than with communities, the Imperial Edict expressed an intent to treat the members of all ethnicities and religions in the Ottoman state with a level of legal and administrative equality absent in the past. Much as such an expansion of rights seemed progressive to European observers who rallied for the rights of fellow Christians in the empire, the centralizing reforms were found threatening both by minority leaders, who lost authoritative powers over their communities, and by Muslims, who lost their status as the predominant nation, or *millet-i hakime*.[16]

While the inspiration for the initial reforms of the Tanzimat clearly derive from Enlightenment documents such as the French Declaration of the Rights of Man and the Citizen and the American Bill of Rights, its role in the Ottoman context has remained quite controversial among historians. On the one hand, the traditionalist school maintains that the Tanzimat represented a period of economic and political liberalization signaling transition to a constitutional state. On the other hand, Marxist historians see the Tanzimat as a sign of increasing ideological imperialist encroachment into the Ottoman Empire on the part of European nations. These views are not mutually exclusive. Rather, the reformers of the Ottoman Empire sought the solutions to long-standing problems through the construction of a radically different order designed to overlay existing systems of governance. In doing so, they selectively adopted European post-Enlightenment forms of order to create a new Ottoman bureaucracy and system of governance. As a result, they inadvertently created numerous economic and physical inroads for European nations who were all too eager for a piece of the coveted Ottoman pie. Yet they also allowed for the invention of a public Ottoman national identity to blockade these paths of colonial incursion.

Although the process of change that the reforms of the Tanzimat engendered has been loosely labeled "Westernization," this designation poses problems on multiple levels. Certainly, no "West" exists that corresponds to the monolith suggested by Ottoman-Turkish imaginings. Rather, a mixture of practices from various schools of thought in Europe, particularly British, French, and German, contributed to a uniquely Ottoman process of modernization.[17] The changes that Ottomans conceived of as Westernization rarely bore anything but a superficial resemblance to their European models. Rather, they represented an Ottoman vision of the West and carried an occidentalist mystique that the empire tried to realize through constant comparisons and bouts of self-deprecation, as expressed in the newspapers and journals of the day. Much as the European practice of Orientalism constructed a timeless, static, and exotic Other that would suit its contemporary needs, Ottoman reformers used the idea of the West to produce a progressive and powerful template through which to induce its own development. One might indeed ask how much of the West that was being emulated truly resembled Europe and how much of this Occidentalization (Batılılaşma) constructed a simulacrum for self-reflection. As Steven Caton suggests in his insightful application of Freud's notion of the uncanny to such Othering, "Not only is the double a supremely ambivalent sign in Freud's formulation of the uncanny; it is also what Freud calls the ego's 'conscience,' [which] is able to stand over against the rest of the ego, which has the function of observing and criticizing the self and of exercising a censorship within the mind."[18] How much of the project of "Westernization," in which museums played a small but immensely symbolic part, constructed a Europeanesque Ottoman identity, and how much of it acted as a conscience, producing a mode of critique and resistance against the demise of the past and against the threats of the future?

The changes brought about by the Tanzimat reflected a newfound need for an interaction between the state and its subjects beyond the collection of taxes and the conscription of armies. Even before the decree, the first empirewide census, conducted in 1831, tried to ascertain the male population of Anatolia and Thrace and counted not only those wealthy enough to pay taxes but also those who were not.[19] Increasingly over the course of the nineteenth century, it became important for the Ottoman government to create channels of communication with its populace in order to foster loyalty and consolidate its power. One of the earliest signs of this shift lies in the publication of an official government newspaper in 1831, the *Calendar of Events* (Takvim-i Vaka'-i). Unlike earlier modes of communication between the government and the populace—such as decrees read in public squares, Friday sermons—these new channels could send a uniform voice all over the empire. The very medium of transmission, published in İstanbul, verified the increasingly centralized control of the state. The range of editorial comment possible in such an organ was limited. Yet despite its relatively small circulation of approximately five thousand copies per issue in Ottoman and three hundred in French, the newspaper had an enormous impact in creating a means of communication between the Ottoman elite and the government. Just as important, it opened the way for the development of a more extensive private Ottoman press in later years.[20]

Although the government quickly recognized the need to produce a populace that could be cohesive as a nation, the composition of that populace was far from clear. Although the *Calendar of Events* was actually published only in Ottoman and French, plans for its publication in Arabic, Persian, Greek, Armenian, and Bulgarian suggest the diversity of the populations and the range of ethnic identities from which the Ottoman state was trying to cull a unitary national identity. Instead, many of these identities would eventually become expressed as independent national affiliations.

As early as 1851 the Council of Knowledge (Encümen-i Danış) began to discuss the structure of the Ottoman language, suggesting a newfound self-consciousness about national identity beyond the functioning of the government. When the first constitutional monarchy (Meşrutiyet) was instituted in 1876, the new constitution (Kanun-i Esasi) established Ottoman citizenship and granted equal legal rights to all members of its populace regardless of ethnicity or religious creed. However, when the parliament convened for the first time, its members soon discovered that their spoken languages were too diverse for effective communication. As a result, the state had to declare Turkish the state language and had to define precisely what constituted that language. With association between language and nationality constructed in nationalist discourse, such a move would soon become an important step toward the formulation of a national identity in the later decades of the Ottoman Empire. Moreover, discussions about simplifying the complex Ottoman written language reflected the government's interest in eliciting a more populist mandate by increasing public access to written materials.

During the same years, Ottomans began to show interest in defining the identity of Turks in relation to the central Asian and Anatolian pasts. For example, Mustafa Celaleddin's *Les Turcs anciens et modernes* (1869) used Greek and Roman sources to prove that many early Anatolian tribes were Turks. This interest suggests a growing concern with defining the Turks as a separate nation under the umbrella of the Ottoman Empire. The work used a technique of analysis that relied on the new theories of Darwinism to construct a modern sense of national cohesion and even to suggest that Turkish had been a "root" language that had influenced ancient Greek and Latin.[21] Thus his work argued that Turks were among the tribes that had founded Western Civilization.[22] His work had a strong influence on the Ottoman authors Namık Kemal and Süleyman Pasha, who were among the first to link the word "Turk" with the Ottoman state rather than use it as a derogatory term for uneducated, nomadic peoples.[23] Instead, these writers wanted to foster patriotism among Ottoman subjects—newly designated as Turkish—by creating links between their (supposed) central Asian forebears and the early Ottomans, and thus link this segment of the population with the ruling family itself. Mustafa Celaleddin's work encouraged Namık Kemal to move away from the Ottoman concept of *millet*s toward the notion of *vatan*, most easily likened to the French concept of *patrie*, or motherland, which would be defined by the borders of the Ottoman state.[24]

Not only were the linguistic and ethnic definitions of the Ottoman Empire under evaluation in the late nineteenth century, but the religious identity associated with the state also came under close scrutiny. İlber Ortaylı suggests that the idea of Islamic civilization was a nineteenth-century development, with no earlier counterparts in the Ottoman Empire: while the appellation *dar us-selam* ("house of peace" in Arabic) designated the Islamic world, it included the diverse peoples that lived within that world in a way that the more modern notion of Islamic civilization does not. Thus he argues that Ottomans of the late nineteenth century began to use the term "Islamic civilization" in reaction to the exclusion of the East from European civilization by Orientalists of the eighteenth century. The birth of Ottoman-Islamic identity came as a direct result of the recognition of multiple nationalities on Ottoman soil and the fragmentation of the empire into new, nationally based states such as Greece and Bulgaria. During the late nineteenth century, the term "Ottoman-Islamic" came to represent a national group that was often produced and promoted through state institutions, in particular educational institutions such as schools and, later, museums.[25]

The heightened concern with education expressed by the reforms of the Tanzimat created the most immediate and effective venue for the creation of communicative links between the state and the populace and the most effective means of making that populace into a citizenry. The prime instigators and promoters of the Tanzimat—Ali Pasha (1815–71), Midhat Pasha (1822–84), and Safvet Pasha (1814–83)—fervently believed that public education should be the primary role of the government and that the lack thereof was the primary cause of Ottoman decline. The Edict of Reforms of 1856 ensured that all schools would be open to the public and regulated by a centralized educational council.

In 1868 one of the government's first moves toward a modern educational system was the establishment of the Galatasaray Lycée, a secondary school whose classes were taught in the French language and which was advised by the French, who hoped to include the Ottoman Empire in their colonial civilizing mission. As a contemporary Frenchman commenting on the Eastern question wrote in 1898, the school was "a symbol of the action of France, exerting herself to instruct the peoples of the Orient in her own language about the elements of Western Civilization."[26]

In 1875 the minister of education, Safvet Pasha, declared the Public Education Regulation (Maarif Umumiye Nizamnamesi), which expressed the need for modern education in the empire.[27] Not only would the public benefit from learning the techniques of Western knowledge and science, they would also learn to be citizens of the Ottoman state through a centrally controlled educational system. Public schools thus constructed an interface between the government and the populace through which people could learn to be citizens—an identity that would not become integrated with Ottoman political experience until the introduction of the first constitution, the Meşrutiyet, the following year.[28] Nonetheless, Safvet Pasha envisioned history education along very traditional lines, emphasizing Islamic and dynastic histories.[29] The declaration of public education thus overlaid a European model to systematize an existing Ottoman ideology.

Even before the institution of public education, in 1869 one of Safvet Pasha's first activities as minister of education was to institute the first Ottoman museum. Although it was as yet a haphazard collection open only to the sultan and his guests, the involvement of the minister of education suggests that from the very first it was conceived of as an instrument of educational significance as well as one that would link Ottoman cultural practices with those of Europe. Like schools, museums provided for public spaces devoted to the construction and projection of the history, culture, and identity of the Ottoman state and its people. Both through its format and through its content, the museum could project a European framework with an Ottomanist and Islamic content and thus model the new state identity as simultaneously Western and Ottoman.

Museums continued to develop under the changing exigencies of the long reign of Abdülhamid II (1876–1909). Economically unstable, the empire was threatened by the protocolonial incursion of European nations, which used the capitulations to control many modern modes of communication and transportation, including telegraph and postal services, banking, and railways. Along with the European technological presence in the empire, Ottoman elites were increasingly attracted by European intellectual models of culture and civilization. Still, they were less interested in emulating a European state than in exploring ways in which the Ottoman state could express itself as European. On the one hand, Abdülhamid II was more interested than his predecessors in constructing an Ottoman identity based on Islamic, Turkish, and early Ottoman traditions. On the other hand, he was eager to produce a national image that would promote the Ottoman nation as a modern state in contradistinction to the Orientalist tropes often representing the empire in Europe and America.[30] Museums played an active role in both of these representational objectives.

Politically, Abdülhamid II faced numerous challenges both within and without the empire. Although he quickly took advantage of the exigencies of the Russo-Turkish War (1877–78) to curtail the constitutional experiment of 1876–77, this short-lived parliament allowed for a forum of self-expression for newly emerging middle-class elites in various parts of the empire.[31] Many of these members of the elite were interested in formulating new modes of identity, which would depend less on the sultanate and the caliphate than on contemporary notions of scientific progress. Several groups, loosely labeled "Young Turks," struggled against the often repressive power structures of the Hamidian state.[32] While Ottoman museums developed as official organs of the state and thus faced notable restrictions on their modes of representation, the sympathies of their administration with the Young Turks rendered the museum an arena of internal political conflict.

While many fought for a parliamentary system, Abdülhamid II envisioned a relationship with his subjects based on the institution of the caliphate rather than on a contractual agreement inspired by Europe. In the Arab provinces in particular, the construction of an Ottoman-based, pan-Islamic identity competed viably with local nationalist movements.[33] Nonetheless, this emphasis on Islam was not designed to supersede the incipient national identity of Ottomanism, nor did it slow the increasingly nationalist identifications of many provinces.[34]

In 1908 the Young Turks succeeded in toppling the throne of Sultan Abdülhamid II. The period after this Young Turk Revolution (1908–10), often referred to as the Second Constitutional Period (İkinci Meşrutiyet), was marked by the increased perception of a state based on a united citizenry, each of whose members bore duties and responsibilities to the state. In addition to rescinding many of the repressive programs of Abdülhamid II, such as the secret police, censorship, and travel restrictions, the revitalized constitution promised increased equality between Muslims and non-Muslims within the empire. Education and science were to be encouraged, and vestiges of the *millet* system were to finally end. The new ruling party, the Committee for Union and Progress (CUP), placed Mehmet Reşat (r. 1909–18) on the throne as a sultan reduced to nearly puppet status.

At first, people of many ethnicities within the empire hailed the reinstitution of the constitution as a panacea to all their economic and political troubles. They quickly became disenchanted. Over the next four years, the loss of Tripoli to Italy, successful nationalist movements in Bulgaria, Serbia, Montenegro, and Albania, and the outright annexation of Bosnia-Herzegovina by Austria and of Crete by Greece resulted in extensive losses of Ottoman lands. While the conservatives in the new Ottoman government reacted by proposing a return to Islam, secularists turned to Turkish nationalism.

It was during this Second Constitutional Period, between 1908 and 1918, that a Turkish national identity began to play a direct role in the cultural politics of the empire. After the collusion of the Arab territories with the British and their subsequent withdrawal from the empire, it became clear that the pan-Islamism advocated under Abdülhamid and by many members of the CUP could no longer serve as an effective ideology for Ottoman identity. Several popular organizations, led by Yusuf Akçura and Ahmet Ağaoğlu, began to use their organization, the Turkish Hearth (Türk Ocağı) to campaign for the simplification of the language to reflect the spoken language of the people. They also claimed to serve the political and economic interests of Turks all over the world as well as those within the sultan's dominions. As part of this project, they hoped to spread information about Turkish heritage to the people. The organization's periodical, the *Turkish Homeland* (Türk Yurdu), established in 1911, set as its mission "to research, make public, and spread Turkish antiquities, history, high and low literature, ethnography and ethnology, early and contemporary events, as well as old and modern Turkish geography."[35]

Even the most ardent supporters of Ottomanism within the CUP began to give up hope that the minorities would be kept within the empire and turned strongly toward Turkish nationalism. Several thinkers, most notably Namık Kemal, Yusuf Akçura, and Ziya Gökalp, had already been theorizing Turkish identity and nationalism. In his 1904 work, *Three Modes of Politics* (Üç Tarz-ı Siyaset), Akçura (1876–1935) tried for the first time to derive the idea of an ethnically based Turkish nation from the aspects of Turkish culture that had remained constant in various pre-Islamic and Islamic Turkic societies.[36] The party actually hired the influential sociologist and writer Ziya Gökalp (1876–1924), who tried to use the trinity "Turkifying, Islamifying, and Modernizing" to define an Ottoman-Turkish present as late as 1918,[37] after which time his work focused on defining a synthetic view of "Turkism" based on Durkheimian and Rousseauian principles.[38] Not only did these competing ideologies of national identity contribute to the late Ottoman vision of self, the Turkist ideologies of the CUP had great influence on the intellectuals and leaders of the Turkish Republic, most of whom were members of the CUP during the last years of empire.[39]

In 1914, soon after the devastation of the Tripolitanian War (1911) and the Balkan Wars (1912–13), the Ottoman government entered into an alliance with Germany and shared in the defeat of 1918. During the following five years, known to Turks as the era of National Struggle (Milli Mücadele), the empire floundered between the competing forces of colonial European nations who had occupied the remaining Ottoman territories in Anatolia; the puppet rule of Abdülhamid's youngest son, Mehmet VI Vahideddin (r. 1919–22); the Allied occupation of İstanbul; and the republican forces led by Mustafa Kemal from Ankara. In 1920, after the San Remo Agreement had created mandates for England and France over Arabic-speaking provinces, the Ottoman government agreed to the Treaty of Sèvres, which allowed Turks territory in central Anatolia with a corridor of access to the Black Sea. The treaty arranged for the rest of the empire to be divided between the Allied forces, including England, France, Italy, Russia, and Greece. Such a division was justified to many by the impossibility of a non-Christian world power. In the words of Lord Curzon,

> For nearly five centuries the presence of the Turk in Europe has been a source of distraction, intrigue, and corruption in European politics, of oppression, and misrule to the subject nationalities, and an incentive to undue and overweening ambitions in the Moslem world. It has encouraged the Turk to regard himself as a Great Power, and has enabled him to impose upon others the same illusion.[40]

The problem was not simply the Ottoman Empire but that an Islamic country had overstepped the bounds of its culture in aspiring—and for six centuries succeeding—as a significant world power. Curzon equated the Ottoman Empire with the power of the Turk, but within what remained of the empire, the government was traditionally Ottoman and did not define itself as Turkish. To the contrary, it was at odds with the forces that derived their identity from Turkish nationalism. Like the Allied forces, they had come to see the idea of the Ottoman state as an outmoded Islamic power; like them, they saw the very empire of which they were citizens as a source of distraction, intrigue, corruption, and misrule.

It was these Turkish nationalist forces who did not accept the Treaty of Sèvres and succeeded in driving out the occupying powers by 1922. With the exile of the last Ottoman sultan at the end of 1922 and the signing of the Treaty of Lausanne in July 1923, the Ottoman Empire gave way to the Turkish Republic, which was formally declared on October 29.[41] Ottoman museums had already set the stage for the formation of a set of new museums, often adapted from the old ones, that would represent a new republican nation with objects culled from several tropes of heritage.

Within this dynamic setting of shifting identity Ottoman museums emerged. How did this originally European institution become a part of the Ottoman environment? The obsession with collection, categorization, and display manifest in the museum reflects its heritage as a child of the European Renaissance, the Enlightenment, and the Age of Exploration. During these eras, the museum of art and the museum of natural history emerged in tandem from early, combined forms in the *wunderkammern* and princely collections of the seventeenth and eighteenth centuries.[42] While these types of collections formed the backbone of the typology of European museums, neither was appropriate for the Ottoman historical experience, and neither form developed in the Ottoman Empire. Rather, the Ottoman museum came to concern itself exclusively with the production of a modern identity through the representation of select histories as appropriate for its needs of national identity production in the late nineteenth century.

The late Ottoman Empire (and the modern Turkish Republic) shared in the belated relation to Western post-Enlightenment institutions characteristic of the colonial (and postcolonial) condition.[43] In adopting the forms of many post-Enlightenment institutions, the Ottoman Empire discarded many of the metanarratives that structured them. Among them, Ottoman museums did not address issues central to the collection and display strategies of their European counterparts. The museum as it developed in France was supposed to represent a world in microcosm. In 1778 the entrance examination of the Royal Academy of Architecture explained, "A Museum is an edifice containing the records and achievements of science, the liberal arts, and natural history."[44] In contrast, disinterested in the acquisition and categorization of encyclopedic knowledge, Ottoman museums did not endeavor to collect and classify a wide variety of natural and man-made objects. Absent from the universalist project of modern imperialism, they did not attempt to produce universal collections. Excluded from the discourse of humanism, they did not "construct the museum as a site where the figure of man is reassembled from its fragments."[45] Although preoccupied with the constitution of modern national identity, Ottoman museums did not use evolutionary models to trace a natural historical development for the modern nation.[46] Interested solely in the production of a history for a modern national identity, they made no attempt to construct a category of fine arts with which to display a national culture. Lacking large local audiences, museums often did not even address the Ottoman populace.

Yet, even devoid of all these characteristics essential to the European museum project, the panoply of Ottoman museums successfully modeled new modes of self-reflection for a burgeoning national identity. Although this identity did not emerge popularly and was only aimed at a popular audience in the last years of the empire, museums adumbrated national symbols of the sort that would become essential to Turkish nationalism of the republican era. The museum practices of collection and display may have relied on European examples, yet the modes of their performance in the Ottoman context addressed local traditions and contemporary needs. As a space of selective collection, self-reflection, and conscientious display, the museum provides a unique venue through which to consider how the Ottoman Empire adopted a European institution and modified it to very specific local needs, ideologies, and aspirations. Although ostensibly pale reflections of the far grander museums of Europe, Ottoman museums avoided incorporating the full range of European museum collections so as to perform their actual function of political resistance to the tides of European imperialism. They produced copies distinct enough from the original that the museum, so essentially European in its origin and aspirations, developed into a mode of resistance to European domination. Over the course of less than a century, Ottoman museums and the tandem practices of archaeology, collection, didactic display, and artifact legislation that grew with them came to represent the Ottoman self-image even as that image entered the chrysalis of war and emerged transformed in the Turkish Republic.

1 Moving toward the Museum

The Collection of Antique Spolia

In 1996 the Turkish Ministry of Culture hosted ceremonies and a conference commemorating the sesquicentennial of museums in Turkey. Celebrations of the centennial anniversary in 1946 had established their definitive birth year. Nonetheless, in 1996 several interested parties debated the suitability of this date. Although the Ottoman government first sanctioned the collection of antiquities in 1846, some people argued that 1723 was a more appropriate starting date. In that year the Ottoman government remodeled the former Church of Hagia Irene, in use as an artillery warehouse, and included a display of valuables in the renovated structure. Others argued that the museum was actually established in 1869, because this was the date when the word "collection" was replaced by "museum," suggesting a greater interest in public display and education. Then again, the Imperial Museum had achieved autonomy as a state institution only in 1889. One could even argue pedantically that all of these dates are inappropriate, simply because a strictly Turkish museum could not exist before the birth of the Republic of Turkey in 1923. Such arguments aside, long before the Ottoman state designated spaces devoted to collection and public display, the limited display of selected objects often represented power and dominion in the empire. Thus the historical roots of the Turkish museum extend, at the very least, to the conquest of Constantinople. The roots of collection in the Ottoman Empire can only be understood in light of pre-Turkic and pan-Mediterranean practices of reuse and display of valuable works of art. Only against this hyperbolically extended backdrop does the extent of the ideological shift embodied by the relatively sudden formation of the Ottoman museum become apparent.

The consideration of the precedents for museums in the Ottoman Empire begs the question of what constitutes a collection and what constitutes a display. In Ottoman lands, two forms of protomuseological display preceded the development of the museum. Both relate closely to the idea of spolia—both in the traditional sense, as the spoils of war, and in the modern sense, used by architectural historians to denote the reused parts of architectural constructions taken from a demolished building.[1] In both cases, the aggregation and maintenance of spolia amount to a form of collection. Their insertion into a new visual context with the express aim of promoting ideological ends renders the collection of spolia highly pertinent to the study of early museum practices.

CONCEALING THE SPOLIA OF CONQUEST

After its conversion into the Imperial Armory at the time of conquest, the former Church of Hagia Irene (fig. 1) retained symbolic value not only through its ecclesiastic architecture but also by virtue of the military and reliquary collections within. From nearly the beginning of the Ottoman reign in Constantinople, the Imperial Armory housed valuables that were captured during the siege of Constantinople, and it continued thereafter to develop as a locus of collection for the spolia of war. The armory also housed important Christian relics inherited from the Byzantine Empire, such as the gold-encased tibia and occipital bones of Saint John the Baptist, today on display in the Treasury section of the Topkapı Palace Museum. In the transfer of ownership from Byzantine to Ottoman rule, these relics came to signify military dominion at least as much as sacred domain. Not only did they retain their religious significance in the eyes of Christian believers, their ownership by the new dynasty acted as a sign of hierarchical religious power within the empire. No evidence exists to suggest that the military or reliquary collections were arranged with any particular order or with an intended purpose of display. Yet the use of the former church to house them served as a constant physical reminder of Ottoman dominion over the formerly Christian city. Lacking the essential function of exhibition, the collections were far from constituting a museum. However, the attribution of value that informed their collection planted the seeds that would make later Ottoman museums possible. Moreover, like relics at many pilgrimage sites in Europe, such relics may well have retained their power even if they were not placed on display.[2] Applying an antipodal psychological model to the nineteenth-century employment of the gaze as a mode of expressing power, the occlusion of these objects from public access would have made them even more powerful in the public imagination.

Fig. 1. The Basilica of Hagia Irene, ca. 1890, with the crenellated outer walls of the Topkapı Palace and the minarets and dome of the Mosque of Hagia Sofia (a former Byzantine church; today a museum) in the background [Grosvenor, 1893]

With the onset of a long series of modernizing reforms in the Ottoman Empire, such relics increasingly became subject to display. As a result of Ahmet III's eighteenth-century reforms of the military, many of the weapons housed in the Imperial Armory became outdated, and in 1730 the building was remodeled and renamed the House of Weapons (Dar ül-Esliha). For the first time, many objects of value were formally placed on display in the armory.

Although several sources provide brief descriptions of these displays, each mentions only those objects that were most interesting to the author. For example, Jean-Claude Flachat, who visited Constantinople in 1766, mentions in his travelogue, "I did not see the arm of Saint John the Baptist there, among the large number of curious objects and rare effects left to the successors of Constantine, much as the Greeks had assured me on numerous occasions that it was kept there encased in gold."[3] As a Christian in a Muslim land, his comments underscore his affinity with the Greek minority population. In contrast, in 1812 the British traveler E. D. Clarke, more interested in technology than in religious artifacts, reported that he "beheld the weapons, the shields, and the military engines of the Greek emperors . . . suspended as trophies of the capture of the city by the Turks." His visit to the building was cut short, so he did not have the opportunity to fully explore the other "interesting remains of the Palace of the Caesars [that] might also be similarly preserved."[4] This comment suggests that like Flachat, he was aware that Byzantine relics were presumably kept in the building. Both of these short descriptions of the House of Weapons indicate that it served as a space of display considered appropriate for the gaze of select visitors, particularly foreigners, yet that their gaze was significantly circumscribed. Indeed, both travelers suggest that they were pulled out of the armory with only a tantalizing glimpse of the treasures held inside.

Centuries later, Ottoman and Turkish historians of the museum also surmised that the House of Weapons served as a precursor to formal museums in the empire. Sermed Muhtar's 1920 guidebook to the Ottoman Military Museum explains that in the eighteenth century "the building was graced with the display of some precious objects, such as old Qur'ans, beard-hairs of the Prophet, ancient weapons, and holy relics."[5] Like the European travelers who described the space earlier, Sermed Muhtar was selective in his interest, as he mentioned only Islamic relics while deeming Christian ones less worthy of note. In contrast, writing during the highly secularist 1960s, the Turkish historian İbrahim Konyalı noted that both Byzantine armor and religious objects were displayed in the armory but did not mention whether those objects had been significant to Christians or Muslims.[6]

The relics housed in the armory—beard-hairs of the Prophet as well as Byzantine relics—not only acted as metonymic souvenirs of holy people and events, but they signified imperial dominion at least as much as religious memory. The Ottoman government had acquired the Christian relics held by the Byzantine emperors during the conquest of Constantinople and had acquired the Islamic relics during the conquest of Egypt and the subsequent assumption of the caliphate. The military instruments on display beside the relics contextualized them, putting the martial implications of their possession in high relief. Although the public could not enter the armory to see the relics, they were far from forgotten. On the contrary, their imprisonment among the arms of conquest made them and Ottoman suzerainty all the more palpable to those outside the former church, left to imagine these embodiments of the holy among the accoutrements of the military. For example, through possession of the relics, the new owners became entitled to partake even in the power of a saint as central to Christianity as John the Baptist. Ottoman control over such an important relic created a vehicle for the transfer of the loyalty of the former subjects of Byzantine rulers. Similarly, the possession of Islamic relics symbolically bolstered both the metaphysical claims of the Ottomans to the caliphate and their territorial claims over most of the Islamic world. The space of the House of Weapons thus used a vocabulary of holy relics to speak subliminally of imperial dominion in a language appropriate for a period when historians used religion as the primary justification for political authority.[7]

Although this collection functioned very much like a museum when exhibited to visitors such as Flachat and Clarke, much of its power relied on its general inaccessibility—a situation antithetical to the premise of exhibition essential to the modern museum. The occlusion of the gaze in this premodern display space suggests a form of imprisonment in which power emerges from concealing objects of value in a monumental structure. The Ottoman state was able to sequester objects from the public gaze while at the same time retaining them in public memory through the use of a major monument as their "prison." While the former Church of Hagia Irene was located on the grounds of the palace, signifying the proprietary role of the Ottoman state, it was located in the first courtyard, which anybody was allowed to enter. People entering this courtyard were able to see the former church and thereby remember it along with the relics within as signs of the conquest. Thus the Ottoman government successfully exhibited its power without resorting to display. This technique has underpinnings remarkably similar to the theories of social control that lay behind the development of the modern prison, whereby outsiders could see the prison as a monument to the power of the government to incarcerate but would not be privy to the punishments within.[8] As a collection that relied more on concealment than on display, the objects housed in the House of Weapons did not constitute a museum even as they served as the seeds of future Ottoman military museums both in content and in purpose.

ARCHITECTURAL SPOLIA UNDER OTTOMAN DOMAIN

The reuse of architectural pieces in contemporary structures constitutes one of the most primitive forms of antiquities collection. As in much of the Mediterranean basin, officials of the Byzantine, Seljuk, and Ottoman Empires collected antiquities by incorporating them into new structures and thus produced new contexts and meanings for old forms. While many scholars have passed over reuse as a convenient way of saving on building costs, Beat Brenk convincingly argues that the expense often incurred as a result of reuse, as well as the prominence of reused pieces in new architecture, suggests an unwritten ideology underlying the practice.

When one considers reuse as a form of collection and display, it bears a striking resemblance to practices later formulated in the modern museum. The collections housed in the Imperial Armory and the House of Weapons presaged the museum in their utilization of a building to house and display artifacts. Yet neither of these collections constituted a museum, as people could rarely if ever see the objects and as these objects were not classified. In contrast, the numerous ancient objects reused in buildings and ramparts lacked the systematic classification essential to a museum. However, as in a museum, reuse allowed for the preservation of objects for their visual appreciation by a wide public. If the museum represents a range of practices that begin with the selection and categorization of objects and proceed with their organization and display, these very different approaches to military and archaeological spolia represent opposite and incomplete moments in the procedures that constitute museum practice.

Unlike precious metals and gems, easily fungible to liquid assets, carved stones do not possess intrinsic value—especially if hidden beneath the soil or irrevocably damaged. Such objects gain value either through aesthetic appreciation or through layers of historical interpretation. Not only does the value of an object vary temporally and culturally, the modes of expression for such evaluation change as well. What constitutes the act of collection and the methods and venues considered appropriate for conservation, observation, or appreciation vary so much that the appropriateness of a particular site for an object in one context may be lacking in another context. Once Europeans had established that the museum was the only acceptable repository for valuable art, they rejected the ancient practice of reuse that was common throughout the domain of the former Roman Empire. Whereas in Europe the practice of reuse had slowly been supplanted by the practice of museological collection, in the Ottoman Empire the sudden introduction of already fully developed practices of museological collection created an ideological rupture in the relationship between antiquities and the visual environment.

Europeans began to collect Greek and Roman antiquities from Ottoman lands during the seventeenth century. By the mid-nineteenth century, the idea of a museum as the most appropriate venue for the preservation of valuable objects had gained common currency throughout much of western Europe. Contemporary historians tend to forget that the practice of archaeological collection for museums was hotly debated in nineteenth-century Europe. Many in the intellectual community argued that museums bracketed and deadened culture by emphasizing its preservation over its production.[9]

Others saw the collection of antiquities as an unfortunate necessity in an era of increasing travel. After traveling to Egypt for the first time in 1873–74, the novelist Amelia Edwards, who later became an important benefactor of Egyptian archaeology, wrote of the newly discovered chapel at Abu Simbel,

> I am told that the wall paintings which we had the happiness of admiring in all their beauty and freshness, are already much injured. Such is the fate of every Egyptian monument, great or small. The tourist carves it over with names and dates, and in some instances with caricatures. The student of Egyptology, by taking wet paper "squeezes" sponges away every vestige of the original colour. The "Collector" buys and carries off everything of value that he can get, and the Arab steals it for him. The work of destruction, meanwhile, goes on apace. There is no one to prevent it; there is no one to discourage it. Every day more inscriptions are mutilated—more tombs are rifled—more paintings and sculptures are defaced. The Louvre contains a full-length portrait of Seti I, cut bodily from the walls of his sepulchre in the Valley of the Tombs of the Kings. The Museums of Berlin, of Turin, of Florence are rich in spoils which tell their lamentable tale. When science leads the way, is it wonderful that ignorance should follow?[10]

For Edwards, the production of a local museum would stem the tide of destruction wrought in Egypt by the confluence of science and art. The museum was made necessary not by the art itself but by the irresponsibility of its Western admirers. Much as Edwards expressed misgivings about the modern science of archaeology, the Jews of Palestine felt that Christian biblical archaeology desecrated holy sites. In 1863, when the French archaeologist Louis-Félicien de Saulcy convinced the public that he had found the site of the Tomb of the Kings in Jerusalem, the Jewish community petitioned Constantinople to halt the excavations.[11]

Those opposed to archaeological collection from the East were a distinct minority in Europe. Many protectionist arguments depended on the perceived inability of non-European races to appreciate and protect the arts of antiquity, recently appropriated as part of the European patrimony. Europeans often perceived the practice of collection from non-European terri-

tories as transferring antiquities from barbaric hands that presumably neglected and even destroyed them into the hands of scholars who coddled,
studied, and preserved them. Collections and the museums into which
they developed reassembled antiquities into a coherent historical network
made up of works culled from diverse ancient sites and repositioned into a
three-dimensional compendium located at home. In these collections antiquities gained a new meaning and value from their situation in a preexisting codified hierarchy set up by the museum institution—a hierarchy
that, although it purported to be timeless, relied on the construction of developmental art historical models during the late eighteenth century.[12]

The collection of antiquities often disturbed the integrity of original
sites or secondary sites of reuse and the meanings invested in them and created a tertiary level of meaning through the new historicization of a given
object. In the European museum, objects could both display the wealth and
acquisitional prowess of their owners and educate the viewer. In addition to
providing information about the objects on display, the museum could help
the viewer to infer and incorporate the ideology and epistemology informing the content and presentation of the exhibit. In particular, the presence of
Hellenic and Hellenistic artifacts in European museums underscored the
notion of ancient Greece as a proto- and pan-European culture. The display
of original sculptures, many of which came from Ottoman lands, not only
emphasized the power of competitive European nations to acquire such antiquities but also suggested the inherent right of European nations to the
layered history of Ottoman territories and, in light of contemporary colonial expansion, ultimately to the territories themselves.

Such collection assumed that antiquities had no value in the visual
world of the Ottoman Empire. To the contrary, accession records of Ottoman museums, read in conjunction with histories of early archaeology,
provide numerous examples of antiquities that had been collected and preserved through the process of reuse long before European interest in them.
These records support the notion that the use of architectural spolia often
had narrative or didactic functions comparable to but ideologically quite
different from those of museum exhibits. Much as hegemony in the
Mediterranean had once been expressed through linguistic eclecticism, the
practice of incorporating spolia into buildings, widespread in the Roman
Empire and curtailed with the rise of medieval Christianity and its suspicion of Europe's pagan past, continued to be part of the local visual environment in the Ottoman Empire well into the nineteenth century.

Long before the emergence of the Ottoman Empire, Christians and
Turks alike preserved antiquities by incorporating them in the stone walls

of public buildings. When Justinian built the Church of Hagia Sophia to commemorate the triumph of Christianity over paganism, he incorporated the spolia of ancient temples into its walls.[13] One of these stones, a circular medallion decorated with a Medusa head, was removed in 1871 from the exterior walls of the mosque and placed in the Ottoman Imperial Museum in response to Ottoman fears that it would be taken to a European museum.[14] Why had the Medusa figure in particular been incorporated in the church walls in the first place? Before Christianity, the figure of Medusa had often been used at temples to serve apotropaic functions. Although the builders of Hagia Sophia may have used the stone as a political statement of Christian hegemony, a cultural memory of its former significance may have contributed to its incorporation in the building.[15] Indeed, in an attempt to diffuse the Christian associations of the structure, Ottoman legends about the building attested that it had been constructed with spolia from structures built by Solomon, one of the most revered prophets in Islamic tradition, on a site originally sanctified by him.[16] The continuing significance of spolia as modes of visual narration attests to their conscious use as a mode of collection and display.

Large ancient Greek architectural pieces were also extracted from the walls of the former Saint George Church and the Saint Sophia Church of Salonica to enter the collection of the Imperial Museum.[17] This suggests that, as at the Church of Hagia Sophia, ancient Greek artifacts were often components of Byzantine religious structures. Because these buildings were designed to last longer than many others, the incorporation of antiquities in their walls may indicate an attempt to preserve as well as display these objects.

In the twelfth century the Crusader knights of Saint John chose to incorporate the friezes of the Halicarnassus mausoleum in the walls of the fortress they built in present-day Bodrum.[18] These friezes depict the defeat of the Amazons by the Hellenic ruler Mausolus. The knights may have simply used these relief panels as decoration, but they may also have wanted to recycle images of conquest to bolster the symbolism of their own fortress. The symbolic value of their use would be more clear if their placement in the fortress were known. However, the archaeologists who removed these panels to European museums did so before the advent of scientific archaeology and thus did not document their precise location on the fortress walls.

Byzantine ramparts had also frequently incorporated antiquities.[19] Turks continued this practice, as can be seen in the fortifications of Rumeli Hisar in İstanbul and in the fortress walls of Ankara. As these structures lack written records, it is difficult to tell when and why some of the objects were incorporated. At the Ankara citadel, a row of horizontally placed Hellenistic sculptures lie in a prominent position near the top of the ramparts in the citadel. While these were clearly placed for purposes of display, it is difficult to ascertain why they lie sideways. Their orientation may serve to make their display more palatable in an Islamic context; alternatively, fallen figures may represent the threat of death that would befall those who might attack the fortress.

Indeed, the incorporation of both contemporary and ancient sculptures into city walls was common in Seljuk cities. Until the nineteenth century, when they were stripped bare by European travelers, the walls of Konya (fig. 2) included a Hellenistic sculpture of a nude male figure in addition to Seljuk relief sculptures.[20] The prominent display of a nude figure outside the fortifications of Konya suggests a visual subsumation of local culture into the then-dominant Seljuk domain. Its prominent location suggests that the Seljuk ruler was interested in constructing a public venue for the display of an object found locally and given considerable symbolic value. Although not housed in a building or labeled, this example of collection and display brings to mind the later use of collected antiquities as signifiers of imperial dominion.

The collection of spolia by Muslims is of particular interest in light of the general assertion that antiquarianism failed to develop in Islamic societies, which Bruce Trigger attributes to an unsubstantiated assertion of Muslim "rejection of pagan pre-Islamic civilizations and their works as an Age of Ignorance, to a tendency to view many features of Islamic history as cyclical, and to a religiously based disdain for works of art that involved the portrayal of human forms."[21] On the contrary, such examples of architectural spolia suggest the physical incorporation of pre-Islamic antiquities alongside the many practices that also often became part of regional religious practice.[22] In contrast, medieval Christians of Europe often destroyed physical reminders of the local pagan past and curtailed the age-old practice of reuse of symbolic sculptures in their new buildings.

The practice of incorporating antiquities in new structures continued under the Ottomans. According to sixteenth-century Italian travelers, Byzantine sculptures of lions had recently been taken from the Blacharnae palace in Constantinople and placed around the gate that opened to the sea.[23] The reuse of specifically Byzantine statuary suggests that their new placement served as a marker of Ottoman imperial dominion, which was underscored by the apotropaic functions and symbolism of power often associated with lions. These sculptures were removed in 1871 as a result of

Fig. 2. City walls of Konya, etching by L. de Labord, late eighteenth century
[Eyice 1978]

railway construction and thereby entered the collections of the Ottoman Imperial Museum.[24] Antiquities were even used in Muslim religious structures. For example, antiquities in the wall of the Bergama mosque attracted European excavators but became part of the collections of the Ottoman Imperial Museum.[25]

Even when their subject matter was overtly Christian, antiquities often remained part of Constantinople's city walls after the Ottoman conquest. Small reliefs depicting Christ, embedded near the Mevlevi, the Edirne, and the Topkapı gates of the city walls, remained part of the ramparts despite their overtly Christian subject matter until approximately 1895, when they entered the collections of the Ottoman Imperial Museum.[26]

During the Ottoman period, people often ascribed supernatural powers to antiquities embedded in the city walls. For example, in 1625 the travelers Sir Thomas Roe and William Petty, charged with collecting antiquities for the earl of Arundel and the duke of Buckingham, contrived a plan to acquire the reliefs from the Golden Gate of Constantinople, which had become part of the walls of the Castle of the Seven Towers (Yedikule). They proposed to "corrupt some churchman to dislike [the figures] as against their law; and on that pretence, to take them down to be brought into some private place; from whence, after this matter is cold and unsuspected, they may be conveyed." They were unable to do so, they said, because the great treasurer announced that they were enchanted and that their removal would cause a great alteration in the city.[27] This story suggests that the European travelers may have had a more absolute vision of the Islamic interdiction against sculpture than did the Muslim elite of the Ottoman Empire.

In a similar instance of magical reuse, the presence of large Byzantine sarcophagi in the courtyard of the Topkapı Palace close to the surface of the earth and divested of human remains has led to suggestions that they may have been purposefully placed on the grounds of the Ottoman palace, perhaps as a means of inaugurating the ground for the new rulers through the souvenirs of the old.[28] This example is of particular interest as the sarcophagi would have worked their magical powers while hidden from public view—not unlike the spolia in the Imperial Armory. At the very least, such examples of reuse attest the Ottoman interest in antiquities, which probably stemmed from existing practices that imbued ancient statuary with aesthetic and even spiritual value.

Magic often provided the justification for the preservation of statues at particular sites. F. S. N. Douglas reported that after its collection by a British museum, Athenians mourned the loss of one of the caryatids from the Acropolis because they saw the statues as sisters who had been magically petrified and who would have been restored to their human selves as soon as the Turkish occupation ended. Another traveler, Hobhouse, assuaged British guilt by suggesting that the Athenians felt that the lot of the statue was probably ameliorated by its removal to England.[29] In a similar legend that emerged soon after the fall of Constantinople, the last Byzantine emperor was said not to have died but to have turned into a marble statue. His body would remain petrified in a cave until a sorcerer released him to reconquer the city. The development of such legends suggests a prearchaeological awareness of underground statues and a supernatural power with which they could be associated.[30] Such magical powers invested sculpture with a type of value quite different from the art historical, aesthetic, pragmatic, and political values ascribed to antiquities as of the eighteenth and nineteenth centuries.

The attribution of magical powers to statuary was certainly not unique to this area; in medieval Europe as well, statues were often either destroyed or reused specifically because of their magical powers.[31] Their reuse in an Islamic context, however, is of particular interest because of the general aversion to three-dimensional figural imagery. The preservation of figural, even overtly Christian antiquities in public spaces testifies to the continuity of preexisting customs well into the Ottoman period. Although the magical powers attributed to the display of these antiquities could never be part of the strategy of modern museums that rely on the post-Enlightenment faith in reason, the production of such mythological narratives as a justification for display parallels the historical narratives often used by museums to justify the display of particular objects in a given setting or category.

As the preceding examples show, the incorporation of Hellenistic sculptures and architectural fragments in buildings of many types probably served practical, aesthetic, and metaphysical functions. The marble stones, already cut to practical dimensions, served as convenient building materials in all types of stone construction. Their incorporation in later structures has frequently been interpreted as a shrewd act of recycling. But carved stones were not placed arbitrarily in the structures, nor were their figural carvings disfigured or hidden. The builders who collected and used these stones wanted them to be seen. Through their inclusion of these stones in walls, builders both preserved them and put them on public display. As in European museums, the collection of antiquities and their reuse suggested the power of ownership and sometimes even of conquest. It encouraged aesthetic appreciation on the part of the public. In contrast to European museums, however, such displays were not informed by classificatory epistemologies. If there was an educational value, it lay in the myths associated with the objects, not in later attempts to place them in graded temporal or aesthetic frameworks.

The advent of modern museological collection in the Ottoman Empire literally tore apart the fabric of this earlier mode of collection as countless antiquities, deemed too valuable to be left in their architectural sites, were removed to European and later to Ottoman museums. These museums further recycled these antiquities by explicating them through narratives of art history and by implicating them in narratives of contemporary imperial history, conquest, and possession. Certainly, this shift in the procedures of collection, preservation, and display was far from unique to the Ottoman Empire. However, the sudden introduction of museums to the empire, as opposed to the centuries of development they had undergone since the Renaissance in Europe, made the collection of spolia for museums a site of conflict in the Ottoman context. This conflict exposes a rupture between the age-old informal modes of collection and the formalized, positivist approach to collecting introduced in the nineteenth century.

The acquisition of spolia, whether military or architectural, is not merely an accidental accumulation of excess objects or a convenient use of existing materials. Rather, their express collection in formats that allowed for interpretation make them precursors of the modern museum. Like the modern museum, the House of Weapons created a central site in which the collection of objects with symbolic significance gave a political message. The incorporation of spolia into the walls of various types of structures also served one of the functions of the modern museum—to display objects to a viewing public who would understand the messages implied. Whereas in the modern museum visitors have labels and guidebooks to construct exhibitional narratives, in these premodern collections myth, legend, and tradition provided the contextual frameworks for the objects on display.

2 Parallel Collections of Weapons and Antiquities

During the late nineteenth century, the Ottoman museum developed out of the collections in the House of Weapons, renamed the Military Storehouse (Harbiye Anbarı) in 1839. Thus the collections remained on the grounds of the Topkapı Palace; all but one would remain there until the end of the empire. This location played an important role in emphasizing the imperial nature of the collections, their relation to the state, and their potential audiences.

The importance of the museum's location came not so much from the immediacy of the royal family but from its proximity to the empire's administrative offices. In 1853 the royal family felt the need for more modern accommodations and moved to the Dolmabahçe Palace on the Bosporus. The Topkapı Palace came to house the family and staff of the previous sultan. Although demoted to a secondary palace, it retained its importance as the home of the Prophet's holy relics, which the sultan visited ceremonially on the fifteenth day of the holy month of Ramazan every year. During these visits, he passed by the developing museum and heard requests concerning its upkeep and development.

More important, although the royal family's residence moved, the administrative center of the empire, the Sublime Porte (Bab-i Ali), remained just down the hill, across from the main gate to the Gülhane Gardens, where it had been since 1654 (see map 2).[1] The proximity of the administrative center ensured that as the panoply of Ottoman museums developed, they would become familiar to an administrative elite whose Europeanizing palates would be most likely to savor the new institution. As a result of increased centralization during the nineteenth century, not only did administrative jobs grow in prestige, the education necessary to participate in the bureaucracy shifted dramatically from one laden with Arabo-

Persian literature and etiquette to one founded in Western languages and practices. Keen on cultivating their interest in poetry and the arts, administrators maintained their ties with European culture in part through the nearby museum.[2]

In addition to these Ottoman visitors, the collections seem to have been accessible to elite European travelers who wrote about the site in conjunction with visits to the defunct palace. The location of the museum provided a well-guarded environment for the collections and ensured that a visitor would be constantly reminded that they signified the taste and power of the Ottoman dynasty that owned, assembled, and displayed them.

Unlike in Europe, where modern museums often emerged from the princely cabinets, or *wunderkammern*, kept by Renaissance nobility, Ottoman museums emerged from collections that had been outside of the range of interest of earlier private imperial collections. Although Mehmet the Conqueror had studied Italian and wanted to participate in many aspects of Renaissance culture, the collections formed during his reign differed considerably from the collections of his contemporaries, most notably the Medici in Florence. Whereas their collections focused on the valuable and the antique and were placed on private display, there is little evidence that Mehmet the Conquerer was interested in his collections for private contemplation or admiration.

THE MAGAZINE OF ANTIQUE WEAPONS

From its inception, the Ottoman museum stood in the transitional zone between an Eastern empire and the impetus of Europeanization. Its founders and first directors were either European or Ottoman citizens with extensive experience in Europe that colored their perceptions and projections of Ottoman identity. While for many years protomuseological collections filled the former Church of Hagia Irene, they functioned in modes that were antithetical to the premises of exhibition of the European museum. As such, they functioned as relatively autochthonous institutions. Once these collections became more museological, they immediately bore the stamp of European institutionality. In 1846 Ahmet Fethi Pasha, the marshal of the Imperial Arsenal (Tophane-i Amire Müşiri) in the Ministry of War, designated the rooms around the atrium of the former Church of Hagia Irene to house two collections owned by the sultan. He thus established the Ottoman Empire's first conscientious museological presentation of imperial collections. From that moment on, each Ottoman museum en-

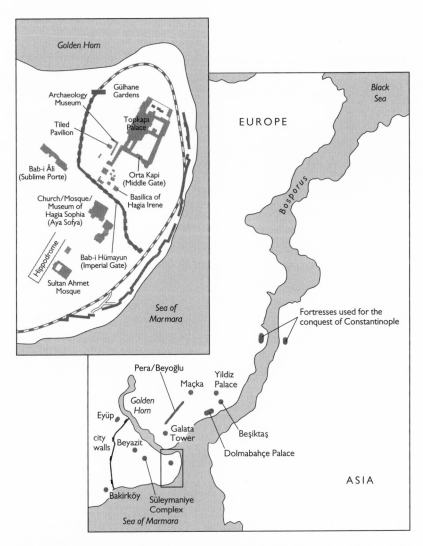

Map 2. Schematic map of İstanbul

tered into a negotiation between its imported format and its nationalist content.

Before his tenure as marshal Ahmet Fethi Pasha had served as ambassador to Moscow in 1833, to Vienna in 1834–36, and to Paris in 1837–39. During this last appointment, he visited London as the official representative of the Ottoman Empire at the coronation of Queen Victoria. He returned to the empire in 1839 for the coronation of Sultan Abdülmecid and to marry the new sultan's younger sister. On his return to Constantinople, Ahmet Fethi Pasha contributed to establishing several modern institutions designed to bolster the Ottoman economy. Among these, he established new steel factories that would carry the empire into the industrial age. He also founded the Beykoz porcelain factory whose goods were emblazoned with the famous insignia Product of Istanbul (Eser-i İstanbul). As modern, European-style institutions, the steel and porcelain factories played an important role in the systematic revolution taking place in the empire. Ahmet Fethi Pasha's familiarity with modern modes of organization not only informed the radical change he led in industry but also influenced his subsequent involvement in Ottoman museums.[3]

As marshal of the Imperial Arsenal, Ahmet Fethi Pasha was in charge of the Military Storehouse, which still contained the collections of the House of Weapons. The earliest archival document that mentions the collections proposes that a space be designated for the arrangement of historical weapons and various objects already in the storehouse, where a museum for the arrangement of antiquities "depicting human and animal forms" already existed.[4] Thus by 1846 a small collection of antiquities had already joined the older collection of weapons and had already been on display. This display became official, however, only under the auspices of the new collections.

Ahmet Fethi Pasha organized the collections by dividing the space of the former church into two parts. To the right of the atrium, a marble portal inscribed with the words "Mecmua-i Asliha-i Atika" (Magazine of Antique Weapons) led to a collection of disused weapons and armor, already stored in the armory. Opposite this portal, a portal inscribed with the words "Mecmua-i Asar-i Atika" (Magazine of Antiquities) led to an assortment of works from the Hellenistic and Byzantine periods, unearthed from various parts of Constantinople and the empire, which had previously lacked an appropriate space for storage or display. Displays in the atrium forged visual links between the two collections. These collections diverged in location and ideological function in about 1880 but until then served similar ideological ends through conceptually separate yet physically intertwined exhibits.

Like earlier assemblies of objects, the primary audience for the new collections was the ruler and selected guests. Although the church-museum of Hagia Irene would eventually become a site visited by many foreign and and native tourists, the initial audience for the collections was initially none other than Sultan Abdülmecid. Soon after his first visit, a chamber supposedly in the style of Louis XIV was built in the narthex of the church as a place of rest for the sultan on subsequent visits.[5] It was for his satisfaction that the museum emphasized the most glorious moments of Ottoman history surrounded by the multifarious relics of conquest. The Europeanesque style chosen to decorate the chamber of the sultan underscores the desire of the ruler to partake in a European ritual of collection and display. In his museum alcove, he acquired an Occidental context in which to relax and contemplate the history of his forebears.

Certainly, the collections did not solely serve princely pleasure. However, in the absence of visitor records, it is difficult to imagine the experience of visiting these early collections or the range of people who had access to them. Ottoman officials of the Sublime Porte were expected to contribute to the collections, so it seems quite likely that they constituted the primary audience. They did not, however, publicly record their visits to the collections. In contrast, several foreign travelers wrote about their visits. The famous French novelist Gustave Flaubert and the playwright Theophile Gautier visited the city in 1851 and 1852, respectively. Their accounts provide the earliest descriptions of the displays. The French archaeologist Albert Dumont came to İstanbul in 1868 to catalog the antiquities collections of the nascent museum. Similarly, the German classicist Anton Déthier, who would become the second director of the museum, described the antiquities collections in 1872. Together, these descriptions provide considerable information concerning the display strategies in the dual collections.

The spaces of the Magazine of Antique Weapons carefully framed specific episodes in Ottoman history to their best advantage while marking the passage of archaic institutions in a glorious—but distanced—history. The artillery collections were located in the vestibule, the main body of the church, and the apse; mannequins depicting the Janissaries graced the gallery; and the atrium served as a transitional space between the antiquities of war and the antiquities of culture, located in the Magazine of Antiquuities (fig. 3).

The visitor entered the former church through the vestibule, where the disorder of heaped kettle drums and cooking pots of the Janissaries reminded the viewer that the corps had been abolished twenty years earlier and that its possessions had become mere curiosities. Flaubert briefly described the exhibit hall after this entryway:

> Nice hall of arms with a dome, vaulted, with simple naves of fusillages in a bad state; on the ceiling, in the upper story, ancient arms and of an inestimable value, damasquined Persian caps, coats of arms, for the most part communal, huge Norman two-handed spears. . . . The sword

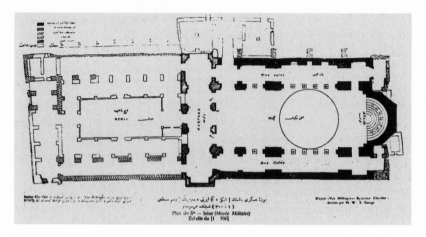

Fig. 3. Basilica of Hagia Irene, ground plan [Sermed Muhtar]

of Mohammad, right, large and flexible like a whalebone, the scabbard covered with green leather; everybody took it and brandished it, except for me. They also showed us, under glass, the keys of cities taken by the sultans. . . . [A]ll the fantastic and heavy artillery of the past.[6]

The only object available to touch was the sword of Mehmet the Conqueror, which visitors were presumably encouraged to pick up, playfully pretending to be the great sultan. The sword thus became the focal point of the exhibit.

Gautier's description, confirming many of Flaubert's observations, attempts to contextualize the exhibit in a contemporary Ottoman political milieu: "Quantities of old halberds, cases of arms, antique cannons, and curiously shaped culverines recall Turkish strategy before the reforms of Mahmoud."[7] In the main body of the church, he continues, "the wide walls [were] lined in close mosaic, with medieval and modern armor of every form and description. Breastplates, helmets, coats of mail, suits of chain armor, battle-axes, maces, scimitars, pikes, though arranged in symmetric order, blend in a strange confusion with tens of thousands of rifles from America which point upward in great stacks from the floor."[8] By juxtaposing the collections of historical and modern artillery in the church nave, the museum bound the memory of the classical Ottoman military to a simultaneous reminder of recent military modernizations.

Gautier points out that the arrangement of these weapons in rosettes classified by type mimicked the arrangements of the French artillery museum, which may indeed have influenced Ahmet Fethi Pasha's techniques of display. The artillery exhibit would thus have acted as a sign of Ottoman progress in the realm of exhibitionary practices as well as in that of the military. Also, the placement of arms in rosettes may have reflected the late-nineteenth-century development and increasingly prominent display of the Ottoman coat of arms (Arma-i Osmani), designed by an Italian artist during the reign of Mahmut II. This coat of arms featured the exalted crown of the sultans, topped by the official seal (*tuğra*), flanked by tomes symbolizing Islamic and modern law, and surrounded by old and new symbolic armaments. Like the museum display, the coat of arms emphasized the continuity of old traditions alongside new reforms. As Selim Deringil points out, however, "the fact that it bristled with weaponry is of course indicative of the actual weakness of the state relative to its peers."[9] Similarly, the symbolic emphasis on military collections during this period may have served as psychological compensation for the actual military weakness of the empire.

As a well-known French intellectual, Gautier would have been an excellent candidate through whom the Ottomans could advertise their Occidentalizing activities, as exemplified by the existence of a museum and by the display strategies of the objects within it. However, in his search for an exotic Oriental empire, Gautier was distinctly unexcited about this exhibit of modern weapons, noting with some disappointment that the Ottomans seemed more interested in this portion of the museum than in the historical displays closer to the architectural apse, for him the crowning glory of the exhibit. Beneath a gold mosaic cross that remained from the Byzantine period, he reports having seen

> the sword of Mehmet II, a straight blade on which an Arab inscription in gold letters gleams upon the blue damascening; an armlet inlaid with gold and constellated with two discs of gems that belonged to Tamerlane; an iron sword, much dinted, with a cross-hilt, formerly belonging to Scanderberg the athletic hero [and in] glass cases . . . the keys of conquered cities; symbolic keys just like jewels, damascened with gold and silver.[10]

The choice of the apse as the focal point for the display emphasized the meaning produced by using the former church as a museum. The apse became transformed from an altar to Christ, memorialized by the mosaic cross that to this day remains visible in the apsidal conch, to an altar to empire, secularly sanctified by the military relics below. The three main relics signified three powerful historical figures: the armor of Timurlane, the Mongolian invader of Anatolia under Beyazit II's rule, represented subsequent reunification of the empire; the armor of İskender Bey, leader of the Albanian revolt of 1443, represented Ottoman power in Europe;

and, most important, the sword of Mehmet the Conqueror represented the preeminent victory of the Ottomans over the Byzantines, already highlighted by the very site of the museum. Nearby, the keys to conquered cities underscored the extent of Ottoman dominion, as each key represented a city wall that had been crossed in battle.

These exhibits remained in place despite the museum's closure during the Russo-Turkish War of 1877–78, when the former church reverted from a museum to an armory. The author Ahmet Midhat recalled that when, as a young recruit, he had been sent to this armory to be fitted with arms, piles of unidentified historical weapons lay in disorder near the modern Henry Martini rifles being distributed to soldiers.[11]

Although the museum remained closed for three decades, former attorney general of the United States, Edwin Grosvenor, was able to visit the exhibits that remained in it (fig. 4). The descriptions and photographs in his work correspond closely with the writings of Flaubert and Gautier, indicating that the museum changed very little during the decades it was closed. It is highly unlikely that the exhibits of a closed museum would have been altered. Those discrepancies that exist in the descriptions probably result from their having seen different parts of the museum or their having chosen to emphasize different aspects. The most notable addition mentioned by Grosvenor is, "in suggestive proximity and equally mute, the bell of Sancta Sophia and the kettles of the Janissaries."[12] He includes a picture of the bell, positioned in front of a fence of muskets and flanked by spiked maces. Its presence beside the relics of the Janissaries emphasized the process through which the Ottomans had aided in the conquest of Constantinople and simultaneously referred the Janissaries to an equally defunct place—the museum—in the annals of history. This small display represented metonymically the overall program of the museum, juxtaposing church and sword, as Grosvenor interprets it, mute and paralyzed and under the surveillance of the Ottoman museum.

Grosvenor indicates that the display in the apse had not changed since midcentury and also describes the displays immediately surrounding the central exhibit. Flanking the apse, the visitor could see the "knightly weapons of the Crusaders and the machines of war of Alexios I Komnenos." (The knightly weapons mentioned here may be the same as the two-handed Norman spears mentioned by Flaubert.) Historical helmets stood guard over the valuable military relics featured in the apse. Like the relics of the heroes featured in the apse, the helmets stood proxy for anonymous soldiers who had fought for the glory of empire.

Fig. 4.   Apse of the former Church of Hagia Irene, as the Magazine of Antique Weapons, ca. 1890 [Grosvenor]

A carefully formulated history informed the arrangement of these collections and led the visitor through a controlled narrative of the Ottoman legacy. The display of the military collections used the existing church architecture to emphasize the production of empire through military conquest. In the apse secular relics displaced the sacred relics that had represented dominion in the eighteenth-century House of Weapons. This shift coincides with the increasingly secularist writing of Ottoman history after the Tanzimat. Whereas earlier historians had focused on religious justifications for Ottoman power, a new generation began to downplay sectarian differences and situate Ottoman history in relation to external events, such as the French Revolution.[13] Reformists often emphasized modern modes of thought that favored a secular scientific understanding of the world over old-fashioned theological ones. The empire may not yet have been ready to construct a model of this transition from the theological to the secular with the use of Islamic spaces, but it could do so effectively using defunct Christian ones.

DISPLAYING THE JANISSARIES

While the historic armor and weapons displayed in the church nave articulated the might of the Ottoman Empire and the modern weapons testified
to its progressive trajectory, the Janissary mannequins in the gallery em-
balmed the romantic and glorious history of the empire in the spatial in-
terstices of the defunct church. When the sultan visited the collections in
1847, he was particularly delighted by the Janissary mannequins displayed
there.[14] Indeed, the mannequins would eventually become the linchpin of
the entire museum display, summarizing the glorification of the past covalent with its dismissal from the trajectory of the future affected by the
museum. If the eighteenth-century Ottoman museum acquired a prison-
like quality through the exclusion of the public gaze, its nineteenth-
century heir realized this carcereal potential by producing actual bodies to
imprison in the liminal space between myth, history, and memory.

Considering that Sultan Mahmut II had controversially abolished the
Janissary orders only a quarter of a century earlier, it is startling that their
representation should have played a large part in the exposition of Ottoman heritage undertaken by the museum. Without question, the Janissaries had once served a central role in the growth and maintenance of the
Ottoman state. It would have been impossible to construct a believable visual narrative of Ottoman military glory without creating a venue through
which the Janissaries would be included in the historical legacy. The Magazine of Antique Weapons thus needed to create a means through which it
could simultaneously celebrate the achievements of the Janissaries and emphasize, even exaggerate, their passage into distant historical memory.

Ahmet Fethi Pasha probably got many of his ideas for the Magazine of
Ancient Weapons from the museums he saw in Europe, some of which had
opened quite recently. The Tower of London armory display, for example,
had been renovated in 1837, the very year of his visit. As part of the official fanfare for the coronation, the tower was probably an important desti-
nation for visiting ambassadors.[15] There Ahmet Fethi Pasha would have
seen equestrian figures and knights represented, as a British guidebook explained, "in effigy" by mannequins displayed throughout the Tower Museum.[16] The armor they wore had been abandoned a century and a half
earlier; the display of these mannequins revived a nearly forgotten history
so that it could be re-collected and reframed in the public eye of the nation.
In contrast, the mannequins in the former Church of Hagia Irene wore
costumes outlawed only twenty-four years before the opening of the new
exhibits. Unlike the historical figures brought to life in the Tower of Lon-

don, not enough time had passed for people to have forgotten the Janissaries. If the British figures seemed to incarnate ever powerful ghosts from the past, the still mannequins of the Janissaries emphasized their recent death.

The historical proximity made their display into a type of embalming rather than a type of homage, akin to the production of wax effigies after the French Revolution. During the Revolution, Madame Tussaud produced wax effigies not only of heroes, such as Marat, but also of enemies, such as the king and queen, their doctor, Robespierre, and several Jacobins. The representation and display of these enemies of the state as if they were alive heightened the violence of their demise.[17] Similarly in the Ottoman Empire, the mannequin effigies of rebellious soldiers violently cut down in the 1820s became memorialized as the loyal forces of the early empire, yet their presentation emphasized their historicity. The use of anthropomorphic sculptures as historical representations suggests just how distant from iconoclastic Islamic mores the Ottoman military had become. Their representation not only marked the Janissaries' passage into history, but also the passage of the traditional Ottoman order—Islamic, Turkic, and imperial—that they had once defended.

By 1852 the mannequins had been moved from the former church to a new site, called the Ancient Costumary (Elbise-i Atika). This new location, in the tent warehouse across from the Mosque of Sultan Ahmet (often called the Blue Mosque) on the Hippodrome, emphasized their passage into history more clearly than their placement in the former church. Close to the site of their bloody abolition, this alternative site served as a monument to their demise at the same time that it celebrated their rich history. No records remain to indicate why the mannequins were moved from one site to another. Those in charge of the collection were probably interested in creating a locational reference for the collection so as to make the political agenda of their display more transparent. Moreover, the new site brought the collection to a spot in the city close to the palace but more accessible and thus more appropriate for a public venue (fig. 5).[18]

Each of the one hundred forty mannequins wore the costume of a particular rank in the Janissary corps, of an official at the Ottoman court, or of an old-fashioned artisan. New costumes for the mannequins were sewn in Vienna, but original weapons were used to arm them. The mannequins were arranged in small vignettes depicting Janissaries in mundane situations. For example, the Janissary manning the entrance stood roasting corn, and one grouping inside showed a Janissary playing a lute as his companions listened. The latter is described by Gautier:

Fig. 5. Janissary Museum, ca. 1880–1916

> This Janissary brigade private seems a jolly rascal; a type of ferocious fraternity resides in his forcefully rendered characteristics accentuated by a long mustache; one sees that he would be capable of humor during murder, and he sits with a the nonchalant posture of a member of a privileged corps for whom all is permissible: legs crossed, one over the other, he plays his *saz* . . . for charming the loiterers of his group.[19]

In front of the Janissary mannequin was a table displaying old coins, which also temporalized him as a figure taken out of the past. Though the soldiers had arms, they were depicted at rest and disempowered. The mannequins were designed to instigate a recollection of the past but to avoid any dioramic reconstruction of either the might of the Janissaries or the violence of the Auspicious Event.

In glass cases the length of the hall "were collected, like types of antediluvian animals at the museum of natural history, the individuals and races suppressed by the *coup d'etat* of Mahmut II."[20] The mannequins represented not only the defunct military orders but also other old forms of dress outlawed for adult males in 1829. As Gautier points out, the mannequins, situated between the world of two-dimensional images and the three-dimensional world of the living, acquired a "cadaverous aspect" that allowed them to indicate the passage of old ways into time immemorial.

It is only twenty-seven years since the massacre of the Janissaries took place, yet it seems as though it were a hundred, so radical is the change that has been worked. . . . The old national forms have been destroyed, and almost contemporary costumes have become historical antiquities. When looking through the glass at these mustached or bearded faces. . . . One feels a strange sensation. . . . [I]n seeking a transition from the statue to the living being, one encounters the cadaver.[21]

The display did not differentiate the mannequins by century but by function, as if the sartorial practices of the military and of civilians alike had remained constant before the eighteenth century. Later periods were only represented in the collection by members of the corps trained by the Comte de Bonneval in the 1730s and by depictions of contemporary military personnel designed to contrast with the historical displays. Through Gautier's interpretation of the museum, it becomes clear that it produced a memorial to a flattened past that conflated disparate events, such as the Auspicious Event and the dress reform, to create a space of memory in stark opposition to a modernized present. Much as nineteenth-century Orientalist practices constructed a detemporalized Orient, the Ottoman Empire used these galleries to construct a temporally neutral Other out of its own past.[22]

The mannequins returned to the galleries of the former Magazine of Ancient Weapons sometime before 1868. As with their first move, the reasons for this one are unclear. Several Hellenistic funerary steles accompanied their display in the new location, transferring the reference to their demise formerly inferred by the site on the Hippodrome to an actual grave marker.[23] The transition to the site of the dual collections also created a single museological unit through which the state could begin to express a relatively holistic vision of its heritage and its vision for the future as bolstered by that heritage.

The dual collections in the former church were not the only venues through which the Ottoman government expressed its increased consciousness of the power of display. Perhaps the clearest expression of the use of Janissary mannequins as a mode of nationalist expression comes from their temporary function in the imperial exhibit at the 1893 Columbian Exposition in Chicago. While most records of Ottoman participation in world's fairs focus on economic and trade ramifications, it used the fairs as symbolic venues as well. In 1893 state council members disputed the wisdom of sending Janissary mannequins to the exposition lest they remind Christians of earlier conflicts between East and West. The official commissioned to package and send the mannequins explained that this would not pose a problem, as the Ottoman state had abolished the Janissary corps and thereby had reached the same level of civilization as Europe. It had an army dressed in modern fashion, which proved its modern countenance. Furthermore, images of the Janissaries were omnipresent in Europe, and the mannequins were seen by every foreign visitor passing through İstanbul, where they were not considered objectionable. In the final decision on this matter, the mannequins were declared not to be dangerous, because historical mannequins were on display in the historical museums of all countries. Moreover, mannequins displaying modern military dress would also be included in the display to ensure that the Janissary mannequins would be relegated visually to the annals of history.[24] Twelve Janissary mannequins stood as both guards and hosts for visitors entering the Ottoman exhibit at the exposition.[25] They also played a central role in the Ottoman pavilion of the 1900 Paris World Exposition.[26] Irrespective of the site of their display, Janissary mannequins served to remind the viewer of the glorious past of the Ottoman state while also forcing the viewer to acknowledge the separation of that imperial past from the future produced through the reforms of the nineteenth century.[27]

Whether displayed alongside ancient weaponry, among displays of defunct sartorial practices, or independently, Janissary mannequins acted as bifurcated signs for a glorious past as well as a modernizing present. Like the institution of the museum itself, the mannequins stood between their referent and the present represented via their display.

THE RISE AND ROLE OF BIBLICAL
ARCHAEOLOGY AND HELLENISM

The collection in the Magazine of Antiquities closely resembled the production of a modern present through the display of an antiquated past evinced by the Magazine of Antique Weapons and the various displays of Janissary mannequins. As in these latter exhibits, the collected antiquities bore more value as signs for participation in European practices than as aesthetic or historical artifacts. This becomes eminently clear on examination of the archaeological practices that allowed for the collection of antiquities in a centralized depository in the imperial capital.

The sudden interest of the empire in local archaeology emulated the rising interest in nationalist archaeology evident in Europe. From the Celts in France to the Vikings in Scandinavia, the archaeological study of the achievements of prehistoric peoples laid the groundwork for the construction of autochthonous ancient ancestors for modern nations. Preceding modern ethnic divisions, the identification of such exalted forefathers proved invaluable in the ideology of national identity formation, historical pride, and unification in much of Europe.[28]

Perhaps more important, the sudden onset of Ottoman collection came in response to increasing European interest in archaeology on Ottoman territories stemming from several congruent interests that came to a head in the mid-nineteenth century, among them biblical archaeology and Hellenism. Although generally considered divergent branches of nineteenth-century archaeological practice, from the Ottoman perspective, both involved Ottoman territories and signified similar originary and thereby proprietary narratives constructed by Europeans about Ottoman lands.

Archaeology provided a new, modern method through which Europe could link its own heritage with that of the biblical Near East through material cultural remains. The territories of the empire included the regions in which biblical events were believed to have taken place: Egypt, Mesopotamia, and, most important, Palestine. Medieval scholars had hoped to link northern and western Europe to the recorded history of the Near East as well as the classical world by inventing imaginative lineages that identified biblical characters as the founders of early kings of European nations.[29] Similarly, modern biblical scholars hoped not only to prove the veracity of biblical stories through scientific methods exercised on Ottoman lands but also to establish a right to rule in the lands that formed much of the basis for European heritage.

Before the modern era Protestantism had mythologized the Holy Land, transforming the physical pilgrimage of Catholicism into a metaphorical pilgrimage of the soul and rendering its real spaces unimportant. With increased opportunities for travel and a growing interest in positive modes of knowledge, Europeans became increasingly interested in the narrative accuracy and the historical veracity of sites used for pilgrimage yet often justified by little more than legend and tradition. (Ironically, as travel to Palestine and Israel has become, yet again, difficult because of to regional fighting, the Orlando Holy Land Experience, which opened early in 2001 and is led by Protestant American interests, has revived the notion of localizing pilgrimage into a series of symbolic sites divested of their contemporary realities.)

The desire for narrative accuracy was not only a requirement of the positivist ethos of the nineteenth century, it also came in direct response to new challenges to the literal interpretation of the Bible. The publication, in 1859 and 1871, of Charles Darwin's two treatises on evolution, *On the*

Origin of Species by Means of Natural Selection and *The Descent of Man, and Selection in Relation to Sex,* led biblical scholars to attempt to develop scientific modes of defense for biblical history. Darwin's theories threatened the biblical worldview by suggesting not only that the history of the earth was much longer than that suggested by the Bible but also that man was not the center of the universe, only a random result of millions of years of arbitrary mutation. Evolution recast the geography of humankind from a predestined narrative of greatness that began in the Garden of Eden and resulted in Europe to one that followed the life patterns of primates.[30] As the debate about the chronological veracity of the Bible in the face of developing evolutionary theories grew during the nineteenth century, the excavation of Near Eastern cites provided material evidence for cultures mentioned in the Old Testament.[31] Biblical archaeology became of the utmost importance in mooring faith back in the geography of the Near East. Perhaps as important, archaeologists could use popular interest in biblical studies to finance their archaeological projects.[32]

In 1865 the British Palestine Exploration Fund set out to map the region and to determine the true sites of biblical events. As the fund explained in its prospectus,

> No country should be of so much interest to us as that in which the documents of our Faith were written, and the momentous events they describe enacted. At the same time, no country more urgently requires illustration. The face of the landscape, the climate, the productions, the manners, dress, and modes of life of its inhabitants differ in so many material respects from those of the Western world, that without an accurate knowledge of them it is not too much to say the outward form and complexion of the events and much less the significance of the records must remain more or less obscure. Even to a casual traveler in the Holy Land the Bible becomes, in its form, and therefore to some extent in its substance, a new book. . . . Much would be gained by obtaining an accurate map of the country; by settling disputed points of topography; by identifying ancient towns of Holy Writ with the modern villages which are their successors. . . . A work is urgently required which shall do for the Holy Land what Mr. Lane's "Modern Egyptians" has done for Egypt—describe in a systematic and exhaustive order, with clear and exact minuteness, the manners, habits, rites, and language of the present inhabitants. . . . Many of the ancient and peculiar customs of Palestine are fast vanishing before the increasing tide of Western manners, and in a short time the exact meaning of many things which find their correspondences in the Bible will have perished.[33]

The fund thus saw modern Palestine as a living example of biblical history and yet also as a blank slate on which it could draw an ancient topography. The behaviors of local peoples were perceived as modeling those of Europe's biblical ancestry, as Europeans imagined the local people—Muslim, Jewish, as well as Christian—were unchanged during the intervening millennia of political and geographic upheaval. Indeed, they saw the investigation of the contemporary Near East not simply as a topographical map but as a chart for lost times—a chart that would make real the Bible, thus reducing the threat that evolutionary theory posed in suggesting the fictive nature of biblical narratives.

The Palestine Exploration Society, founded in New York in 1870, added the defense of the Bible to the program of illustration promoted by its British predecessor.

> The work proposed by the Palestine Exploration Society appeals to the religious sentiment alike of the Christian and the Jew. . . . Its supreme importance is for the illustration and defense of the Bible. Modern skepticism assails the Bible at the point of reality, the question of fact. Hence whatever goes to verify the Bible history as real, in time, place, and circumstances, is a refutation of unbelief. . . . [T]he Committee feels that they have in trust a sacred service for science and for religion.[34]

Like the British Palestine Exploration Fund before it, this American archaeological society saw Palestine as a site of living history, in which the past and the present could merge in a single body of knowledge.

Not all biblical archaeology, of course, was undertaken in Palestine. Like the lands of the eastern Mediterranean, European archaeologists divested the region near the Euphrates and Tigris Rivers from its modern inhabitants. While since the tenth century this region's inhabitants had referred to the region as Iraq, by the mid-nineteenth century Europeans had increasingly made use of the modern term Mesopotamia (derived from ancient Greek) to differentiate between the region's pre-Islamic history, affiliated with European heritage, and the Islamic present, which had superseded it. As Zainab Bahrani points out, modern historians continue to identify the two non-Muslim groups of the region, Greeks and Jews, as the primary links between modern and ancient cultures, excluding the regional legacy of the Islamic world from the construction of Western Civilization.[35]

As biblical archaeology used scientific methodology to make the Bible as positivistically credible as evolutionary theory, it also lent credence to a biblically based interpretation of history that saw successive empires—Babylonian, Persian, Hellenistic Greek, and Roman—transferring the center of power and creativity westward from the Near East to Europe. Along the same lines, in the 1880s the Swedish archaeologist Oscar Montelius developed a diffusionist chronology for human civilization that placed the dawn of civilization in the Near East. Although this view was highly controversial, it appealed to many Christians as an affirmation of the biblical view of world history threatened by Darwinian thought.[36] Moreover, it supplied a link between the ancient Near East and the West while relegating that link to the second millennium B.C., after which the modern Near East had declined and left its full inheritance first to ancient Greece and then to western Europe and North America.[37] This Eurocentric interpretation of history, in turn, became the premise for the organizational strategies of many universal survey museums. Moreover, as Trigger points out, "a view of prehistory which saw the Western European nations rather than the Arab peoples as the true heirs of the ancient civilizations of the Near East helped to justify Europe's colonial interventions in that region."[38]

An even greater impetus to archaeological activities in the empire was the rise of Hellenism in Europe during the eighteenth and nineteenth centuries. An important aspect of Hellenism was its political incarnation, philhellenism, and the international support that it garnered for the Greek War of Independence (1821–32). Numerous American, British, and German Hellenophiles joined the war effort of the 1820s, including probably the most illustrious among them, Lord Byron. In 1832 Greece wrested its independence from the Ottoman Empire. According to the narrative of philhellenism, after nearly two millennia of imperial rule—first under the Byzantines and then under the Ottomans—a newly defined Greek nation could reunite with its glorified ancient heritage and, led by monarchs of German and Danish ancestry, revive the traditions that had inspired western Europe to greatness. Yet Hellenism had to be invented in Europe as the cornerstone of Western Civilization before it could be imported to Greece as a nationalist movement. A combination of the real and imagined culture of the ancient Greeks became, in various guises, a heritage to which all could lay claim. While within Greece archaeology served an "ethnogenetic" function whereby "the tracing of the antiquity of the ethnic constituent of a present nation restores a pseudo-historical sense of continuity and legitimizes the present," outside Greece as well the ancient past could serve any number of modern claims to cultural hegemony via participation in ancient traditions.[39] Moreover, the construction of ancient Greece, through texts as well as artifacts, as the site of the childhood of Europe served to disassociate the modern inhabitants of Greece from their local archaeological heritage and lent even more credence to the European imperial project.

Had Europe never discovered, invented, rediscovered, and reinvented the ancients for changing political and philosophical needs and tastes over the course of the past half millennium, the shared culture of the civilization in which we live would be remarkably different. Before embarking on a study of how the Ottoman Empire came to adopt one of the end results of this obsession with the ancients—that of the collection and organization of their material remains—it is essential to consider, if only briefly, the processes through which Europeans began to use ancient Greek artifacts as emblems of modern identity. Hellenism became a pan-European endeavor that spanned the course of many centuries and found varied forms of expression in different countries.

In Italy people began to excavate archaeological artifacts as early as the fifteenth century. In the early sixteenth century Raphael became the first legal inspector general of antiquities.[40] By the seventeenth century several members of the British aristocracy had burgeoning collections of Greek and Roman antiquities.[41] Although an awareness of ancient Greek and an appreciation for the classics had been a staple of Western education since the Renaissance, "until the late eighteenth century, most educated [western] Europeans regarded their culture as Roman and Christian in origin, with merely peripheral roots in Greece."[42] However, in the face of the growing strength of France in the late nineteenth century and its self-styled affiliations with the Roman Republic, associations with ancient Greece began to appear as a mode of cultural resistance in both Germany and Britain.

The publication of Johann Winkelmann's *History of Ancient Art* in 1764 revitalized Europe's peripheral interest in Greek art through the classics. More important than his actual interpretations of individual works, his analysis suggested a utopic world that could be seen and even reconstituted outside of Greece through the aesthetics of ancient works of art. The aesthetic observations he made became models for the political ideals that ancient Greece was supposed to represent. He was the first to conceive of art as a national-cultural product and thus began a tradition through which the display of art in national museums could signify national success and progress.[43]

As Suzanne Marchand explains, "the elective affinity Germans of the late eighteenth century discovered between themselves and the supposedly noble, naive Greeks became a constantly recurring motif" as Hellenism became an integral part of the Prussian educational system in the early nineteenth century, even despite some local opposition to the adoption of a foreign national culture.[44] By idealizing both domains, Germans came to conflate modern Germany with the ancient Greek world. By the end of the nineteenth century, for example, the archaeologist Ernst Curtius could justify large-scale archaeological expeditions to Greece by simply explaining that "Germany has herself inwardly appropriated Greek culture."[45]

Similarly, in England ancient Greece became a model for nineteenth-century citizens. An 1826 guidebook to the British Museum even suggested that England could itself be ancient Greece reborn. As Inderpal Grewal points out, "Greek art was interpreted as validating and inscribing English values. . . . Classicism was believed to be the apotheosis of all art forms, one that was seen as part of the European heritage. It stood as proof of the superiority of the West over the barbaric East; as such it presented one more reason for the civilization of the East through European colonization."[46] As in Germany, the aesthetics of ancient art suggested political and cultural models for contemporary emulation. Ancient statues came to represent not a foreign culture but a modern and local one. Hellenism eventually spread back to France where, in claiming to have given birth to the art museum as a public institution, that country proclaimed itself the inheritor and embodiment of classical civilization.[47]

Aside from encompassing the patrimony of the modern Greek nation, the European gaze on the continuity of Greece in its locational exile in western European cultural traditions permitted classical archaeology to develop as the supposedly "neutral" center of the history of art.[48] This ideological need for the ancients played a vital role in informing the disciplines of architecture, archaeology, and art history, which worked in tandem to unearth and to analyze the aesthetic remains of the ancients for the consumption and elucidation of the modern world. As Stathis Gourgouris points out, the rise of Hellenism coincides with the rise of Orientalism. Its discourse produced a just, logical, and dominant image of the West in opposition to the lascivious, curious, and dominable East. Thus it provided a means of producing a beloved, idealized self for the colonial Other.[49] The construction of an imaginary Orient was well mirrored by the construction of an equally imaginary ancient Greece: much like Jerusalem, however, Winkelmann and the German intellectuals who shared his romantic, Protestant traditions felt no need to experience Greece as a true location. As Richard Jenkyns explains, "To the German mind, Hellas became a sort of heavenly city, a shimmering fantasy on the far horizon."[50] As the disci-

pline of Orientalism developed, it similarly depended on absence: "It allowed the European to know the East better than those who actually lived
there could. The fact that Sacy, Renan, and others could do this without
setting eyes on the regions they studied only reinforced the message that
the European's power of the East was justified by their knowledge of it."[51]
The simultaneous invisibility of the counterutopic East and the utopias of
Jerusalem and Greece that resided within it produced the equally protean,
equally undefinable but mirror images of East and West on which both the
narratives of Hellenism and Orientalism relied. The physical counterparts
to these imaginary utopias—modern Greece and Palestine in contradistinction to the Ottoman Empire—all had to contend with constructing
identities in an era from which they were epistemically excluded.

If, as Gourgouris suggests, "colonial mastery is implicated within a
scopic economy," Europe art-historically colonized the past of ancient
Greece even as it encouraged the formulation and institution of Greece as
a modern nation.[52] Greece may have gained independence from the Ottoman Empire, but it did so only under the guidance of European monarchs who had refashioned themselves as ancient Greeks and thus shunted
aside the more fragmented histories and assorted progeny of the ancients.

Indeed, without the extensive theorization and imagination of ancient
Greece already under way in Europe, the directors of modern Greece's national cause would have had a hard time resurrecting ancient Greece as a
symbol for the modern state and might have chosen other primary tropes
for unification. The Greek Renaissance of the 1770s depended heavily on
the direct translation of French Enlightenment texts and thus translated
the neo-Hellenic image produced by the European Enlightenment into a
neo-Hellenic image for modern Greek culture. Whereas in Europe ancient
ruins only signified a romantic past, for Greeks they came to delineate a
symbolic present. Ancient monuments became ready-made national symbols culled from the past but given content via Europe.[53]

In light of the important symbolic role of antiquities in Europe and in
Greece, what was the Ottoman Empire to make of the considerable collection of Hellenistic antiquities lying under its own soil? On the one hand,
the appropriation of these statues as a part of the national patrimony could
represent the Ottoman Empire as integral to the cultural heritage already
on display in the museums of Europe. On the other hand, these very statues had been adopted as national symbols by a newly independent
province—the existence of which served as the concrete representation of
"civilization in predetermined confrontation with [Ottoman] barbarism."[54]
The Ottoman Empire could not simply appropriate the ancient Greek past

in the footsteps of its European counterparts, in part because its history actually did bear the remains of that legacy, physically and politically. Although the empire could not adopt the symbolism of classicism or Hellenism, it used the collection and display of antiquities to create symbolism out of the very act of possession.

Europe's affinity with ancient Greece left the newborn nation of Greece in an awkward double bind. Identifying ancient Greece as the "childhood of Europe," Winkelmann gave the patrimony of Greece to western Europe, leaving only more modern sites of heritage to the modern Greeks. Michael Herzfeld suggests that "the West supported the Greeks on the implicit assumption that the Greeks would reciprocally accept the role of living ancestors of European civilization." As Greece tried to nationalize its archaeological narrative, he continues, "unlike their European patrons, the Greeks were not seeking a return to a Classical *past;* they were instead seeking inclusion in the European *present.*"[55]

Ironically, the situation was not very different in the Ottoman Empire, from whose lands many material treasures of the Greco-Roman and biblical pasts emerged. Like modern Greece, the late Ottoman Empire (as well as modern Turkey) sits in an ambiguous position: "neither wholly 'us,' those who practice academic research, nor entirely 'them,' those who are practiced upon."[56] However, whereas Europe cast modern Greeks and the modern inhabitants of Palestine alike "in the role of living ancestors for European civilization," the Ottoman Empire and modern Turkey (as well as modern Arab nations) received no role at all.

In contemporary historiography the legacy of classical and biblical archaeology has been meted away from the Republic of Turkey (the chief heir to the cultural legacy of the Ottomans) and given to Greece and Israel, respectively. Consider, for example, the unintended double meaning of Stephen Dyson's critique of classical, as opposed to anthropological, archaeology: "While young Turks in anthropological archaeology have been slaying their ancestors, the dutiful in classical archaeology have been worshipping theirs."[57] Turks have been written out of the story of rediscovering the ancient world via the modern to such an extext that the fact that the historical Young Turks were indeed fighting classical archaeology rarely surfaces in rewriting the historiography of the discipline. Indeed, in this sense the conflation of ancient Greece and the modern nation-state has been successful. In the eighteenth and nineteenth centuries, however, it was the Ottoman Empire in which Europeans traveled to access both regions. It was the Ottoman Empire whose laws had to be circumvented to export antiquities, and it was the bureaucrats of the Ottoman Empire who had to be tricked into acquiescing. While both ancient Greece and the Holy Land had long been imagined as shining utopic visions, their production as physical locations and their subsequent cartographic and archaeological exploration coincided with the very material growth of European colonialism. As Ian Morris explains, "If philology gave western academics the tools to possess ancient Greece and to trace a line of power from it, archaeology took the matter one step further. By filling national museums with Greek statues and vases, governments could show their commitment to Hellenism and their civilized status, and also the strength of their power over ancient Greece"[58] and, I would argue, the Holy Land to which Britain would soon lay claim.

The dual nature of the biblical and Greek heritage for Europe was not lost on Ernest Renan, a French intellectual of the late nineteenth century who was as contemptuous of Constantinople as he was laudatory of Athens and Jerusalem. "If there is such a thing as one miraculous history, there are at least three," he wrote. "Judea's lot was religion, Greece's truth and beauty, Rome's might."[59] Clearly, that Rome was not Constantinople. In a letter of 1865 he writes:

> Constantinople is certainly a marvel in its way. It is the city of painters and the picturesque. Its ensembles are without equal in the world. But this is all. With the exception of Saint Sophia and one or two Byzantine remains, there is not a single beautiful building, nothing which bears analysing, bad taste carried to its extreme; everything is made to satisfy an ephemeral caprice and for show. . . . This city appears to me like a city of monkeys, a sort of perpetual capital, founded by this worthy Constantine, for ignominy, intrigue, and baseness.[60]

As a prime theorist of nationalism, Renan without a doubt promoted a hierarchy of nations, in which the Ottoman presence because of its Islamic nature acted as poison for the histories of its territories embedded in the miraculous. The ultimate contrast, for him, against the Islamic absence of reason, which he expounded in his 1883 lecture, *L'Islamisme et la science*, was "the Greek achievement, that is to say science," which would "continue forever," along with the "mark of Israel [that] will be eternal."[61] How could the Ottoman Empire respond? Beyond Namık Kemal's extensive defense against the lecture, what could the empire do on a public stage?[62] Archaeology allowed the empire to use the vocabulary of Europe's cultural capital in order to re-vision its position in relation to that capital and thus in relation to culture defined as European. In the words of Frantz Fanon, "to speak means to be in a position to use a certain syntax, to grasp the morphology of this or that language, but it means above all to assume a culture, to support the weight of a civilization."[63] Archaeology was the syntax that let the Ottoman Empire assume—take for granted—its participation within Europe and thus to respeak and in so doing unravel the narratives of its civilization.

Whereas biblical archaeology provided a narrative of scientific legitimacy for Christian conservatives in Europe, Greek antiquities provided an entrée into the birth of Europe. Much as "many Greek intellectuals were as keen as those in the West to promote a Hellenist reading of antiquity, which gave Greece a special place in Europe,"[64] members of the Ottoman elite hoped to become acknowledged as a seminal site for European culture rather than be excluded from the narratives of its supremacy. Moreover, an association with ancient Greece would link the empire with modern science and distance it from the narrative of irrationalism associated with religion, particularly Islam, which had not entered a secular phase, in contemporary European discourse. If, as one archaeologist suggests, "archaeology, especially in its modernist form, has been formed on the premise of a sense of loss, its subject matter conceived to be the recovery of tradition and a sense of community in contrast to the feeling of disenchantment for the world in which they live,"[65] then for the Ottomans, the archaeological recovery of a Greek past could compensate for the modern Ottoman loss of power. Moreover, it could recast the tropes of modernity being borrowed from Western Civilization within a new originary mythology for the empire.

As in Greece, this fascination with the ancient world ran the risk of perpetuating the Ottoman reliance on Western approval of their use of Greek heritage. The ways in which the Ottoman Empire used its practices of archaeology and museum display served to allay this risk, constructing instead a peculiarly non-European mode of speaking the Greek past into an Ottoman territorial present.

Still a primary locus of Orientalist fascination, the Ottoman Empire of the nineteenth century was attempting to reconfigure its identity as congruent with European practices and institutions. The collection of antiquities and the development of a museum to house them played a symbolic role in representing the new cultural aspirations of the Ottoman state. The Greco-Roman heart of European civilization, the neoclassical architecture of humanism, became usurped as indigenous to Ottoman territory and entered a parallel construction of Helleno-Byzantine heritage. On the one hand, the Ottoman Empire used its a priori ownership of Helleno-Byzantine antiquities to include itself in the club of nations that traced their cultural heritage to the ancients and thus constructed a shared experience of "Western Civilization." On the other hand, it displayed its qualifications as a modern European state through its possession of a contemporary cultural institution like the museum.

Between the mid-nineteenth century and the early twentieth, the modes through which the Ottoman Empire expressed the value of archaeological antiquities traced an ambivalent path between the simultaneous assimilation of European values and the growth of nationalist consciousness. Soon after the establishment of the dual collections in the armory, antiquities stole the center stage of the Ottoman museum from military memorabilia. Thereafter Helleno-Byzantine artifacts formed the backbone of the Imperial Museum enterprise. The collection of the material remains of other cultures—such as the Hittites, Assyrians, or Phoenicians—could have, at least in part, marked the new interest in local subterranean material culture. It did not. The collection of non–Greco-Roman artifacts from Ottoman lands would have emphasized the links between the Ottoman Empire and the East, at a time when many Ottoman statesmen were coming to regard their empire as geographically European.[66] The collection of the artifacts of other Anatolian peoples was as yet tangential to the primary task of collecting Helleno-Byzantine artifacts that could capitalize on the actual and symbolic value of their Greco-Roman counterparts in European imaginings, writings, and collections since the eighteenth century. Perhaps just as important to the collections ultimately included in the Ottoman Imperial Museum was timing: by the time antiquities gained cultural and political value in the empire, many of the ancient antiquities from Eastern territories, such as Ninevah and Egypt, had already left the empire. When, near the turn of the century, major non–Greco-Roman finds—such as the Ishtar gate of Babylon, discovered by Robert Koldeway—came to light, they did not fit with the existing collections of the Imperial Museum, which already emphasized the empire's Greco-Roman heritage.

This issue of timing was perhaps convenient, as the primary goal of the museum was to render the empire closer to Europe. As Frederick Bohrer points out, "Assyrian and other nonclassical antiquities . . . embody particularly the exotic. For the more strongly we cling to the Greco-Roman tradition as that of our distant forebears, the more we delimit other antique cultures as foreign."[67] The collection and display of Helleno-Byzantine artifacts from Ottoman territories showed Europe that the empire was a primary repository of the heritage claimed by the Occident and thus automatically interjected the empire into a collective, pan-European experience of cultural memory. Moreover, by controlling the acquisition of archaeological goods, the Ottomans effectively regulated European access to a heritage that many European nations claimed.

For the first time in the empire, heritage became inextricably linked to the land rather than to government or religion. Anything that had been produced on Ottoman soil eventually was incorporated into the Ottoman legacy, much as the histories of all peoples having lived on Turkish soil would someday enter the historical narrative of the Republic of Turkey. This process began with the collection of Helleno-Byzantine artifacts. By adopting the practice of collecting these artifacts, the Ottoman Empire attempted to acquire the cultural capital, and the cultural heritage embedded in that capital, that Europe claimed through the ownership and appreciation of such works. Through laws, excavations, publications, and museum displays, the valuation of antiquities began to express a hybrid Ottoman national identity, at once belonging to and in conflict with the sultan and at once part of and in opposition to Europe. This identity became increasingly tied to Ottoman territories and to the objects that had been made on those territories, as can be seen in the successive antiquities laws of 1876, 1884, and 1906 discussed in later chapters.

THE EARLY YEARS OF ARCHAEOLOGY IN OTTOMAN TERRITORIES

The general interest in particular pre-Turkic Anatolian and Thracian cultures became increasingly concrete with the growth of antiquities collection and the development of formal archaeology over the course of the nineteenth century and its predilection for ancient Greek artifacts. In 1784 the French ambassador to Constantinople, the Comte de Choiseul-Gouffier, sent an agent to Athens with an official permit allowing him to draw and make casts of antiquities, indicating that the Ottoman government already kept track of European interest in antiquities. However, the comte's interests far surpassed the permission he had received. He instructed his agent, "Take everything you can. Do not neglect any opportunity for looting all that is lootable in Athens and the environs. Spare neither the living nor the dead."[68]

In 1800 Lord Elgin's similar disregard for Ottoman possession of antiquities coupled with his interest in the Parthenon marbles led to one of the earliest conflicts between a European collector and the Ottoman state. In that year Lord Elgin, acting consul of England to Constantinople, assembled a team of artists to aid him in documenting the architecture and sculpture of the Athens Acropolis. As soon as they had set up their scaffolding to take casts of the monuments, the military governor of Athens attempted to curtail their activities by declaring all military installations—including the Acropolis—closed to foreigners. Lord Elgin successfully circumvented this order through an appeal to the sultan. The original decree issued by the sultan is missing, but the Italian translation sent to Elgin's team remains. According to this decree,

> the said five artists dwelling in that place shall be employed in going in and out of the citadel of Athens which is the place of observation; or in fixing scaffolding around the ancient Temple of the Idols, or in modeling with chalk or gypsum the said ornaments and visible figures; or in measuring the fragments and vestiges of other ruined buildings; or in excavating when they find it necessary the foundations in search of inscriptions among the rubbish. . . . And that no one meddle with their scaffolding or implements nor hinder them from taking away any pieces of stone with inscriptions and figures.[69]

Although classical scholars in Europe had only recently begun to incorporate the practice of archaeological collection into the study of the ancients, this directive suggests that the Ottoman government already had a good idea of the types of activities in which they might be interested. The ability of collectors to make models and take measurements on Ottoman territories depended on explicit permission from the central government. Although no law prohibited the export of antiquities, there was still a need to receive permission for their removal. If Ottomans had not recognized a value in antiquities, the removal of the carved stones would have carried no more meaning than the removal of clods of dirt and would have elicited no concern. Even with the permission granted by the decree, Lord Elgin's team encountered local resistance and was only able to affect the large-scale export of the Parthenon's friezes by bribing local officials with cut glass and firearms.[70]

Like the Parthenon marbles, the Aigina sculptures left the empire under contested circumstances. In 1814 an excavation team led by the British traveler C. K. Cockerell set out to collect marble antiquities from the island of Aigina, south of Athens, without permission from the central government. They worked at night, telling the locals who tried to keep them away that they had decrees permitting their work. As they uncovered marbles, they immediately loaded them on to a ship waiting in the harbor. Thus when local officials laid formal claim to the antiquities, they were easily removed from the empire before officials could confiscate them.[71] Although not governed by express legislation, the excavators were aware that their actions were not sanctioned. Once the marbles had been exported from the empire, French, Bavarian, and English agents chased the shipment around the Mediterranean as each nation sought the marbles as a physical manifestation of their archaeological and territorial power.[72]

The value that had begun to be associated with antiquities was expressed not only through obstacles to their export but also through their use as gifts to Europeans. As early as 1838 Sultan Mahmut II gave a group of reliefs from Assos to King Louis-Philippe of France as a gesture of friendship.[73] Even after the institution of increasingly strict antiquities laws, such personal gifts from the sultan to European monarchs would continue to underscore the right of the ruler to dispose of the goods of the country at will, thus using them to attest his personal ownership of the Ottoman territories and their products.

With the establishment of the Magazine of Antiquities in 1846, the Ottoman government declared its interest in and appreciation for antiquities through an institutional format learned from Europe and thus legible to it: the museum. The founding document of the dual collections defined the antiquities neither in terms of their periodization nor in terms of their historical or aesthetic value but in terms of their appearance—as "depictions of humans and animals, and other various antiquities."[74] Presumably the objects collected were valued not so much for their historical or cultural worth but for the political significance they gained through European appreciation.

At these early stages of museological presentation in the Ottoman empire, terminology provides insights into Ottoman perceptions of the developing institution. The term *mecmua* means both "collection" and "magazine," much as it did in nineteenth-century English. The word has no inherent implication of exhibition. However, the document cited above that established the new display spaces refers to them as *müze*, or museum. While at times some other terms, such as *numunehane* (sample-house) or *müzehane* (museum-house), were occasionally—and apparently arbitrarily—used to refer to the museum, this word adopted from French remained the primary reference for the new institution. The use of *numunehane* is of particular interest, as it suggests that the Ottoman understanding of the museum was more as a space of erudite sampling and organization than one of display.[75] However, its use seems to have been exceptional. As for the term *müzehane*, it seems to refer to the museum as institution more than to the specific physical museum building and collections. The Ottomans could have adopted a word from the existing language, much as the Arabs adopted the word *mathaf* as a locus for valuable and rare objects, or they could have continued to use the term *mecmua* to refer to the developing institution. That they ultimately chose neither of these options indicates that the museum was perceived as an institution to be learned from existing European examples and adapted to Ottoman needs. Still, that the collections were not yet designated as a museum suggests that even in Ottoman eyes they still lacked some of the attributes that such an institution would require.

The collection of antiquities by Ottoman officials increased slowly after the establishment of the Magazine of Antiquities. In 1847 a governor in the province of Jerusalem sent sketches of "reliefs on antique marble" and attempted to identify them historically. In addition to making such reports to the capital, he arranged for the collection of antiquities around Jerusalem in a local storage area. Similarly, officials in Aleppo sent a list of works to the capital that cited ceramics, statues, and coins that had been found in that province.[76] When the French traveler Maxime de Camp tried to acquire a statue in Aydin in 1850, local officials confiscated it. He was only able to make a plaster cast once it was in the burgeoning antiquities collection in the capital.[77] In June 1851 a functionary of the Ministry of Public Works sent the statuette of a nymph found at Seisebil in Crete to Constantinople. In March of the same year, an inscribed stone was reported found at Varna (in modern Bulgaria); the following year, when the German traveler Heinrich Petermann passed through, he could only find a copy of the inscription written on the wall of the café, as the piece had been incorporated into the imperial collections.[78] These incidents suggest that a mechanism for the collection of antiquities may have been established in conjunction with the institution of the magazine and also indicate that officials sent to various parts of the empire had received instructions concerning the centralized collection of antiquities.

By this time Europeans had grown accustomed to the practice of requesting official permission to excavate and export antiquities. For example, on hearing of the traveler Charles Fellows's tour to Lycea on the island of Rhodes, the trustees of the British Museum tried to arrange for a decree that would help in the export of sculptures. Denied permission at first, by 1841 he was allowed to remove "the sculptured stones, lying down, and of no use, at a place near the village Kinik." In the absence of any mechanism to stop him, Fellows took this as a license to excavate and remove an entire temple to the British Museum.

Similarly, when C. T. Newton applied for a decree to excavate the Halicarnassus mausoleum in Bodrum in 1852, his permission was slow to arrive, so he began exploring in 1855 without a permit. After determining the foundations of the mausoleum (and digging through the dirt floors of two homes in the process), he was still very eager to remove the lion sculptures embedded in the Bodrum castle walls that had initially spurred him to ask for the decree. Instead of granting him permission, however, the local commander received orders to remove the lions that Newton had requested (fig. 6) and to send them to the Imperial Museum. As I discuss in chapter 3, the exhibition of these lions in the Imperial Museum would become symbolic of Ottoman control over antiquities. Nonetheless, the nascent possessiveness of the Ottoman government over antiquities was still erratic: only one year later Newton received permission to excavate at Didima and exported twelve statues to the British Museum. Similarly, the Ottoman government gave the railway engineer John T. Wood free rein to export any antiquities he might find during his excavations at Ephesus.[79]

When archaeologists failed to follow the stipulations of excavation and export permits, the Ottoman government often stood in the way of their activities. When Newton applied for a decree to permit his excavations in 1869, he learned that the Ottoman government was upset that the British Museum had never given it any of the duplicate statues found at the excavation of Cyrene by Smith and Porcher. To help Newton obtain the new decree, the British Museum returned some of the sculptures and gave a small collection of vases and figurines to the Imperial Museum.[80] Such an exchange implies that the value of antiquities was perceived as interchangeable. Excavation did not serve to contextualize artifacts in a historical framework but to acquire beautiful pieces with which to decorate museums.

By the time Heinrich Schliemann excavated Troy in 1870, the Ottoman government had established a consistent pattern of granting foreigners permission to excavate at their own cost provided that half of the antiquities found would go to the Ottoman government. In similar arrangements, the Russian excavator Ispandoni and the English excavator Kastos were each granted half of their finds. In contrast, when imperial subjects happened on valuable antiquities, common practice seems to have allotted them a reward of one-third the value of the find.[81] Although Turkish sources do not cite either practice as an officially legislated law, the visiting archaeologist Albert Dumont made reference to both in 1867, indicating that they were well known among European archaeologists.[82] When Schliemann broke such an agreement and secretly exported all of his finds to Greece in 1874, the Ottoman government used the court system to sue him for its half of the Trojan antiquities and received monetary compensation. Although Schliemann was able to receive additional per-

Fig. 6. C. T. Newton with Hellenistic lion sculptures at Halicarnassus [Stoneman]

mits for excavation, the museum always hired armed guards to watch his sites and excavation teams.[83]

Museum catalogs rarely mentioned how objects arrived in the museums of western Europe. The politics of acquisition becomes neutralized by the production of legends about real archaeologists, such as Lord Elgin and Heinrich Schliemann, as well as through the glamorization of the archaeologist in film. From the 1932 Hollywood horror film *The Mummy* to the 1981 *Raiders of the Lost Ark*, archaeologists recover the hidden past of civilization in exotic and dangerous third world lands.[84] Such public narratives divest museum objects of their geographic heritage, so that once in the museums objects of ancient art lose any connection to the physical world and context from which they have been exhumed. Invested with modern interpretations of the ancient world and divested from their physical origins, ancient sculptures have in large part become the cultural property of western Europe.

DISPLAY STRATEGIES IN THE MAGAZINE OF ANTIQUITIES

A 1910 account relating the foundation of the Magazine of Antiquities suggests that the collection was used as an institution for the indirect representation of the sultan. It relates that as Sultan Abdülmecid was hunting in the outskirts of İstanbul, his horse stumbled on some inscribed stones. When Abdülmecid learned that these gilt inscriptions commemorated none other than Constantine, founder of the city, he commanded that they be removed to a place of honor, as such a name should not be left in the dust.[85] The earliest catalogs of the museum collections, published many years later, in 1869 and 1871, show no records of such stones. While these stones may not have been real, the story symbolizes the initial function of the magazine to link the contemporary ruler with the power of antiquity, as embodied in objects.

The growing European interest in the antiquities found on Ottoman soil spurred the Ottoman government to shift the modes through which it collected and appreciated ancient works. Thus the government began to encourage the active collection of antiquities by provincial officials and to sanction the collection of antiquities in the capital. As members of the elite sent objects to the magazine, those in charge of the collection placed them haphazardly, extending the role of the military storehouse to antiquities. No acquisition records were kept at all until 1850. Between 1850 and 1869, when the first director was appointed to the collections, the few records that were kept mentioned little other than the year of acquisition, the province from which the object was acquired, and sometimes the name of the donor. At this stage the magazine functioned as a private collection for the pleasure of the sultan, with no pretense to public edification. In viewing the collections, the sultan could frame himself as a European monarch, with new types of interests absent from the lives of earlier sultans. The specific contents of the collection were irrelevant to their primary function—to display the sultan as a modern, or at least Europeanized, ruler through the fact of his collection of antiquities.

Flaubert and Gautier had remarkably little to say about the small antiquities collection. Flaubert summarized it briefly: "There is also at the palace a museum of antiquities: a statuette of a comedian with a masque; a few busts, a few pots, two stones with Egyptian characters."[86] Gautier seemed slightly more impressed by the small collection: "Of particular note, to be taken as a sign of progress: there are assembled in the courtyard that precedes the ancient church of St. Irene, transformed into an arsenal, and which is part of the palace, diverse antique objects: heads, torsos, bas-reliefs, inscriptions, tombs, the rudiments of a Byzantine museum, which could become curious through the addition of daily discoveries."[87] Although the collection was quite new, it was shown to these European visitors as a sign of the cultural modernization and Westernization of the empire. Unimpressed by the modern displays of weapons, Gautier mentions the Magazine of Antiquities not with admiration for the objects within but as a "sign of progress"—the very reason for its institution. The implication of progress through the identification with antiquities holds an irony that exposes the primacy of form over content in the quest for the modern.

The first catalog of the Magazine of Antiquities, compiled in 1868 by Dumont, provides an invaluable record of the early display strategies of the collection. The deficiencies he perceived illuminate his expectations for the Ottoman museum as much as they describe the actual displays in it. Whereas he expected an antiquities collection organized according to taxonomic typology and strictly sequestered from other types of collections, he instead found a mix of objects whose display failed to address the tenets of art historical identification, labeling, and order in vogue in Europe.

> The statues, inscriptions, and bas reliefs in the halls of St. Irene are displayed with no order; many, hidden by objects that have no relation to archaeology, can only be examined unsatisfactorily. . . . [The] [m]obile labels, very easy to move, only give the vaguest information about the origins of objects found outside of Constantinople. One can only wish that the Ottoman Porte will find a European archaeologist to classify all these antiquities.[88]

Responding to the absence of internal cohesion he perceived in the display, Dumont chose to organize his article according to a typological categorization that he saw as appropriate for the collection. Nonetheless, his description provides an idea of what types of objects were located in which parts of the former church. The magazine consisted of a large closed hall with glass cases; an exterior courtyard to the right of the entryway; the gallery, which housed the museum of the Janissaries, as well as some antiquities; and the courtyard preceding the entrance to the museum. The exterior courtyard had only one antiquity, a sarcophagus attributed to Phedre and Hypolite. Other antiquities—including the head of the serpent monument from the Hippodrome, two colossal heads of Medusa, statues of Venus and Diana, Roman portrait sculptures, and several relief panels—were housed primarily in the closed hall of the magazine. A few funerary stelae were displayed alongside the Janissary mannequins in the gallery. These funerary stelae shown in conjunction with the Janissary mannequins, as well as the placement of sarcophagi outside of the museum, seem to have augmented the overall program through which the two collections acted in conjunction. The main exhibit hall, however, seems to have contained a haphazard selection of antiquities with an independent exhibitionary logic based on contents, not on preexisting typologies.

Dumont's description serves as a rudimentary guide to the spaces of the magazine. Déthier's brief description, published in the same year, pays more attention to the provenance of the works in the collection but gives no indication of their arrangement. He describes the room devoted to the collection of antiquities as full to overflowing with "a sarcophagus brought from Salonica with depictions of Hypolite brought in for its protection . . . four inscriptions from Dreros on Crete, a large bronze disk depicting the Phoenician goddess Astarte brought from Lampsacus, and . . . [of particular importance] a piece of a relief from the Mausoleum depicting Amazons." He continues: "In the same section there are a group of inscriptions in cuneiform that were sent by Midhat Pasha from Baghdad, four stones with inscriptions that have been understood to not be hieroglyphs brought from Hama as a gift from Sabri Pasha, a bronze statue of Hercules, a bronze statue found in pieces in Tarsus and among them inscriptions stemming from the Byzantine protective corps of the Princes Got and Bauvacier."[89]

This wide variety of provenances suggests that even before formal orders had been distributed to the provinces, progressive members of the Ottoman elite were already eager to participate in the formation of an imperial antiquities collection in the capital. In particular, the participation of Midhat Pasha, one of the prime reformers of the Tanzimat, in the collection of antiquities underscores the drive toward Westernization that fueled the formation of the early collection. The early inclusion in the museum collection of one of the friezes from the Bodrum mausoleum underscores the nascent interest in removing antiquities from sites in order to preempt European acquisition efforts: this panel was probably one of the works that had been recovered from Newton.

Although Dumont's primary interest was in the archaeological collection, the proximity of the antiquities and the military collection made it impossible for him to entirely ignore the weapons pervading the building. As often as not, items in the poorly documented antiquities collection were partially hidden behind military objects or mannequins of Janissaries. Dumont indicates that about one-third of the antiquities were located not in the section set aside for antiquities but in the Janissary gallery. Initially posited as separate entities accessed through opposing portals, the two collections instead intertwined to produce the covalent meanings implicit in the museum's agenda.

Dumont interpreted what he saw as the museum's shortcomings as the best efforts of novice collectors and curators. Yet these apparent failures point to the differences between his (European) approach to the collections and that of its Ottoman owners. To Dumont's chagrin, the labels that occasionally accompanied the antiquities only mentioned provenance insofar as the objects came from various regions in the empire. For the Ottomans arranging the exhibit, unlike for Dumont, the ownership of these objects, rather than their accurate situation in a narrative of classicism, was of primary importance. For the Ottomans, these antiquities acted less as relics of antiquity than as signs of modernity, signaled by participation in the act of collecting antiquity that already consumed intellectuals in the West. They did not seek to produce a representative or encyclopedic sampling of ancient art. They did not propose to construct the type of taxonomically complete collection that contemporary European and American museums craved. Rather the eclectic collection in their possession marked their control over these antiquities, particularly when juxtaposed to symbols of military dominion. As Gautier had inadvertently surmised, for the Ottomans, the primary function of the magazines was to serve as a sign of progress, not a reference for erudition.

The program of linking contemporary lands to Helleno-Byzantine pasts was central to the initial program of the dual military and antiquities collections. Sarcophagi placed strategically around the former church reinforced the relationship between the military collections and the Byzantine heritage of the city suggested by the commingling of the artillery and antiquity collections. The sarcophagi exhibited immediately outside the church building underscored the themes of antiquity and artillery played out in the collections. Gautier reported, "Near to the church, two or three porphyry sarcophagi, decorated with the Greek cross, which must have contained the corpses of emperors and empresses, deprived of their damaged lids, collect water from the sky."[90] These had been discovered only a year after the institution of the collection, in the second courtyard of the palace, and were soon moved to the exterior of the former church. Dethièr reports that a number of sarcophagi were also located in the courtyard between the two marble portals.[91] In 1892 Grosvenor recognized these sarcophagi as imperial. He identified the three sarcophagi outside the church as belonging to Emperor Theodosius the Great, Constantius II, Saint Helen (removed from her tomb in Rome), and Saint Helen's son the emperor Constantine.[92] As for the sarcophagi in the atrium, they were now accompanied by the chain (fig. 7) designed by the Byzantines to close off the Golden Horn to invaders but circumvented by the Ottomans. The kettle drums of the Janissaries stood in front of the sarcophagi, again layering the intertwined themes of cultural and military domination.

Even before visitors to the collections entered the defunct church, they were greeted by sarcophagi identified with the chief characters in the his-

Fig. 7. Chain commemorating the conquest of Constantinople, on display in the atrium of the former Church of Hagia Irene [Mordtmann]

tory of the city. Although the accuracy of the attributions is questionable, these sarcophagi constructed a conceptual frame for the display. Byzantine sarcophagi in the museum's atrium represented the physical death of the Byzantine rulers, just as the chain lying before the sarcophagus represented the metaphorical death of their empire. This atrium, located between a collection of weapons and a collection of antiquities, visually delineated the military and cultural processes through which the Ottoman Empire had laid claim to preceding cultures. Nearby, the bell of the former Church of Hagia Sophia lay dormant, again testifying to the imperial changing of the guard. Thus the museum told a story claiming participation in European culture through a remote history of possession and conquest. Even without the taxonomic guise that Dumont desired, the collection of antiquities in this context served to represent the state primarily to foreigners, who at the very least became aware of the empire's nascent attempts to establish modern institutions symbolic of European-style modernity. The absence of such a taxonomic or scientific focus in the collections served to underscore the ideological objectives of the museum—

not to gain power through the ownership of universal knowledge, but through the possession of history and its territories.

Under a single roof, the Magazine of Ancient Weapons and the Magazine of Antiquities represented the state by displaying a military history of imperial conquest alongside a shared heritage with the West, represented by Helleno-Byzantine antiquities. The museum thus incorporated these past civilizations into the Ottoman in two complementary guises—through the relics of military conquest and through the symbols of cultural adoption.

In Europe the appreciation and collection of Greco-Roman antiquities followed centuries of intense interest in classical studies, particularly philosophical and philological. In contrast, intellectuals of the Ottoman Empire did not become aware of the ancient world until their increased contact with western Europe in the late eighteenth century. While the Ottoman interest in the classics would never rival that in Europe, the education of Ottoman subjects in France led to an increased awareness of both classical writings and their path of transmission through medieval Arabic sources. In conjunction with a newfound interest in the classics, popular journals began to publish articles discussing ancient thinkers and their philosophies. To maintain the guise of Islamic propriety, they often emphasized that ancient knowledge had only been maintained through Arabic translations of scientific texts.[93] The adoption of Helleno-Byzantine antiquities as part of the Ottoman patrimony, literally emergent from Ottoman lands and communicable to Europeans only by permission of the Muslim state, paralleled the idea that the scientific knowledge that had led Europe to greatness relied on its passage through Islamic texts. Similarly, the possession of Hellenistic antiquities relied on its passage through the Islamic territories of the Ottoman Empire and reframed European reliance on the East in a secular context.

Increased contact with Europe during the nineteenth century made elite members of the Ottoman government aware of the importance of Greco-Roman artifacts to the cultural practices of Europe. The Ottoman adoption of the Greco-Roman legacy, an ideological tool for Greek independence, subverted its original use: it transformed Hellenism into a means through which the Ottoman Empire could partake in the Western heritage and at the same time declare its territorial sovereignty.

The museum thrust the public representation of the Ottoman Empire into a modern time frame demarcated by the very act of collection and the strategies of display. No matter how jarring a visitor such as Dumont found the disorder of objects, Ahmet Fethi Pasha did not feel the need to create a taxonomy for the objects in the museum, except for classifying the two collections in opposition to each other. Although after his extended stay in Europe he was probably conscious of the organizational strategies of European museums, his purpose was to impress the museum audience with the fact of Ottoman ownership rather than to participate in the positivist ordering of knowledge in vogue in Europe. The superficial emulation of the museum institution allowed it to produce a spatial discourse that contextually transcribed the Greco-Roman past already incorporated into the European heritage. In forging continuities between Ottoman and European histories, Ahmet Fethi Pasha followed a trend seen among historians of the Tanzimat, who were interested in linking the history of the empire with the events of European history. The spaces of the museum in the former Church of Hagia Irene participated in this framework for Ottoman history, situating it both in a Turkic tradition—that of Mehmet II, Timurlane, and İskender Bey— and in a European one—that of a Hellenistic and Byzantine heritage.

The meanings invested in the spaces of the museum at the former Church of Hagia Irene developed over the course of its existence, increasing in complexity with the addition of new objects that allowed for the more explicit exposition of political themes in the guise of suggestive histories. During the early years of the dual collections, the Ottoman government learned how museum display could produce specific visions of history for a visiting audience. As they expanded their museums, they would incorporate this knowledge into programs of display planned from the inception of each museum.

3   The Rise of the Imperial Museum

After the initial efflorescence of the dual collections in the former Church of Hagia Irene, the archaeological antiquities came to the fore as the military antiquities received less attention and finally, in 1877, were closed to the public. Why did the Ottoman museum shift its attention from a military to a Helleno-Byzantine heritage at this juncture? There were two primary reasons. First, the new constitution enacted soon after Sultan Abdülhamid II acceded to the throne allowed for broader inclusion of cultures under the Ottoman umbrella, which could be facilitated by an emphasis on antiquities. Second, the celebration of military history after the loss of the Russo-Turkish War in 1877 would have touched on the fresh wounds of incipient powerlessness, whereas an appeal to the distant past, embodied by antiquities, could construct new ways of incorporating a European identity into the empire without chafing against the recurrent concerns of politics and war. By framing the Ottoman relationship with Europe in a cultural guise, the museum created a new type of space in which to argue issues of territoriality and policy. To do so, it used a new language of archaeological ownership that could circumvent the recent memory of humiliating military defeat.

THE HELLENO-BYZANTINE HERITAGE
IN THE IMPERIAL MUSEUM

The upsurge in the importance of antiquities began well before the reign of Sultan Abdülhamid II. During his visit to Vienna in 1867, Sultan Abdülaziz visited the Abras Gallery, where he saw a large collection of antiquities. This is the activity that the French journal *L'Illustration* chose to depict in its article on the sultan's sojourn (fig. 8).[1] Although we cannot know

Fig. 8. Sultan Abdülaziz visiting the Abras Gallery in Paris [*L'Illustration*]

whether this was a definitive moment in the sultan's decision to support the institution of the Ottoman Imperial Museum and to enhance its collections, the image suggests that Greco-Roman artifacts were one of the main signs of European civilization to which the sultan was exposed in Europe. The use of this image in the report on his visit also suggests the symbolic nature of his adoption of European customs: wearing Western dress, he participated in the very European activity of museumgoing, as if to expunge the image of the supposedly foreign, mysterious, and threatening Oriental empire that he ruled and thereby represented.

The Ottoman interest in antiquities began to accelerate soon after Sultan Abdülaziz's visit to Europe. In 1869 Grand Vizier Ali Pasha renamed the Magazine of Antiquities the Imperial Museum (Müze-i Hümayun), with consequences both for the subsequent arrangement of the institution and for legislation concerning the collection of objects to be housed in it. Both words of the new title bear significance in relation to the museum's developing functions. As an "imperial" museum, the institution became representative of the entire empire as a conglomeration of various territories metonymically represented by antiquities. *Müze* implied new cultural functions similar to those of European museums. As an institution participating in the supposedly universal science of archaeology, the new museum marked the state as a participant in an international elite culture. The word "museum" also implied an educational function similar to that of European museums: it was a place where the public—in this case, the Ottoman elite and foreign tourists—could learn about state power through the appreciation of antiquities in a carefully orchestrated setting.

As if to underscore the educational subtext of the new institution, it was the minister of public education, Safvet Pasha, who took the first step toward the official consolidation of Ottoman antiquities efforts. In conjunction with the announcement of the new museum, he issued a memorandum to various regions of the empire—Aydin, Sarıhan, Adana, Hüdavendigar, Konya, Trablusgarb, Salonica, and Crete—in which he requested the careful packaging and transportation of all antiquities to the capital. Rather than rely on donations as the Magazine of Antiquities had, the new museum would actively seek new acquisitions by making use of the Ottoman administrative network. The governors of distant provinces, particularly Salonica and Crete, were among the most avid respondents, eager to send antiquities to the capital at every opportunity.

The recent events in Greece may have made these governors aware of their precarious position as provincial administrators in territories that might soon break off from the empire. Thus they hoped to collect antiquities as a sign of their imperial possession of these territories, much as European nations asserted their dominion through collections acquired in colonial territories. Using the administrative network for the acquisition of antiquities underscored the role of the centralized state and asserted that the appropriate location for the ancient history of all Ottoman territories was in the capital—not in provincial sites and certainly not in foreign collections. Thus the interest in antiquities became a venue through which the central government could assert its territorial rights at the moment of conflict. Provincial administrations, in turn, could respond with a show of allegiance in which the control of antiquities became a sign of cooperation.

Safvet Pasha instructed local governors that they should acquire "any old works, otherwise known as antiquities, by any means necessary, including direct purchase." His reference to the underground discovery of "a grave in the form of a lid made of stone and a sarcophagus surrounded with writing and also images of people and animals made of stone" indicates that the directive was spurred by an already mounting interest in antiquities throughout the empire. This directive served as the first attempt to construct an empirewide policy for the handling of antiquities. In it Safvet Pasha suggested that the person preparing an object for transport should take note of its condition, the location of its discovery, and the value placed on it locally. The item should then be purchased, packaged, and sent to the growing museum collection in the capital.[2]

Although Safvet Pasha's involvement in the issuing of such a significant edict clearly suggests an educational intent behind the institution of the museum, even the Ottoman elite was only recently coming to understand and participate in the cultural practice of antiquities acquisition. Safvet Pasha's first edict failed to attract the attention of regional governors. It was only after he sent out a second missive in 1870 that regional governments began to send shipments of antiquities.[3] During these years, the press became active in popularizing the idea of antiquities collection among the elite. The newspaper *Terakki* reported on the museum's acquisition of statues from across Marmara and from Tekirdağ in 1869 and 1870.[4] These early reports indicate that an effort was under way to inform the educated public about the state's nascent policies of antiquity acquisition.

The antiquities entered the Imperial Museum under the directorship of E. Goold, who had recently been appointed to the newly established post. The appointment of Goold, a teacher at the Galatasaray Lycée, underscores the link between the two institutions as establishments designed to educate the same elite group of Ottoman students. Goold emphasized the intimate relationship between the project of public education and the mission of the new museum in the latter's 1871 catalog, dedicated to the grand vizier Ali Pasha, one of the Tanzimat reformers. Goold wrote, "The foundation of the Imperial Museum of Constantinople as an annex to the new development of public education is due to the intelligent initiative of Your Highness."[5] In keeping with the egalitarian and progressive ambitions of the Tanzimat, the Imperial Museum was designed to serve a new class of citizenry with a new relationship both to historical heritage and to the state.

What, precisely, was the museum to teach? In his directive to the provinces, Safvet Pasha defined the museum in the artillery storehouse as resembling those in Europe. Similarly, the directive stipulating the establishment of the museum begins with a reference to museums in Europe: "It is not right for a museum to not exist in our country when the museums of Europe are decorated with rare works taken from here."[6] The museum was established to lay claim to Ottoman territories through objects that emerged from the land. Ironically, the founders of the museum used the emulation of a European institution to counteract the physical incursion of Europe onto Ottoman territory. Through asserting its ownership of antiquities, the empire could reaffirm symbolically its control over its territories. Moreover, the museum would teach its visitors to be European through their participation in the European cultural practice of aesthetic appreciation: they too would have a museum "decorated" with antiquities. With its new name, Imperial Museum, its focus was not on these antiquities but on the concept of empire that the antiquities could represent. In shifting its designation from "collection" to "museum," the institution acquired the bivalent task of glorifying the empire through the metonymic devices of antiquities and situating that empire as part of Europe through the practice of their display.

One of the first tasks the museum undertook was the first complete inventory of its collections. Goold attempted to identify all the objects in terms of what they represented and the period in which they were most likely produced. Although the original inventory filled 288 pages, the list was abridged for publication. Goold's 1871 catalog enumerates only 147 of the objects that were exhibited in the museum at that time, with ten illustrations by Limonciyan, an Armenian member of the museum staff. It fails to provide a clear provenance for most of the antiquities but describes each at length and notes its donor. Most of the citations refer to donations prompted by Safvet Pasha's 1869 decree. Among them are donations from Carabella Effendi, assistant to the governor general of Tripoli of Barbary; Ali Riza Pasha, assistant to the governor general of the province of Africa; Salih Efendi, lieutenant in the Imperial Marines; Abdurrahman Pasha, governor (*mutasarrif*) of Menteş; Sabri Pasha, governor of Salonica; and Kostaki Pasha Adossides, governor of Lasit on the island of Crete.[7]

The inclusion of artifacts from such a wide variety of locations suggests a relationship between the capital and the provinces that was constructed through the transportation of antiquities to the capital. The catalog reflected the provenance of the objects in the museum only by reference to the donor, so that each official who participated in the quest for antiquities acted as a link between the territory under his command and the capital. Each official who sent antiquities became a participant in the practice of collection and thereby performed an act symbolic of his allegiance to the state. Each province came to be represented in the collection through antiquities that had been located in it. The appropriate place for valuable antiquities was neither at its site of origin nor in European collections nor incorporated in new structures but rather in the Imperial Museum. Thus the museum came to designate Ottoman territories much as European museums that garnered their collections from colonial territories used artifacts housed in their capital cities to underscore imperial possessions. In effect, the museum allowed the Ottoman Empire to mimic exhibitionary colonial institutions of much younger European empires.

As museum director, Goold also engaged in some archaeological activities. In July 1869 he was sent to the ruins of Kyzikos on the peninsula of Kapıdağ and brought back a number of antiquities. His activities were reported in short newspaper articles, indicating that there was an attempt to bring the museum to the attention of the public.[8] In Trablusgarb and Bursa, Carabella Efendi eagerly excavated and sent everything he found, ranging from antiquities to whalebones, back to the museum. Thus from the first years of its institution the museum actively participated in the removal of artifacts from their sites and in their centralized collection. While at this point archaeology served simply to accelerate the process of acquisition, it would later evolve into a program designed to foil the colonialist subtext of European collection.

With the death of Ali Pasha in 1871, Sultan Abdülaziz appointed Mahmut Nedim Pasha to the post of grand vizier in an attempt to wrest control of the government from the men of the Tanzimat.[9] Mahmut Nedim Pasha immediately fired all of Ali Pasha's staff, including Goold. He also eliminated the post of museum director and hired a painter named Teranzio to watch over the collection without giving him an official title. The closing of the museum at this stage marks its importance vis-à-vis the reforms of the Tanzimat, perceived as threatening the stability of the empire and the absolute control of the monarch. The museum was important enough as an institution embodying the aims of the Tanzimat to warrant closure. Only a year later, Mahmut Nedim Pasha lost his position to one of the primary Tanzimat reformers, Midhat Pasha.

Under Midhat Pasha's administration, the new minister of education, Ahmet Vefik Efendi, an ardent supporter of the Tanzimat and a fan of French culture, quickly reestablished the museum. He appointed the German Anton Philip Déthier museum director, in which post he served from 1872 until his death in 1880. Since 1847 Déthier had been working on various antique inscriptions in the environs of İstanbul, which he published in 1864.[10] Unlike Goold, who had no qualifications to run the museum other than being European, Déthier had studied history, classics, philology, archaeology, and art history at Berlin University.

THE ANTIQUITIES LAW OF 1874

One of Déthier's first accomplishments as museum director was the establishment of new legislation for the regulation of antiquities trafficking. Although the new law was ostensibly designed for Ottoman protection, it essentially legalized much of the antiquities export that for so many years had been periodically and erratically interrupted and discouraged. In contrast to the 1869 edict, which emphasized the internal procedures for the recovery of antiquities, the first antiquities law, issued in 1874, primarily addressed foreign nationals. The law was written "in response to the insufficiency of the decree concerning antiquities that was established in conjunction with the institution of the Imperial Museum, and . . . that for some time inside of the [empire] people of various countries have been collecting attractive and rare works the protection of which needs to be kept in mind."[11] The simultaneous publication of the law in both French and Ottoman ensured its universal accessibility, while its content underscored the still ambivalent nature of the empire's museum enterprise.

As the mode of appreciation for antiquities shifted to a European-style institutional framework, their value became expressed in terms of protection. Just as Europeans had justified their tactics of antiquities acquisition as precautionary measures against Turkish negligence, the Ottomans justified their new laws as precautionary measures against European pilfering. The establishment of a museum of Ottoman antiquities did not simply denote the internal adoption of a European institution and the cultural practices invested in it. Rather the collection of antiquities in the Imperial Museum strengthened resistance to the incursion of European cultural practices, including the unauthorized collection of antiquities.

Ironically, the relationship between the Ottoman state and European archaeologists inverted the relationship between the strategic use of space by a landowner and the tactical use of space by a temporary invader postulated by Michel de Certeau.[12] Although the Ottomans owned the land in question, they did not pay attention to sites until the incursion of Europeans, who thus had the opportunity to set up the boundaries and rules of archaeologically significant spaces and established localized control over them. Through its enactment of legislation, the Ottoman government failed to reestablish strategic control over the territories and antiquities in question; they could merely tactically maneuver in the spaces already chosen, mapped, and exhumed by Europeans. Their maneuvers may have limited the number of antiquities that Europeans were able to take from Ottoman soil, but their failure to institute archaeological programs to compete with the European usurpation of land made them repeatedly concede the strategic upper hand.

The new law provided only a brief definition of an antiquity: "Every type of artifact that remains from the past is among antiquities. There are two types of antiquities: (1) coins and (2) all other kinds of works that can or cannot be carried."[13] This definition is not only remarkably short, it presents a very odd categorization. For the first time in the empire, it mentions coins as antiquities, valuable in a historical sense rather than in a monetary or metallurgic one. While the European practice of archaeology had in part grown out of the study of numismatics, in the Ottoman Empire the consideration of ancient coins as visual evidence to be collected, organized, and analyzed only came in conjunction with the adoption of the practice of archaeology.[14] However, unlike antiquities, coins had always been perceived to have value. The inclusion of coins as a separate type of antiquity may reflect the shift in the type of value that the government was trying to assign to them.[15] Reevaluated as artifacts, coins would become more valuable for their historicity than for their fungibility. Indeed, before long a numismatics collection would become a small department in the growing Imperial Museum.

Other antiquities were simply defined as old objects that could or could not be carried. In the event that they could be carried, they could be collected and exported. If not, they de facto belonged to the state, as did land. This unusual categorization for antiquities suggests that the idea of Ottoman territory extended only to the land itself, not to the portable objects on or in it. Unlike the British concept of the treasure trove that had been adopted for the collection of archaeological artifacts in the mid-nineteenth century, the royal title to the land was not interpreted to extend to treasures beneath it. Much as the people living in the Ottoman empire had not yet acquired citizenship, the objects on and in the land had not yet become implicitly Ottoman.

The law showed more concern for the ownership of antiquities after their discovery:

> Wherever antiquities are undiscovered (lying upon the ground), they belong to the state. . . . As for the antiquities that are found by those with research permission a third belongs to the excavator, a third to the state treasury, and a third to the landowner. If the excavator and the landowner are the same, this person will receive two-thirds of the finds and the state shall receive one-third. . . . The division of antiquities will occur according to the desire of the state and according to the nature or

the value [of the finds]. . . . The state is responsible for the preservation of sites that cannot be moved and for the appointment of an administrator to such sites.[16]

The law required the permission of landholders to excavate on their land and prohibited the excavation of public places of worship, roads, and cemeteries.

Despite the accelerated development of the Imperial Museum during these years and the increased concern over control of the antiquities trade, the first antiquities law was designed to propagate and legitimate much of the ongoing export of antiquities. The laxity of the law was exacerbated by the many exceptions allowed by the sultan's personal directives. For example, in 1879, when the French attempted to export antiquities they had excavated on the island of Semadirek thirteen years earlier, they appealed the law prohibiting the wholesale removal of antiquities from the empire. The sultan granted the French consul's request that the pieces become a gift from the empire to the French government, and the law was effectively circumvented.[17]

In the tradition established by Goold's partnership with Carabella Efendi, Déthier continued to hire a number of agents in various provinces to collect antiquities for the museum. In Salonica a Greek man named Yuvanaki; in Bandırma, the Armenian Takvor Aga; and, after 1874, Dervish Hüseyin of İstanbul aided in augmenting the museum's acquisitions. The staff associated with the museum was in large part Greek and Armenian, not Jewish or Muslim. When the assistant director, Limonciyan, resigned in 1880, he too was replaced by a Greek, Nikolaki Ohani Efendi. Although the museum was designed as an institution that would aid in educating the predominantly Muslim Ottoman elite to become European, it was initially operated almost exclusively by foreigners and by members of Ottoman Christian minorities.

In part this restriction was built into the skills considered desirable for work at the museum. When an antiquities school was proposed in 1875, its guidelines stipulated that entering students already know French, Greek, and Latin well enough to translate them into Turkish—skills that Christian, rather than Muslim or Jewish students, would be likely to have already acquired. An article in the newspaper *Şark* applauded the notion of training Ottoman subjects as archaeologists but complained that this restriction in particular would unduly restrict the applicants: "The point of studying Greeks, Romans, and various peoples is to become a scholar. People will want to attend the school not because they already are scholars but because they wish to become scholars."[18] With abnormally rigid prerequisites and requiring year-round ten-hour workdays compensated with an unusually small stipend, the plans for the school were poorly conceived and the school never opened.[19]

Although the museum had not yet begun to sponsor its own full-fledged archaeological expeditions, the collection had long since been expanding beyond the capacity of its marginal spaces in the armory. With the acquisition of eighty-eight cases of antiquities from Cyprus in 1873, the museum needed a larger building. Although Déthier considered the construction of a new museum, this was deemed too costly. In its stead, the Tiled Pavilion—built in 1478 as the first building of the Topkapı Palace—was chosen as a less expensive venue for housing the antiquities collection. Arrangements for the transfer of the building from the personal treasury of the sultan (Hazine-i Hassa) to the Ministry of Education began in 1873. In 1875 repairs and remodeling began to transform the pavilion so that it could "preserve and display the beautiful works that Europeans value highly."[20]

The museum administration hired a European architect by the name of Montrano to transform the pavilion that had architectural characteristics reminiscent of central Asian styles into a European-style museum. Originally the front of the pavilion was composed of a portico facade of fourteen narrow columns and was entered from staircases underneath the frontal arcade. To facilitate entry of museum pieces as well as visitors, a two-part staircase was added to the front of the pavilion and the original stairwells were made into coal depots. All original wall stoves were covered, chimneys were removed, and some windows were shut off. Tiled niches were covered by wood frames and shelving. Much of the glazed brick architecture was plastered over.[21] The early Ottoman architectural legacy of the building was physically toned down to make it look more like a European neoclassical museum building that would be an appropriate venue for the display of Hellenic artifacts.

A museum commission was established in 1877 to oversee "the completion of the repairs to the Tiled Pavilion that [were] being made into a museum, the transport of the antiquities and coins already in the collection to the new space without being damaged, to conserve antiquities outside of the museum in their present state, to make a path for excavation and research, to make the museum into a place of spectacle that [would] attract everybody's attention, and to categorize and organize the existing works."[22] For the first time, this document makes reference to the museum as a place of public spectacle, with a mission to attract visitors, not merely to exist for the glory of the sultan, and to organize antiquities, not merely to house them. Although the collection had become a museum in 1869, it was only after its move to the Tiled Pavilion that it acquired the didactic functions that distinguish a museum from a collection. This was quite common for collections in Europe. For example, whereas the Louvre had been open to the public since 1793, the British Museum had severe restrictions on the number and physical appearance of its visitors through much of the nineteenth century; its doors opened to the public daily only in 1879.[23]

In 1873 newspapers reported that Minister of Education Cevdet Pasha and Déthier were planning for the museum to open to the public.[24] The newspapers expressed the hope that more space would allow for better organization and for public access and would provide information about the antiquities through the publication of catalogs in both Turkish and French.[25]

The constitution of the commission suggests that the museum was designed to attract European visitors more than Ottoman subjects beyond the limited elite audience already working at the Sublime Porte. In addition to the museum's director, Déthier, the commission included two Armenian members of the museum staff (a guard, Köçeoğlu Kirkor Efendi, and the administrator of coins, Sebilyan Efendi), one Muslim-Turkish member of the education board (Mustafa Efendi), two Levantine (Europeans living in the Ottoman Empire) bureaucrats (Messrs. Mosali and Delaine), and the Ottoman chief of the Sixth Municipality (Osman Hamdi). Although the museum was located in the first—predominantly Muslim and commercial—district of the city, the only municipal chief to participate in the commission was that of the sixth district—the primarily European district of İstanbul, including Pera.[26] The spectacle designed so near the palace seems to have been a day trip deemed more appropriate for tourists than for locals.

Indeed, the museum was conceived as an advertisement for the changing aspirations of the Ottoman state. Münif Pasha, then minister of education, spelled out the objectives of the new museum in a speech delivered at the museum's opening, on August 17, 1880.

> The opening of a museum in İstanbul similar to those in other civilized countries was the hope of our progressing nation. We are all thrilled by the elimination of this deficiency—a great work of our royal sultan—which serves as an example of the devotion and care spent on the expansion and development of institutions that are traces of civilization, efforts worthy of monarchs.[27]

His speech suggests that, as before, the primary value of the museum resided in its similarity to European institutions. As a sign of civilization, the museum redefined the relationship of the empire both to Europe and to history.

Münif Pasha pointed out that the museum drew parallels between the Ottoman world with two separate civilizational references. On the one hand, the institution allowed the empire to participate in the traces of European civilization, measured by the appreciation of antiquities. On the other hand, it served as an atlas to earlier civilizations that had lived on Ottoman soil:

> There is no need to go on at length about the benefits of such museums. They show the level of civilization of past peoples and their step-by-step progress. From this, many historical, scientific, and artistic benefits can be obtained. Everybody knows the great effects of archaeology on European Civilization.

What were these great effects of archaeology? To reify national identity. To gain historical depth and transform this into material wealth. To justify possession—and then to claim it. To produce a determinative narrative of progress and thus to ensure the hierarchical position of modern Europe in relation to the narrative of history. If archaeology could do this for Europe, what could it not do for the Ottoman Empire?

Not only did the new museum serve as a link between the previous civilizations of the empire and the Ottoman present, the experience of methodical progress evidenced in their artifacts was designed to project an indigenous example of progress for the Ottoman Empire. For the most part, progress in the nineteenth-century empire was conflated with Europeanization, and the primary debates concerning progress considered how technology could be adopted without cultural bastardization. The museum implicitly provided an alternate interpretation of progress. As the artifacts showed, progress was not simply a European prerogative but was native to Ottoman soil. In fact, the progress of cultures to which Europe traced its own roots stemmed from Ottoman territory.

> In the past, we did not appreciate the value of antiquities. Among the Europeans, a few years ago an American took enough antiquities from Cyprus to fill an entire museum. Today, most antiquities in European and American museums are from the stores of antiquities in our country.

Thus the speech emphasized the idea that Europeans had built their progress on objects native to Ottoman soil, made by civilizations native to

Ottoman lands. To take those objects away would perhaps reduce the imbalances of progress between East and West that they represented.

An intellectual ploy commonly used to defend Westernization suggested that European progress, based on knowledge of the classics, relied on texts and sciences that had been studied in the Islamic world during the Middle Ages in Europe, where they had been forgotten. Similarly, by emphasizing the reliance of Europeans on Ottomans in the arena of antiquities, the minister of education reclaimed the patrimony of those antiquities. In light of contemporary debates, he implied that the oversight of previous generations with regard to antiquities was analogous to the European disregard for classical texts during the Middle Ages.

The speech proposed two primary roles for the new museum. It was to provide instruction on the idea of historical progress through its displays, and it was charged with counteracting the European usurpation of material culture that was beginning to be seen as rightly Ottoman. The museum would simultaneously educate Ottomans about progress and teach Europeans a new respect for the empire:

> Until now, Europeans have used various means to take the antiquities of our country away, and they did this because they did not see an inclination toward this in us. For a long time this desire has been awakened among Ottomans and recently even a law was passed concerning antiquities. Since the foundation of the Imperial Museum is the greatest example of this, we can now hope that the Europeans will change their opinions about us.

Even if today the Europeans spend vast sums to excavate in Greece, the finds are not taken to their countries but remain in Athens.

> Since every part of the Ottoman nation was once full of antiquities that belonged to the civilized peoples who lived here, if these had been valued in time, İstanbul would have the greatest museum in the world. Nonetheless, many antiquities have been collected and valuable things were among the things that were found.

As a result of negative experiences in the past, the Ottomans had learned the value of the antiquities they would now collect in the museum. The museum would thus physically showcase their progress to Europeans, who would learn to respect the Ottomans as equals and as participants in a contemporary culture that collects, as well to respect them as heirs to the cultures whose artifacts were being collected. Just as Europe readily accepted Greece's claim to its own heritage, Münif Pasha hoped that they would learn to see the Ottoman Empire as a descendant of the ancients in its own right.

The minister's speech ended by emphasizing the physical connection between the site of the museum and the antiquities to be housed within:

> Even this building that we are in today is an antique. This building, among the great works of Mehmet the Conqueror and a fine example of the architecture of that period, is very suitable to this purpose.

Although many historians today consider the use of the Tiled Pavilion an arbitrary choice based on the availability of space, clearly it could not have been the only empty building suitable for housing a museum. Indeed, the minister's speech suggests that it was a carefully considered site, chosen to forge links between the apogee of Ottoman glory brought to mind through the conquest-era architecture, the glories of past civilizations as evidenced in their art, and the progress of the empire evinced by the very establishment of a European-style museum.

Nonetheless, the modifications made to the building served to erase many of the signs that marked it as "Oriental," such as elaborate tilework and wall stoves. While the history denoted by the building was central to its significance as a museum, it was perhaps equally important to render the structure less distant from European models of how a museum should look. Moreover, the choice of an early Ottoman building with frontal columns—the only building of its kind in Istanbul—may have made an obtuse reference to the neoclassical style often chosen for European museums. The visual link between a distinctly Eastern-Ottoman building and a type tied to classicism would only have underscored the inherent links between Ottoman and classical civilizations that the museum was designed to emphasize.

Anton Déthier died in 1881 without having the opportunity to curate the exhibits of the new museum building. The ministry of education asked the German consulate to help it find a new European director, and the museum began to negotiate with Doctor Millhofer of the Berlin Museum. However, before his contract could be written, the son of the vizier Edhem Pasha, Osman Hamdi, was hired instead. Osman Hamdi's biographer, Mustafa Cezar, suggests that the Ottoman administration was beginning to see the development of the museum under Abdülhamid II as an act of God and therefore felt the need to hire a Muslim rather than a Christian as its director.[28] Although the desire to hire an Ottoman subject may have been couched in such religious terms common to the era of Sultan Abdülhamid II, the selection of an Ottoman director suited the contemporary drive to assume control of antiquities as part of the Ottoman historical and cultural legacy.

OSMAN HAMDI AND THE EFFLORESCENCE
OF THE IMPERIAL MUSEUM

The growth of the the Imperial Museum as a barometer of Ottoman cultural self-perception and projection, from a small collection into an institution with empirewide implications, depended to a great extent on the efforts of a single man who embodied many of the intellectual aspirations of his age. Educated as a lawyer and an artist in France, Osman Hamdi took on the roles of painter, educator, museum administrator, legislator, and archaeologist in his native land. Through his instrumental role in bringing many new cultural activities to the Ottoman Empire, Osman Hamdi laid sturdy foundations for the subsequent maintenance of antiquities as a measure of the patrimony and sovereignty of the country. His work framed and guided the self-image of the empire through its museological project.

Osman Hamdi did not arbitrarily fall into the position of museum director from a background of anonymity. Rather his position as the eldest son in an important bureaucratic family gave him the many educational and familial advantages that led him to direct one of the prime signifying institutions of the late empire. His father, İbrahim Edhem, was born in the Greek Orthodox village of Sakız. After being captured as a prisoner of war during a village revolt, he was sold as a slave to the chief naval officer, Kaptan-ı Derya Hüsrev Pasha, then head of the Ottoman Navy, who would also soon serve as vizier to the sultan. Lacking his own family and children, Hüsrev Pasha raised several children who had been bought as slaves or orphaned. In 1829 four of his children, including İbrahim Edhem, were among the first Ottoman students sent to France to be educated. After studying metals engineering in Paris and Vienna, İbrahim Edhem returned to the Ottoman Empire, where he served in several official posts—as an army engineer, as the French tutor of Sultan Abdülmecid, and, briefly in 1856, as minister of foreign affairs. He served as ambassador to Berlin in 1876 and to Vienna between 1879 and 1882. While his tenure as vizier to the sultan in 1877–78 was relatively brief, he left the position in the sultan's good graces. After serving as minister of the interior between 1883 and 1885, he retired in İstanbul. İbrahim Edhem's close relations with the royal family, as well as his appointment in various departments of government, paved the way for his son to have the connections and education necessary to construct a new attitude concerning the arts in the empire.

Osman Hamdi was born in 1842 and grew up in a household that was both well integrated into the imperial bureaucracy and one of the most Western-oriented families in the country. He was brought up as an Ottoman, loyal to the Ottoman state, but the many letters to his father written in French suggest that he probably spoke French at home. Nonetheless, of İbrahim Edhem's four sons, Osman Hamdi was the only one to pursue an education in France. By following this family tradition, he was well suited for a variety of positions in which his fluency in French culture would serve as an asset. His brothers served the state in various capacities but did not play a central a role in reformulating the empire as a European state. While his brother Mustafa became a customs agent and his brother Galip İbrahim became the first Ottoman numismatist, his youngest brother, Halil (Edhem), followed in Osman Hamdi's footsteps as assistant director at the museum after 1892 and as director of the museum after the latter's death in 1910. He later played a significant role in the transition of Ottoman cultural institutions in the Turkish Republic and served as a member of parliament from 1923 until his death in 1935.

In 1860 Osman Hamdi traveled to Paris to study law. However, he soon decided to pursue his interest in painting instead, left the law program, and trained under the French Orientalist painters Jean-Léon Gérôme (1824–1904) and Gustave Boulanger (1824–88). A member of the royal family, Şeker Ahmet Pasha, joined him in Paris two years later to study with the same artists, and presumably the two men became friends. At the 1867 Paris Exposition Universelle, Osman Hamdi exhibited three paintings. None seem to have survived, but their titles—*Repose of the Gypsies, Black Sea Soldier Lying in Wait,* and *Death of the Soldier*—indicate typical Orientalist subjects befitting a student of Gérôme and Boulanger. During his stay in Paris, Osman Hamdi married a Frenchwoman and had two daughters with her. They accompanied him to İstanbul when he returned in 1869. The following year he was sent to Baghdad as part of the administrative team of Midhat Pasha, who would later become an important reformer of the Tanzimat. After a one-year stint in Baghdad, Osman Hamdi returned to serve in the Office of Foreign Affairs associated with the palace.

Osman Hamdi's interest in the arts became closely tied to his father's high-level administrative positions in 1873, when the latter served as head of the commission for the Ottoman delegation to the Vienna International Exposition and made his son commissioner for the exhibit. Osman Hamdi aided in the collection of materials for two books that his father published in association with the delegation: the *Usul-u Mimari-i Osmani*, published simultaneously in French as *L'architecture ottomane*, and the *Elbise-i Osmani*, published in French as *Les costumes populaires de la Turquie en 1873*. The former work consisted of a compilation of fourteen plans and elevations of Ottoman architectural styles through the centuries. The latter consisted of forty-two plates by the İstanbul-based photographer Sebah of regional costumes throughout the empire. Whereas the former emphasized the historical virtuosity of the Ottoman architectural tradition, the latter emphasized the breadth of the empire's territories. Many of the costumes pictured in the book were brought to the exhibit in Vienna. Despite Osman Hamdi's efforts, the costumes remained in Vienna. Osman Hamdi's work in Vienna was not only his first experience in constructing collections with which to represent the Ottoman state, it was also his first experience arguing for the retention of objects as symbols of Ottoman identity. It also changed his personal life: while in Vienna, he met another Frenchwoman, who accompanied him to İstanbul and changed her name to Naile on his separation from his previous wife. The nationality of his wives underscores Osman Hamdi's close personal identification with the Western world even as he professionally represented Ottoman interests.

After his return to İstanbul, Osman Hamdi was appointed to several positions in the Department of Foreign Affairs. With the deposition of Abdülaziz in 1876, he became the director in charge of foreign-language publications in İstanbul. The following year he was appointed director of the Sixth Municipality. On September 3, 1881, he left this post in order to receive his appointment as museum director.[29] Osman Hamdi used his position as museum director to develop the museum and to rewrite the antiquities laws, to create nationally sponsored archaeological expeditions, and to institute a school of the arts.

While Osman Hamdi endeavored to retain archaeological antiquities in the country, he quickly recognized the need to create local appreciation of such works. In 1882 he instituted and became director of the Academy of Fine Arts (Sanaii Nefise Mektebi), which provided Ottomans with training in aesthetics and artistic techniques without leaving the empire. Like students in France, the students of the new school were trained to draw and sculpt by copying ancient sculptures and friezes. Thus the school created a new artistic elite with an intellectual investment in the collection and maintenance of antiquities.

Throughout his professional career as museum and academy director, Osman Hamdi continued to paint in the style of his teachers, Gérôme and

Boulanger. Both of these artists favored the depiction of Orientalist subjects using luminescent light and clear lines evocative of a warm and exotic Middle Eastern climate. In their use of colorful costuming and intricate architectural settings, Osman Hamdi's paintings reflect a particularly strong influence from the paintings of Gérôme.[30] However, whereas Gerome presented a romanticized, salacious East with a deceptively transparent realism, Osman Hamdi adopted the style of his master to represent a glorified and dignified vision of Ottoman heritage. If his works resemble the Orientalist vision of his masters in the timelessness of his settings, they also offer a contrast in that this timelessness enhances the Ottoman image while providing a subtle commentary on his own role as the mediator of the empire's artistic heritage.

Osman Hamdi made no direct reference to the museum in his paintings: he did not depict museum spaces, nor did he attempt to contextualize antiquities in ancient sites. While his works often situate him in an imaginary Ottoman past, they also serve as an allegorical representation of his efforts at the Imperial Museum. He often seems to have chosen his subjects with reference to the experiences of his day job as museum director. In examining the cultural implications of the new museum, his paintings become documents of its director's hopes, intentions, and frustrations in relation to the projects in his charge.

While the trope of the painter in Oriental garb was common to many Orientalist artists, Osman Hamdi's liminal identity as both an "Oriental" and a participant in European cultural practice gives this use of self-portraiture an irony not lost on the artist as he repeatedly depicted himself in the idyllic serenity of the Ottoman past. His interest in costume charades was already clear when he was in charge of the Ottoman exhibit at the 1873 Vienna exposition. There, as part of the festivities, he removed his Western-style clothes in favor of a romantic view of himself as the quintessential Ottoman (fig. 9).[31] Since the eighteenth century, shifting costume had been one of the primary games of identity and identification played by Europeans with an interest in the Orient. As an Ottoman, Osman Hamdi chose to wear the sign of his nation as a European activity, in effect taking back the clothes of othering that such playfully exotic costumes represented.

Osman Hamdi's Oriental garb is particularly significant in light of the Ottoman displays at the exposition. Unlike many other displays of foreign cultures shown at European exhibits, the Ottoman display did not showcase the colonial power of European nations.[32] Rather it served primarily as an advertisement for Ottoman goods. The cultural aspect of the display,

Fig. 9. Osman Hamdi in Oriental garb at the Vienna Universal Exposition, 1873
[Cezar]

including Osman Hamdi's costume exhibit, served to familiarize Western audiences with the traditions of a foreign nation while maintaining control of that history. At the same time, however, by adopting the tropes of colonialist representation that were dominant at world expositions, the Ottoman Empire began the practice of representing its past as an ethnographic Other, both within and outside the empire. In particular, the designation of national costumes that spanned the empire helped to define a visual identity for a nascent concept of Ottoman allegiance. Even though such costumes had been outlawed with Sultan Mahmut II's dress reform of 1826, they came to represent Ottoman identity as a historicized and exotic entity for international consumption. Like the Janissary and military mannequins exhibited in Chicago, by dressing every day in a frock coat, Osman Hamdi exhibited his modern interests and education; by donning period dress for the camera, he took control over the place of the Oriental within an Occidental frame.

Similarly, Osman Hamdi's usurpation of European practices, such as painting, to cultural self-representation established his control over a visualization of historical memory. Unlike the characters in the paintings of European Orientalists, Osman Hamdi's subjects were never engaged in bloodshed, nor were they languid spectators in a glorious environment. Rather they tended to be scholars, musicians, merchants, or people praying, washing, or socializing—active in their own lives, neither lasciviously on display nor embroiled in battle. In many of his paintings, scenes appear to show slices of life, snapshots of distant and indeterminate times. The opacity of the stories into which paintings lead the viewer begs a symbolic reading of the images.

Although he had a French education, always dressed in European clothing, and led a Westernized lifestyle, Osman Hamdi unfailingly chose to represent himself in his paintings in anachronistic Ottoman garb. In the early piece *The Painter at Work* (fig. 10) he depicts himself painting his wife, who reclines fully clothed on a divan with her back turned to him, contemplating the view outside. In direct contrast to the European Orientalist trope of a nude woman exposed to the artist outside the picture frame, his model does not present herself physically or mentally either to the painter or to the viewer. Not only do both characters in the painting wear traditional Ottoman garb, they live in palatial apartments decorated in an anachronistic style. In real life Osman Hamdi and his family wore European-style clothing and lived in a wood frame house just outside of İstanbul. One might ask whether, in adopting the atemporalizing effects of European Orientalist painting in his self-portrait, he accepted the conven-

Fig. 10. Osman Hamdi, *The Painter at Work* (n.d.) [Cezar]

tions for depicting the Orient and thereby acceded to the European vision of the Orient; whether he romanticized the Ottoman past in portraying himself with self-conscious anachronism; or whether he used the historicizing tropes of Orientalist painting to suggest a new way of looking at history in the Orient.

This question has implications not simply for Osman Hamdi as a painter but for his vision as director of the Imperial Museum project. In the painting he works in a space not merely anachronistic but also somewhat museum-like. Ceramics line the shelf on the rear wall, which is also adorned with artillery arranged around two display shelves, one of which holds a wrapped dervish headpiece. Here Osman Hamdi presents himself as both a painter and a collector—his real occupations—projected into an anachronistic Ottoman time and space even as he engages in a European activity. The juxtaposition reveals a consciousness of his liminal position, both as an individual and as the director of an institution that, in his own words, had "the privilege of living in a state of perpetual crossing."[33] In repeatedly presenting himself as an Ottoman in his self-portraits, Osman Hamdi simultaneously adopts the image of the timeless Easterner as the strongest mode of denoting his Ottoman self and incorporates his daily Europeanate practices into a redefined Ottoman identity.

As Linda Nochlin notes, "It might be said that one of the defining features of Orientalist painting is its dependence for its very existence on a presence that is always an absence: the Western colonial or touristic presence."[34] In other words, Orientalist painting produced a voyeuristic space by allowing the viewer to enter secretly to observe a forbidden scene—an irony not lost in its frequent depiction of Oriental harems. The word "harem" does not, after all, mean a space of wanton luxury and women but rather the forbidden or private spaces of the traditional Islamic home.

In contrast to the exposure of the harem theme common in colonial-era representations of the East, Osman Hamdi's painting does not offer access to or conquest of secret spaces as does Delacroix's *Women of Algiers*, winner of the French Salon competition in 1834, four years after the French conquest of Algeria.[35] In Hamdi's painting, which takes us into the private space of his own home, the woman faces away from us. We as viewers of the scene may be sneaking up on the artist and observing him but in a sense are denied access to both figures, whose faces we cannot see. Osman Hamdi's model poses instead for the Ottoman artist who, in effect, comes to control the action of the scene.

As Nochlin notes, "Gérôme's Orientalist painting managed to body forth two ideological assumptions about power: one about men's power over women; the other about white men's superiority to, and hence justifiable control over, inferior, darker races."[36] If the former was not of great concern to Osman Hamdi, the latter clearly was. While his painting may reinforce the trope of female passivity against male activity, it passes this activity to the hand—literally, the skilled and painting hand—of the Oriental rather than the Occidental artist. If Delacroix's work expressed French colonial power by exposing the hidden and private spaces of the Orient to the colonizing gaze, Osman Hamdi's work refused to give that power to the Occidental artist or, for that matter, archaeologist. One might compare this transfer of power from the Occidental to the Ottoman painter to the dynamic between the powerful male hero and the passive female heroine in classical Hollywood cinema. In her germinal feminist critique of classical cinema, Laura Mulvey argues that "in-built patterns of pleasure and identification impose masculinity as 'point of view' " for the viewers of films.[37] As such, through a combination of scopophilia—pleasure in viewing the passive female character—and narcissism—identification with the active male character—the viewer comes to possess the female object of desire through the active onscreen possession of the male protagonist. Furthermore, the realist conventions of classical film "portray a hermetically sealed world which unwinds magically, indifferent to the presence of the audience, producing for them a sense of separation and playing on their voyeuristic fantasy."[38] Similarly, in European works of Orientalist painting, the knowledge that the Western male artist—Delacroix, Ingres, Gérôme, Boulanger, or any of the other artists who reveled in exposing the Oriental harem—provided scopophilic access to Eastern women and passed this visual conquest on to the painting's audience.[39] Working in the same realist tradition as classical film, "part of the strategy of an Orientalist painter like Gérôme is to make his viewers forget that there was any 'bringing into being' at all."[40]

By eliminating the moment of voyeurism and using the painting as a window, the artist gives the scene to the viewer. In positing an Ottoman painter depicting a clothed model, Osman Hamdi stole back that act of conquest by reinserting an Ottoman actor, the painter, into the scene. While the gender hierarchy remains intact—the woman is still a passive object of the man's vision and depiction, as well as the repository of all that is private and owned by culture—the doubled sense of othering that comes about from the imperialist gaze of Orientalist painting is negated.

With Osman Hamdi at the helm, the Imperial Museum developed from an almost arbitrarily assembled collection of antiquities into an institution capable of representing developing state ideologies. While he retained his role as museum director and school administrator until his death in 1910, the administrative, archaeological, and legislative activities of his first ten years as museum director set the stage for the subsequent development of the museum. Seen together, such efforts highlight Osman Hamdi's interest in framing the archaeological museum as a nationalist Ottoman enterprise and his recognition of the need to develop a place for the museum in the public psyche.

One might ask why, at this juncture, antiquities were able to play such a pivotal if subtle role in the expression of Ottoman identity. Among other reasons for practicing archaeology, the archaeological historian Bruce Trigger suggests that nations might adopt the practice "to enhance the group's self-confidence by making its success appear natural, predestined, and inevitable, to inspire and justify collective action, and to disguise collective interests as altruism."[41] Indeed, European archaeologists came to the empire to make their claim to Ottoman territories appear natural. By uncovering the Helleno-Byzantine heritage of Ottoman territories and including these artifacts in museums that used them to write European narratives of progress, they made the Ottoman claim to the empire's territories appear spurious.

While the 1874 law was a step in opposition, its very weakness pointed to the difference between the discourse about antiquities on Ottoman territories and that of countries with similar treasures that attempted to restrict the export of antiquities. The antiquities legislation of both Greece and Egypt were (at least on paper) more restrictive than the 1874 law. The Olympia Treaty of 1874 between Germany and Greece made official the already highly restrictive attitude of the Greek government toward the exportation of antiquities.[42] In Egypt, French interests tried to restrict antiquities export as early as 1835.[43] However, despite the establishment of an antiquities storehouse in Cairo, politics soon forced the donation of the nascent antiquities collection to Archduke Maximilian of Austria. By 1858 the French Egyptologist Auguste Mariette, acting in the official post of conservator of Egyptian monuments attempted to curtail all unauthorized excavations by establishing an antiquities service museum.[44]

Why was the development of antiquities legislation so much more adamantly restrictive in Greece and Egypt? As in the Ottoman Empire, foreign archaeologists in these countries were eager to procure antiquities for European museums. While in both cases Europeans often saw their own claim on local heritage as stronger than local, nationalistic patrimonies, hegemonic European discourse still constructed a binding relationship between Greek and Egyptian territories and the artifacts found on archaeological sites in them.

In contrast, the Ottoman Empire was considered an imperial power that had imposed its governance on preceding peoples, usurping the land and the antiquities beneath. The ancient Greek heritage underlying much of the Ottoman territories had already been appropriated by Europe and incorporated into the nationalist patrimony of modern Greece. As the former colonial master of Greece, the Ottoman Empire was implicitly divested of this heritage. Similarly, the growth of local nationalisms in Egypt and Mesopotamia localized ideological claims to archaeologcial sites. This staking out of cultural territory, first by Europeans and then by local national projects, was as much a part of the initial strategic nature of the European archaeological project as the physical staking out of sites and removal of objects. Just as the first antiquities law only allowed the Ottomans to tactically maneuver in spaces set aside by Europeans, the subsequent Ottoman adoption of the Hellenistic legacy could only allow for a tactical manipulation of the boundaries of civilization and culture already requisitioned by Europe.

Like colonized nations gaining their independence, Ottomans had to fight against the supposed objectivity of the scientific practices of archaeology and reinsert their presence into the narrative of civilization that this science helped to write. As Frantz Fanon pointed out, "For the native, objectivity is always directed against him."[45] While the Ottoman Empire was never colonized, the fight against objective truths produced by early archaeological practice here was similar to that required by the processes of cultural decolonization—to construct a viable competing narrative for knowledge already deemed objective and thus absolute.

Archaeological activities helped to justify European hopes of imperial possessions in previous Ottoman territories. Europeans often disguised their activities of antiquities collection as a form of altruism without political motivations. In light of this, Ottoman archaeological expeditions responded to the European incursions in order not only to reclaim artifactual rights, but, more important, territorial ones. Thus the development of the museum and the legislative practices associated with it spoke not only verbally in the language of heritage and history but also physically in the language of conquest and territory.

4 The Dialectic of Law and Infringement

Not only did the museum function as an ideological bridge between European and Ottoman heritage, under Osman Hamdi it also served as a battleground for possession of the physical elements of that heritage. The antiquities legislation of the Ottoman Empire developed as a dialectic negotiation between the writing of the law and a series of subsequent infringements that resulted in more detailed versions in 1884 and 1906. Each successive law not only addressed the deficiencies of its predecessor, it also reflected new values that had become associated with antiquities in the interim.

THE FAILURE OF THE 1874 ANTIQUITIES LAW

Given the numerous loopholes in the 1874 antiquities law and the absence of enforcement, midcentury amateur and professional European archaeologists alike saw the Ottoman Empire as a garden of antiquities ripe for harvesting. However, discomfort with the export of antiquities was growing both within the museum administration and in public discourse. The negotiation involved in several archaeological transactions of the early 1880s underscores the mounting dissatisfaction with existing legal practices.

For example, the German railroad engineer Carl Humann began his exploration of Bergama in 1867 and began excavating in 1871. Through his work for Grand Vizier Fuad Pasha, whom he advised on railway and road routes, Humann gained many valuable connections in the Ottoman bureaucracy. By 1880 he acquired the property of the excavation site and arranged for the Ottoman government to sell him its one-third share of the antiquities for only twenty thousand francs. Between 1881 and 1886 Humann sent hundreds of tons of antiquities to the German Museum of

Antiquities in Berlin, including the altar of Zeus that was subsequently reconstructed inside the museum.[1]

Legal as this transaction was, correspondence between Osman Hamdi and the director of the German Museum of Antiquities, Alexander Conze, suggests Osman Hamdi's unhappiness about the number of antiquities leaving the empire. In 1882 Conze wrote to Osman Hamdi that he had sent a number of publications on the excavation at Bergama in order to maintain good relations with the museum in Istanbul. He also promised a plaster cast of an Apollo statue found at the site. In exchange he requested a stone that was inset in the exterior wall of the Bergama mosque. Rather than reply directly to the request, however, Osman Hamdi merely acknowledged the receipt of the plaster cast and asked for copies of all the great statues of Bergama.[2] His curt reply resounds with the irony of needing to ask for copies, the originals of which he perceived as rightfully belonging to his museum. Conze's letter alerted the museum to the importance of the piece in the mosque wall. In response, an adjunct of the museum, D. Baltazzi Bey, removed the stone from the Kurşunlu Cami, and it entered the Imperial Museum collection in 1885.

Osman Hamdi also arranged for broader preemptive strikes against German archaeological enterprises. For example, in 1882 Conze told Humann that he was looking for funds for new excavations at Nemrut Dağ (fig. 11) and at Sakçagözü.[3] The following year, Osman Hamdi collected funds from the Ottoman Bank, the Eastern Railway Company, and the Haydar Pasha Railway Company so as to perform the excavations under the auspices of the Imperial Museum. The finds were spectacular, but they were impossible to transport, so photographs and models were made instead.[4] The finds were published in French so that Ottoman archaeological activity could become visible on the European stage.

With public interest in antiquities preservation on the rise during these years, the Ottoman Museum began to have more opportunities to advertise its acquisitions. In 1878 the newspaper *Tercuman-i Şark* reported on Schliemann's acquisition of a second excavation permit for Troy. "God willing," the author opined, "this time Baron Schliemann will not smuggle the valuable antiquities to Athens and our museum will make use of them."[5] The newspaper continued to report on the excavations in subsequent issues. Similarly, in 1880 the newspaper *Vatan* reported on the finds at Kargamış by the British excavation team Smith and Henderson.[6] Although the law had yet to clearly define an antiquity, an attitude of proprietorship over antiquities was beginning to take hold in the empire.

Fig. 11. Osman Hamdi on site at the Nemrut Dağ excavations, 1883 [Cezar]

THE ANTIQUITIES LAW OF 1884

The revised Antiquities Law (Asar-i Atika Nizamnamesi) of 1884 attempted to rectify most of the former law's omissions, in part in response to large-scale expropriation of finds such as was occurring at Bergama.[7] A directive from the office of the vizier to the council of the Ministry of Education explained the need for drafting new antiquities legislation:

> According to the antiquities law for the antiquities excavated and removed with an official permit, only one-third go to the state and the other two-thirds to the excavator and the landowner, allowing foreigners and consulates to apply for their own benefit. The persistence of this situation leads to the continued transport of rare and fine works to Europe, even though in other countries the excavators of similar works can only export plaster casts while the originals are left at local museums. This procedure is common in all places, . . . so it has been suggested to the Ministry of Education. In the aforementioned regulation, from now on only a copy of works will be given those who want to excavate on imperial lands, and the original will be taken for the Imperial Museum.[8]

The directive does not present any inherent economic, aesthetic, or historical value in the objects as justification for the new regulation. Rather, it cites the practice of other countries as the sole impetus for the modification of Ottoman law. The law did not develop either to reflect or to foster growing indigenous interest in antiquities. Rather, it addressed a lack apparent only in comparison to the Western world. Such phrasing suited the interests of the government, which cared more for the political value of the antiquities than for their inherent artistic or cultural value.

In contrast to the 1874 law, the new regulation began with a precise definition of antiquities:

> All of the artifacts left by the ancient peoples who inhabited the Ottoman Empire, that is, gold and silver; various old and historical coins; signs engraved with informative writings; carved pictures; decoration; objects and containers made of stone and clay and various media; weapons; tools; idols; ringstones; temples and palaces, and old game-areas called circuses; theaters, fortifications, bridges and aqueducts; corpses, buried objects, and hills appropriate for examination; mausolea, obelisks, memorial objects, old buildings, statues and every type of carved stone are among antiquities.[9]

This definition suggests five broadly conceived categories of antiquities: objects with intrinsic material value, such as coins; carved objects of any material, with inscriptions or designs; architectural spaces, enclosed or not; deliberately buried objects, such as corpses and grave sites; and deliberately placed memorials, such as obelisks and statues. Unlike in the earlier law, where the mobility of an object determined the state's interest in it, in the new law the historicity of the object produced its value. The new definition of antiquities reveals a much more archaeologically informed understanding of objects in that it placed value on a wide variety of pieces with varying material worth. For example, whereas a coin has an immediately apparent economic value, an ancient corpse (presumably a mummy) has a historical value through which it may also acquire an economic value. A similar reformulation of the archaeological project had taken place in Germany in the late 1870s; there archaeologists, who had initially been interested solely in the aesthetics of sculptures, began to place value on other types of objects as evidence for the understanding of material culture.[10]

In addition, the new law asserted that "all types of antiquities extant or found, or appearing in the course of excavation or appearing in lakes, rivers, streams, or creeks," automatically belonged to the state and made their destruction or removal illegal. Thus not only did the word "antiquity" become more clearly itemized and defined, all antiquities became identified as automatically part of the Ottoman patrimony.

In contrast to earlier legislation, according to this law, both portable and stationary antiquities automatically entered the domain of imperial property. Moreover, these objects were now explicitly associated with the peoples who had lived on Ottoman territories. The tactical relationship established by the Ottomans to European archaeologists who had staked out Ottoman territories began to change. By adopting the former peoples of the Ottoman Empire, the Ottomans usurped the European claim on the Hellenistic heritage. They started to claim the land by claiming the ancestral origins associated with archaeological objects. In a literal sense archaeology deepened the Ottoman claim on its territory. In an age of nationalism, when the notion of indigeneity as a legitimizing force was gaining credence, such a claim bolstered the Ottoman bid for nationhood based not simply on their conquest and centuries of rule but also on their adoption of the peoples who had lived on Ottoman soil via the arts they left behind.

Following this lead, the new law began to recognize the integral value of sites in relation to objects. Article 4 of the new law provided that "individuals and groups do not have the right to destroy and move antiquities under their own land or spaces." No longer was theft the sole mode of destruction; modern archaeologists were also concerned that they should be able to fully and accurately document their sites. The act of arbitrarily disturbing an archeological site constitutes a destructive act. Once an area had been determined as an archaeological site, it became illegal to build within a quarter kilometer of it without a permit. It was also illegal to lift the stones lying on the ground in such an area. In addition, the law forbade taking measurements, drawing, or making molds of antique stones, as well as constructing scaffolding around ruins.

To enforce the new restrictions, the law gave the government the power to expropriate private property for archaeological purposes. According to the 1874 law, the land could be owned by the excavator, who would then receive its bounty as if it were an agricultural harvest. In sharp contrast, in the new law the substrata of the land took precedence over its surface: if the government owned all archaeological objects and they happened to be under private property, then the government automatically gained a right to that property. In effect, the law limited property rights to the surface of the land and excluded anything that might be found underneath or discovered by happenstance. In Ottoman tradition, all land implicitly belonged to the sultan. Although this was no longer appropriate in the modern age following the liberalization of the Tanzimat, the claim to all substrata of the land reinforced a similar ideology—that ultimately all territory belonged to the state, even if it took thousands of years to reemerge through archaeology.

No individual could assume ownership of an antiquity without a permit—without the government explicitly relinquishing that object. Similarly, no object could be exported from the country without the express consent of the Imperial Museum, and the law stipulated procedures to limit such exports. The excavator and a representative of the museum were to keep two notebooks of finds, updated and signed daily to prevent the secreting of antiquities before they had been recorded.

The procedures for excavation reflected a new understanding of the relation between archaeology and site topography. According to article 10 of the 1884 law, the first step in asking for an excavation permit would be to delineate the boundaries of the site through the production of a map. This new procedure probably reflects German influence on Ottoman regulatory procedures. Since the excavation of Athens in the mid-1880s, an unofficial alliance had developed between German archaeologists and military cartographers. This was cemented in 1892, when excavations planned in Germany required that the work would be supervised by a team of military cartographers and civilian excavators.[11] Many of the primary projects of archaeological societies developing at the time, such as the Palestine Exploration Fund, were topographic. Similarly, in the Ottoman Empire maps became a prerequisite for the acquisition of an excavation permit.

Certainly, antiquities collectors had produced and used maps and the process of mapping to gain access to sites for many years. In the eighteenth century, the interest in Greek antiquities and the picturesque could not be dissociated from an interest in the landscape topography of Greece, particularly Athens. With the publication of numerous travelogues by members of the early-nineteenth-century Society of Diletanti, a society of travelers to Greece, the spaces of the ancient world began to be measured by the time taken to travel from one site to another.[12] The publication of Wordsworth's *Greece* in 1839 established the locations of all the literary sites of ancient Greece. But as long as the main purpose of the discovery of antiquities was the collection of individual artifacts that could be identified stylistically and appreciated aesthetically, there was no reason to wed objects to the specific sites on which they had been found. It was only with the development of scientific archaeology, with its covalent consideration of aesthetically pleasing objects as well as fragmentary items of daily use as markers of material culture, that site cartography came to play an important role in the archaeological process.

In the Ottoman Empire, the excavation of new sites often began through the cartographic activities of European rail- and road-building concessions. In 1864 the British railway engineer J. T. Wood began excavating at Ephesus. In the same year Carl Humann began to plot modern transportation networks throughout Asia Minor in the service of Grand Vizier Fuad Pasha. Both archaeologists used the transportation concessions of their nations to gain a foothold for archaeological activities. While they produced maps of the sites, the Ottoman government was not privy to the site maps that allowed for their excavations. By the time Schliemann continued his excavations of Troy in 1882, however, the military authority of the Dardanelles supervised the mapping of the region commissioned from a German engineer named Wolf.[13] This suggests that the Ottoman government had by that time gained an awareness of the strategic importance of cartographic site maps which would ensure the requirement of such maps by the 1884 law.

Regulated cartography came to be a standard part of the archaeological process. While attempting to map Palestine in 1885, Claude Reignier Conder, who had previously surveyed with utter impunity, complained that the Turks who oversaw his expedition regarded it with suspicion and finally forbade his work.[14] An 1885 permit for Humann's mapping of the valley of the Bakır stream to the town of Çandırlı specified that the local government receive a copy.[15] In addition to benefiting the state by providing a new awareness of local topography, a preliminary delineation of the site and its contours would prevent the arbitrary and dilettantish collection of antiquities from the uncharted landscape. The inclusion of a provision for maps in the 1884 law suggests that its Ottoman authors conceived of archaeology as a science rather than as a means of satisfying the desires of wealthy foreign aesthetes. It also denotes a shift in the strategic and tactical relations between foreigners and Ottomans, respectively, to archaeological sites that had been governed by the 1874 law. By partaking in the information gained through the production of maps, the Ottoman government ceased to relinquish control of sites to European archaeologists. Nonetheless, by not producing its own maps, the government continued to take a reactive stance to the archaeological activities encroaching on its territories. Archaeological mapping soon became so universally recognized for its strategic significance that during World War I, the maps of the Suez region that had recently been commissioned by the Palestine Exploration Fund were financed by the intelligence service of the British forces. Subscribers to the *Palestine Exploration Quarterly* received copies of the report of that survey, which the authors assured would not strategically benefit the Turks.[16] Yet the maps themselves remained a military secret.

As with the 1874 law, the passage of new legislation in 1884 did not ensure its enforcement. However, increasing public awareness, evidenced by scattered newspaper and journal articles, made it more controversial to allow antiquities to flow freely to European museums. Although the authors of these articles did not express concern for the antiquities themselves, it is clear that they were aware of the issues of sovereignty and ownership that informed their collection. The sudden burst of articles that coincided with the opening of a new building for the archaeological museum points to an increased desire to include the public in the museum's activities. For example, an 1891 article reports:

> In the region of the island of Milo where the famous Venus de Milo statue that now beautifies the Paris museum was found, another fairly worthwhile ancient statue has emerged. It depicts a participant in the gladiatorial games, but its legs are broken. According to scholarly opinion, this statue is believed to be one of the statues that belong to the group of the Venus de Milo. As soon as the government heard of the statue's discovery, it gave the order that a troop of soldiers be posted to guard the site.[17]

The relationship of this statue to the Venus de Milo determined its value in Ottoman eyes. Having made reference to the statue that had been taken by France seventy years earlier, the article emphasizes the responsible action of the current administration—protecting the site from further looting. Not only does the article point to an instance in which the law was followed, it suggests an educational process through which the public would take note of antiquities and see them as shared national treasures in need of state protection. Moreover, it implies that the state treasures of the Louvre, an institution that bespoke the cultural preeminence of France, were actually in large part Ottoman.

Also during the early 1890s, a series of short reports in the literary journal *Servet-i Funun* attempted to advise the reading public (probably for the most part in İstanbul) of archaeological activities around the empire. An article concerning the excavation of a site near the main city of Rhodes emphasized that a group of citizens who had found antiquities had immediately made a report to the police commissariat, which had taken charge of the actual excavation of a number of representational reliefs.[18] This news not only kept antiquities in the public eye but also served as a means to alert the public as to the proper procedure pertaining to the discovery of antiquities.

Despite the growing Ottoman interest in antiquities, European archaeologists continued to export valuable finds. When the German archeologist Carl Bendorf received permission to excavate in Ayasuluğ (Ephesus), an article in an Ottoman journal described the Temple of Diana as "one of the finest and most beautiful examples of ancient Greek [art], just as the city of Ephesus was once one of the most glorious and ornate cities." The article continued, "The emergence of its ruins will be an event of great historical importance, and we hope that the efforts to be made in this endeavor will be fruitful."[19] Despite the publicity of these finds, the antiquities discovered here would soon enter the collections of the Vienna Museum.

Other articles about excavations in Switzerland, Sicily, Egypt, and Athens framed the practice of archaeology in an international arena.[20] By collecting and displaying antiquities, the Ottoman state acquired status through its participation in an international cultural practice. Moreover, the French discovery of early bronze pieces between the Tigris and Euphrates Rivers in 1892 provided new insight into the history of humanity: its beginnings were on Ottoman soil.[21] Articles describing the museum at Versailles, the Vienna Museum, and the Louvre also contextualized the role of museums in the cultural centers of Europe, implicitly showing the need to have a similar institution in the Ottoman capital as well.[22] Even Cairo had its Museum of Antiquities, images of which were also featured on the pages of *Servet-i Funun*.[23]

At times the growing public interest in antiquities created a stumbling block to their donation to foreign governments. For example, in 1896 the minister of education wrote a memorandum stating:

> Antiquities have been determined by experts to be worthy of attention. Therefore, the immunity requested by the French consul in the name of the French Louvre Museum in relation to seven valuable works now located at the Imperial Museum [cannot be granted] so as not to act as an example. . . . If there are any that are double, and one of these does not have value among those pieces which are not important [it can be given], and of those that are not double, a plaster mold can be taken, as specified in the antiquities regulation.[24]

Not only were these objects not from a specific excavation, they had already become part of the Imperial Museum's collection. Undoubtedly, their conferral to the Louvre would have left a tell-tale trail of deliberate illegal activity by government authorities.

Efforts to control the apportionment of antiquities to the Imperial Museum and to foreign museums often depended on the latter's interest in promoting Ottoman cultural aspirations. The emphasis on Hellenistic and Byzantine artifacts in the Imperial Museum reflected its agenda of exhibiting Ottoman participation in European culture and rendered other types of collection peripheral. In 1892 the Louvre requested that the sultan give it seven objects located in the Imperial Museum because they were related to pieces the Louvre already possessed. Osman Hamdi judged that five of the pieces, broken cuneiform tablets, were indeed more valuable in terms of completing the Louvre collections than in terms of their inclusion in the Imperial Museum's collection. However, two of the pieces were bronze statues, bore no relation to the aforementioned pieces, had no duplicates, and thus were of value in the collection of the Imperial Museum. The sultan's officers followed this advice, and only the five tablets were sent to the Louvre.[25] The items considered without value were from the Hittite rather than the Hellenistic past and thus lacked the cultural capital that most intrigued the museum administration. Uninteresting as this was during the Ottoman period, it was precisely this heritage that would become the cornerstone of archaeological nationalism some fifty years later, during the early years of the Turkish Republic.

Although the 1884 law expressed a much more developed consciousness of archaeological value, it often proved too weak to implement. The prescriptions for granting permission to excavators were followed, but the mechanisms designed to conserve antiquities for the Imperial Museum often were not enforced. Bureaucrats often were able to create paths for the export of works as they emerged from archaeological sites before their documentation. Moreover, the close personal ties between Sultan Abdülhamid II and Kaiser Wilhelm I of Prussia and Emperor Franz Joseph I of Austria allowed for the circumvention of the antiquities law at the whim of the sultan.[26]

Only three years after the institution of the new law, the German engineer-cum-archaeologist Carl Humann received special permission to continue to export his finds from the Ottoman Empire. "As to the permit already in the possession of the Director of the Berlin Museum Humann," the permission explained, "the ninety antiquities that he discovered in the region of Zincirli in the province of Adana, which according to procedure belong to the Imperial Museum, should be left to him and in return he should pay for the transportation of the Imperial Museum's portion to İstanbul."[27]

In 1888 officials again gave Humann five to ten pieces from the same dig because their inscriptions were worked on poor grades of stone. The pieces taken for the Imperial Museum were to be left in the garden and the transportation costs paid by Humann.[28] Similarly, in 1885 potsherds from Troy were not considered valuable enough to be kept in the collection of the Imperial Museum and therefore were given to the Berlin Museum. As the document explains, "Because nobody other than Schliemann would want to buy the broken potsherds in storage in the museum and because they are not worthy of display and are not important . . . their sale is considered appropriate for fifty or sixty liras."[29] Although the law had expressed an ideological shift to a scientific mode of archaeological collection, in which all objects were considered interpretable parts of the material legacy of a culture, the Imperial Museum of the Ottoman Empire still considered the acquisition of artifacts according to their appropriateness for display.

Germany was not alone in benefiting from exemptions from the new antiquities law. Because of a favorable political situation at the time, an 1896 decree of Sultan Abdülhamid II gave the Austrian ambassador to Constantinople the right to freely select, at his discretion, from the finds at Ephesus as a mark of friendship between the sultan and the Austrian monarch.[30] The following year, in an attempt to halt the shipment of the second crate of antiquities from İzmir, the minister of public education objected vehemently to this concession of antiquities to the Austrian government.

> The antiquities that were to be selected and chosen from the aforementioned excavation site within the first two years by the consul for the Austrian Emperor were to be restricted. However, from the beginning to the end of the excavation M. Bendorf, who was charged with the excavation, has taken all that has appeared, and even pieces that had already been taken [for storage] to the school in İzmir, and sent them all directly to the Vienna Museum. . . . And of the works that, according to the decree, were to come to the Imperial Museum, I have only been able to obtain a notebook. . . . The Vienna Museum has opened a new section because of its ownership of a wonderful bronze statue of Hercules, the likes of which does not exist in any museum in the world, the published value of which is thirty to forty liras, and the spiritual value of which is beyond reckoning. Even if the importance of the works that appeared this year is not as great as those of last year, they are still worthy of display in museums. Already M. Bendorf has arranged for all of them to be transported to the Vienna Museum. Although the agreement only included the finds of the last two years, it was extended for a year. . . . As for the works that are going to be excavated in the upcoming season, permission has not been granted for their removal. . . . Because the Imperial Museum is particularly bound as a prosperous sign of [the sultan's] dignity in this glorious age for the future progress of the high [sultanate], it must undertake the monopolization of the excavation of a site like Ayasulug, which encompasses one of the richest architectural and sculptural ruins. Even when the [previous] antiquities law was in effect, only one-third of what they excavated and exported belonged to the excavators. For the Imperial Museum to not partake in this . . . does nothing but underscore the void nature of the new regula-

tions. . . . Thus an order must be given that works that belong to the Imperial Museum be delivered to the museum bureaucrat at the site and that the excavators only be allowed to take pictures and molds [of the works].[31]

The Ministry of Education objected to the export of the antiquities not only because of their status as a gift but also because the museum was deprived of knowing precisely what was being exported. Thus, while the sultan continued to use antiquities as items of barter, the museum came to express an increasing interest in maintaining antiquities as historical signifiers whose meaning depended on their contextualization within the empire.

Despite all objections, between 1896 and 1906 seven consignments of antiquities were sent to Vienna from Ephesus. Nonetheless, the minister's letter provides insight into numerous concerns relating to the museum in this period. It denotes a strong disjunction between the sultan and the Ministry of Education. Whereas the sultan considered antiquities part of his private domain and thus retained the ability to dispose of them at will, the ministry perceived the museum as the branch of the government responsible for maintaining antiquities within the empire. It thus expressed a preference for a uniform reign of law over the arbitrary enforcement of law by the monarch. This disjunction reflected the shift from a monarchic order, in which the ruler owned all Ottoman territories, to a parliamentary one, in which the people on the land would be represented by the government. The author of the above letter—quite probably an irate Osman Hamdi ghostwriting for the minister—emphasized the role of the museum as a mark of the empire's progress and its participation in the modern age through the amassing of antiquities. While he did not directly refer to the actions of the sultan as anachronistic and embarrassing, he strongly implied that the free flow of antiquities from a rich Ottoman site to a foreign country was an oversight of both material and symbolic dimensions.

Conveniently for Europeans, the sultan had more reservations about Osman Hamdi, director of the Imperial Museum, whom he suspected of sympathizing with the Young Turks, than about the European governments with whom he could barter seemingly useless stones. Even though Osman Hamdi was in charge of monitoring the excavation and export of antiquities, he was forbidden to leave Istanbul for more than a decade because of his political leanings. This created a palpable disjunction between the interests of the museum and the state it purportedly represented.

The sultan's disinterest in antiquities seems to have been famous among archaeologists of the late nineteenth century. For instance, Theodor

Weigand, director of the German Archaeological Institute in İzmir, eagerly took advantage of the sultan's willingness to use antiquities to forge alliances with Europe. Covetous of Austria's export of their prize finds at Ephesus, Germany began machinations for special privileges at their excavations, especially at Bergama. In peace negotiations with Greece the previous year, Germany had sided with the Ottoman Empire against France and Russia, bolstering its standing with the empire. The claim that France and Russia, as well as Austria, had benefited from special archaeological privileges supported Wiegand's claim that an antiquities treaty with the Ottomans was necessary and possible. Rather than apply to the appropriate administrative body, however, he suggested that the consulate, which would be involved in the negotiations, reformulate the special dispensation as a personal favor requested by the kaiser. In 1899 Germany arranged for a secret treaty with the Ottomans allowing Germans to keep half the antiquities found at any authorized excavation. However, concern over criticism of the sultan, as well as fear of compromising the image of German colonial neutrality, prevented the overt use of the agreement. Not only were legislators becoming aware of the value of antiquities, their objections suggest that the Ottoman bureaucracy included enough members conscious of their value to produce a political force that might criticize the sultan for making such an agreement.

The controversy surrounding these massive infringements of the law resulted in some self-regulation on the part of European archaeologists. For example, Wiegand opted for a policy of carefully wrought diplomacy concerning the distribution of antiquities. Realizing that Osman Hamdi could easily sabotage the sultan's infringements of the antiquities law, he arranged for antiquities to be apportioned to competing museums on site, preventing either side from appropriating all the desirable pieces. He even went so far as to return less valuable antiquities that Humann had secreted away from Priene, justifying his actions through a scientifically disinterested desire to publish the material, as well as a less noble desire to curry favor with the Ottoman authorities.[32]

The competition for antiquities extended beyond the rivalry between Germany and Austria. In 1898 the director of the British Museum sent the Imperial Museum a letter expressing concern over the increasing favors that the Ottoman government was conferring on Germany. The British Museum was concerned that Ottoman authorities might transfer excavation rights to German hands without warning despite the extensive work already undertaken by British archaeologists such as Austen Layard at Nimrud since 1882. In his letter, the director suggested that while the Ottoman government certainly had "an exclusive right to the terrain in question," "the importance of the work already executed at Ninevah by archaeologists in the service of the British Museum establish[ed] a moral title [to the excavation] which should be considered in their favor by the Ottoman government against the intervention of a foreign society."[33] The competition between British and German museums was played out on Ottoman territories under the control of the Imperial Museum, which expressed Ottoman territorial sovereignty through its power to grant or deny excavation permits.

Although, as already noted, reliefs with Christian subject matter from the city walls entered the Imperial Museum collection as of 1895, in 1900 Wiegand used the supposed Ottoman disinterest in non-Hellenistic antiquities to arrange for the export of "works dating from Christian times" to the Berlin Museum:

> During his visit last year to the capital of the sultanate, this request was conveyed by M. Wiegand and this request was recently repeated, that the desired stones consist of seven capitals now on the streets of İstanbul, and one stone from Salonica and one stone from the village of Alaçam on the coast of the Black Sea which are now being sent to the Imperial Museum. There is no harm seen in the gift of these nine stones.[34]

Unlike the works requested by the Louvre Museum and retained by the Imperial Museum in 1896, these stones already entering the Imperial Museum collection were released to the Berlin Museum through the personal intervention of Wiegand. Thus the breach reflected not so much a change in policy as a personal favor for an old friend.

The carefully wrought diplomatic balance of such archaeological exchanges began to sour with the removal of the Mschatta gate to the Berlin Museum. In 1902 the Byzantinist Joseph Strzygowski interested the director of the Royal Museums, Wilhelm von Bode, in the ruin of a castle (then thought to be Sassanid) known as Mschatta, located in the Syrian desert (today in Jordan). Bode, fearing that the imminent completion of the Hijaz railway would cause the monument to be plundered, made a direct appeal to the kaiser to acquire the castle's monumental gateway at all costs. The Deutsches Archaeologisches Institut (DAI) and the embassy in Constantinople also entered into the bargaining for the gate. On seeing photographs of the gate, Osman Hamdi refused to capitulate. A 1903 order from the Department of the Sultan discusses the export of the ruins:

> The export of some stones from the building known as Mschatta, located in the valley of Balga in the village of Salat in the province of

Syria, has been requested by his highness the German emperor for the Frederick Museum which is to open in Berlin. The report of the high council [*meclisi vukela*] of June 4, 1903, concerning this matter requires that it be shown that these stones do not have a religious purpose and that it become understood that they have various designs. Even if it would be necessary to maintain them as part of the sultan's privy because of their status as antiquities, and even though it would be good to transport them to the museum in the capital, the most important matter is to make certain that the aforementioned stones are not religious antiquities. The honored German emperor, like his grandfather, has made manifest numerous times works carrying charity and friendship. Since the aforementioned imperial highness follows in the footsteps of his grandfather, upon the request of the aforementioned emperor, the council has decided to grant the petition made by the German consulate.[35]

This decision recognizes several aspects of the antiquities in question. First, it raises the question of whether these were religious—presumably Islamic—antiquities, implying that religious ruins might require more careful conservation. Indeed, increasing religious conservatism was one of the hallmarks of Abdülhamid II's reign, as was reflected in the museum collections. More to the point, however, the decision recognized the Imperial Museum as the appropriate place for the stones but deemed it necessary to give them to Germany because of that country's history of good works benefiting the Ottoman Empire. The concession of valuable antiquities to Germany carried with it an implicit obligation for Germany to continue an economic and political alliance with the Ottoman Empire and served as a reward for such actions. The German consul arranged for the gate to go to the Berlin Museum as a personal gift from the sultan. In a show of Germany's appreciation, he also arranged for Kaiser Wilhelm to give the sultan a team of black thoroughbred horses.[36]

Soon after this exchange, the involved ministries began to tighten their enforcement of the antiquities law. Reports of infringements rather than requests for exceptions began to circulate in the bureaucratic paperwork. For example, the following request, addressed to the prison administration, emphasizes the need to enforce existing laws in the very region of the Mschatta affair.

In parts of the imperial territories in which historical importance is evident, such as Syria and Phoenicia, many people are selling the antiquities they search for among the ruins to foreigners who are travelling in the region. Because many of those in Europe who are involved with the science of antiquities are discussing this, the Imperial Museum hereby informs the internal affairs administration and the administrators of the coast guard that in the case of permission to export the aforementioned works they must show heightened attention and inform the Imperial Museum when works need to be returned.[37]

By 1905 local authorities were apparently heeding this request and had become quite cautious about smugglers: "Because recently antiquities have been stolen by smugglers from the ruins of Rikka in the province of Aleppo, a royal decree resulting from the greed of the aforementioned locals has been rumored. However the encoded order telegraphed by the Ministry of Education has not arrived. Therefore the need for instructions is hereby expressed."[38] The crackdown recorded in both of these documents alludes not so much to the activities of foreign excavators but to those of locals who were engaged in selling antiquities to foreign tourists.

Objections to the continuing export of antiquities by licensed excavators increased. In 1905, seven years after the Austrian government had received its special dispensation, the minister of education registered a complaint about the administration of antiquities at Ephesus:

> Concerning the antiquities that appeared at the excavation done at Aya-sulug in the name of the Austrian Museum[,] . . . a special regulation was processed [in 1313/1898], such that after this date all the many valuable antiquities emerging from this site were sent to Vienna without even a single work or a photograph being sent to the Imperial Museum, definitely violating the regulations pertaining to the Imperial Museum and the clear protection of the law.[39]

Similarly, the museum attempted to block the British export of antiquities, confusing the director of the British Museum, D. S. Hogarth, who had apparently never encountered such measures. "The two cases of marble fragments are still at Smyrna," he wrote in a personal letter to Osman Hamdi. ". . . I don't know if it is true that the Ottoman administration has prevented [their] exportation."[40] Apparently, the law had been so neglected that its sudden enforcement came as a shock.

By the end of the year, in anticipation of the new law of 1906, the government issued an order to rescind any permits previously granted to foreigners:

> Some of the provisions of the Imperial Museum regulations, in particular the third article related to excavations, have been found insufficient for the future progress of the Imperial Museum's acquisitions and activities. Until the completion of the drafting of amended legislation and its enactment, the directorship of the aforementioned museum indi-

cates that nobody, be they of foreign or Ottoman nationality, shall be granted a permit for excavation.[41]

Excavators suddenly lost their permits and, with them, their relatively unhindered ability to remove antiquities. In no uncertain terms, the directive stated, "In order for the drafting and enactment of certain principles and regulations concerning the guardianship of the Imperial Museum, the exploration by a group of foreigners who are currently exploring Baghdad and nearby regions needs to be prevented and [an order] has been given that nobody should be given an excavation permit."[42] Similarly, Robert Koldeway, who had been excavating the Ishtar Gate in Babylon since 1898 and had exported his finds since 1902, abruptly lost his permit in March 1905 when he refused to remit the packed cases of finds from Assur that the museum's agent, Bedri Bey, attempted to confiscate.[43]

Under the 1884 antiquities law, the Ottoman Empire assumed rightful ownership of antiquities in their domain. As the political and economic strength of the empire diminished, antiquities ceased to serve as an appropriate bargaining chip with which to make deals and placate European allies. Their symbolic value, not only as ties to a shared heritage, but also as markers of continued sovereignty, began to take precedence over their value as gifts. At the same time, the rule of law in relation to antiquities began to supersede the personal will of the sultan in their collection and distribution.

Osman Hamdi's frustrating experiences with the export of antiquities belied his high hopes for the role of the museum as an educational institution for the Ottoman public. In *The Tortoise Trainer* (1906; fig. 12), he depicts himself as an educator frustrated by the systems around him. He stands near the upper-story window of an Ottoman public building, body bowed, watching his pupils eat the leaves he has fed them. In one hand he holds a flute with which to instruct them. Around his neck hangs a leather prong with which to punish them. Unfortunately, his pupils lack ears with which to hear his flute and have hard shells protecting them from any leather whip. Although this painting bears no explicit references to the museum, it may serve as an allegorical reference to Osman Hamdi's role as an educator in Ottoman society. He has the tools with which to teach, but the pupils available to him are not capable of receiving his instruction. He stands as the patient father of frustration, watching his minions do all that they can without learning anything at all. It was at this moment of frustration that a new system of legislation had to step in to turn the tortoises into appreciative subjects of cultural education, or at the very least into sentient and responsible administrators willing to build enforceable laws.

Fig. 12.   Osman Hamdi, *The Tortoise Trainer* (1906), oil on canvas,
223 × 117 cm, collection of Erol Kerim Aksoy [Cezar]

THE ANTIQUITIES LAW OF 1906

By the time the third antiquities law was drafted, the Ottoman government not only had a more clearly articulated understanding of and appreciation for antiquities, but the Imperial Museum had taken a primary role in their administration. The revised antiquities law, passed on April 23, 1906, began with a consideration of the administration of antiquities rather than with their definition. Thus it foregrounded the processes of executing laws over the reasons for their existence, which by that time were implicit. The law established a central commission for antiquities, composed of the museum director, his assistant, and two museum guards. It also stipulated that local administrators of the Ministry of Education would be responsible for local museums, from which they would monitor local archaeological activity and relay information to the central commission.[44] In this manner the law finally provided for a mechanism for its administration and implementation. For the first time, the law explicitly designated the museum as having a plurality of roles: the institution responsible for the administration of antiquities; the only appropriate site for their collection and display; and the primary governmental organ responsible for antiquities preservation.

The new law delineated the rules of antiquities ownership more clearly than its predecessor. It stated simply, "The fine arts and the evidence of knowledge and science and literature of ancient peoples who once resided on lands under the administration of the Ottoman government without exception are antiquities." Moreover:

> All antiquities either known to exist or found on land and property belonging to the government in the aforementioned imperial territories or properties belonging to individuals or groups are the property of the Ottoman government. The right to find, conserve, collect, and place these objects in the Imperial Museums belongs solely to the government. This article includes objects mentioned and not mentioned, and fine Islamic arts.

This new definition of antiquities relied on a more conceptual footing than did that in the earlier laws. With a more contemporary understanding of scientific archaeology, the law explicitly recognized objects other than fine arts as antiquities and saw them as signs of earlier cultures. The law also provided for an overhaul of the concept of possession, wherein ownership of these objects relied not on the inherent Ottoman-ness of the territories but on their administrative prerogative.

Nonetheless, despite the modern underpinnings of the law, its wording often lacked the careful organization and categorization one might expect in an era suffused with positivist epistemology. For example, the law described in great detail the wide assortment of objects that could be construed as antiquities:

> For example, mosques and charities and holy buildings, abandoned lice-infested temples and synagogues (that is, the places of worship of Jews) that are now in disuse, basilicas (a type of church), churches, monasteries, burial towers, commercial inns, fortresses, towers, city walls, houses, theaters, bridges, horse squares, circuses (the place used in Roman times for carriage races and games), amphitheaters (the place used for plays and wrestling), baths, built sea-shores, wells with and without walls, cisterns, roads, obelisks, aqueducts, *höyüks* (burial hills), burial chambers with or without visible engraved surfaces, sarcophagi made of all sorts of materials that are or are not inscribed, poles, coffins, painted or gilt images or *nakab* [face veil with eyeholes], reliefs, stelai (funerary stones, memorial stones, and memorials on poles), statues, statuettes, figurines (little clay statuettes), wells with inscriptions and reliefs, leather and papyrus (a type of leaf with brands on it), parchment (writing on leather), and handwriting on paper, worked flintstones and weapons, mechanisms and tools of all materials and vases and equipment for measuring, and decorations, rings, jewelry, scarabs (a thing made of clay in the shape of a bug), weights, water jugs, medallions, molds, engraved stones, things carved of wood, inlaywork, and things made of ivory and bone are included. . . . Old walls and the ruins of buildings and any type of broken parts of buildings and old objects, scattered bricks, stone, and glass and broken pieces of wood and ceramic are among antiquities.[45]

The haphazard organization of this seemingly all-inclusive list could appear to be an accident of inexperience. Yet its author, Osman Hamdi, had received training in French law and was no doubt familiar with various legislative strategies. The arbitrary organization in this list, as well as the alternating use of great specificity with great broadness, suggests that he may have chosen disorder as a stylistic device to convey the potential breadth of what could constitute an antiquity. Published as a small pamphlet, the new law had a didactic presence: it not only admonished the reader to behave responsibly in relation to antiquities but also educated him as to what types of things could be considered antiquities. The range—from anything handwritten on paper to a circus; from things found frequently in the empire, such as inscribed stones, to things found rarely, such as scarabs; from the familiar objects, like weapons, to the remote ones, like flintstones—indicated that almost anything could be construed as an antiquity. The phrase "mentioned and not mentioned" em-

phasized the breadth of the category of antiquities suggested by this haphazard list. In essence, the law reserved the right to transform any object
of historical or cultural curiosity into an antiquity and thereby to protect
it. Like the apparent lack of organization belittled by Dumont in the Magazine of Antiquities, the lack of organization here may well have reflected
strategic opacity rather than negligence or ineptitude.

While the 1884 law had for the first time defined the objects made by
the ancient peoples of Ottoman territories as subject to Ottoman administration, the new law expanded this mandate to objects of a more recent
past. In addition to promoting a sense of cosmopolitan internationalism
through the display of Greco-Roman artifacts, the museum's new Islamic
collection would reflect a burgeoning sense of national pride in the familiar arts of the Ottoman world. Notably, the list of objects begins not with
ancient objects but with relatively modern if somewhat picturesquely disused sites of worship—not only Islamic but Jewish and Christian as well.
The inclusion of these sites laid claim to a more recent history and recognized the religious and cultural multivalence of Ottoman heritage. Moreover, the interest in these sites shows a rising consciousness that objects
and architecture of periods with extensive written sources form an important part of the historical record, which it is the state's duty and prerogative to preserve, protect, document, and in certain cases collect.

Whereas the museum had initially been designed primarily to house an
Other to be subsumed within the Ottoman self, the new Islamic collections
would provide room for reflection and celebration of the autochthonous
and variegated Ottoman self. This increasing interest in Islamic heritage
reflected Sultan Abdülhamid's policies, which emphasized the caliphate
and the role of the sultanate in protecting the rights of Muslims both in
the empire and in recently independent regions, particularly in eastern Europe. The inclusion of Islamic works also reflected an increasing consciousness of the Islamic world as a unified whole that could be represented
through the objects it had produced.

Such an interest in local heritage, and its collusion with nationalist
endeavors, corresponds with the increasing interest in Europe in local, as
opposed to Greco-Roman, archaeological heritage. In 1890, for example,
a German branch of the DAI opened with the express purpose of
studying Germany's own history, conceived as beginning with the first
settlers of German lands, rather than human or Western history, conceived as beginning with the first writings of the ancients.[46] Increasingly,
the interest in the cultures of one's own land became part of the concep-
tualization of nationalist heritage. In the case of the Ottomans, the inter-

est in antiquities had begun as a desire to participate in European visions of Western culture and had developed into a means of tracing national history through antiquities. The expanding definition of an antiquity marks the moment when the Islamic history and the ancient histories of the Ottoman Empire became part of a continuous heritage, belonging exclusively under Ottoman administration.

Despite the anticipated crackdown on antiquities export, abrogations of the new law began almost immediately. The German consulate voiced its complaints about the new law only a few months after its passage.[47] In response, Germany successfully acquired special dispensation to export a considerable amount of antiquities: "The imperial decree that has been shown to the sultan—which explains that what the German Consulate has requested is not the adjustment of the new antiquities law, but that half of the antiquities to be found belong to the imperial government and half to the Berlin museum—has received the support of the sultan."[48] While a direct consular appeal to the sultan had again been effective, unlike earlier exemptions, this provision technically was limited to a single use and could not be guaranteed comprehensively. Nonetheless, German archaeologists continued to export important finds from the empire, including the monumental market gate of Miletus, which they exported in 1908 by taking advantage of the confusion caused by the Young Turk Revolution.

Not only did the abrogation of the law by European institutions continue (although to a lesser extent than before the 1906 law), locals often participated in smuggling antiquities, particularly in the eastern portions of the empire. In 1910 reports from Syria indicated that members of two tribes there were aiding Frenchmen involved in the construction of the Hijaz railway in collecting antiquities from Mada'in al-Salih[49] In response to such problems, the government arranged for the translation of anti-smuggling laws that were in effect in England and in Italy.[50] Reports of smuggling both by locals and by foreigners persisted in the following years, indicating that public awareness of antiquities as a commodity had grown and also that the government had begun to take a more regular interest in supervising its exchange across borders.[51] During these years, eastern Anatolia and the Syrian provinces emerged as sites of considerable unrest and resistance to the Ottoman government. The smuggling activities of local tribes reflect their collusion with European forces who would later lay claim to Ottoman territories and also their dire need of money and supplies.

The 1906 antiquities law was so comprehensive that it not only stayed in effect for the rest of the Ottoman era, but was adopted by the Republic of Turkey and remained in effect with only minor modifications until 1973. While the museums of the republic reflected new understandings of national identity, the transmutability of the 1906 law suggests that its content already reflected important changes in what constituted the Turkish-Ottoman national identity as it would be expressed through museum display. Particularly, it emphasized the idea of indigenousness as the primary criterion in the national acculturation of artifacts into modern museum settings and narratives. Moreover, as in Greece during the same era, this understanding of archaeological value paved the way for an ethnogenetic understanding of Turkish history, such that "the tracing of the antiquity of the ethnic constituent of a present nation restores a pseudo-historical sense of continuity and legitimizes the present. . . . Somehow if one has defined the start (past) and the culmination (present) of a trajectory, all that goes in between is, in some miraculous manner, insignificant."[52]

The politics of the successive acts of legislation that treated antiquities as a cultural commodity suggest that the museum served as a locus of tension between Europeans who sought antiquities, an Ottoman intellectual elite who fostered the museum, and the sultan, who technically was the sole owner of the collection. The disputes played out in the arena of antiquities reflect the ongoing tension between the supporters of a constitutional monarchy and the totalitarian preferences of Abdülhamid II. By emphasizing the rights of the state to own antiquities over the rights of the sultan, the museum administration established the idea of a democratic museum—a repository for the collective valuables of the citizenry as represented by the state—long before the idea of representative government had gained currency in Turkey.

5 Technologies of Collection

Railroads and Cameras

The process of antiquities collection in the Ottoman Empire unfolded in the context of the acquisition of technologies and practices that were new and exciting not only in the empire but in the entire world as well. The reformulation of archaeology as a large-scale science depended heavily on new modes of transportation, such as the railroad, both for people and for cargo. Similarly, photography provided new modes of documentation and transport of information. Together, these technologies transformed the ways in which cultures could be recorded and disseminated.

The Ottoman Empire acquired these technologies, invented in Europe, at the cost of its financial—and, many feared, cultural—independence. It participated in the growth of archaeological practice and the territoriality implicit in it only through the imported technologies that were exceedingly dependent on Western imports and financing.

RAILWAYS

The establishment of railways across the Ottoman Empire marked a spatial and transportational contest over territorial hegemony played out through the multivalent contest over antiquities. The physical construction of the railbed created disputes over the ownership of culturally valuable properties. The historian Morris Jastrow, writing during World War I, took note of the political ramifications of activities such as history, philology, and archaeology that had once been framed in the guise of disinterested science:

> As an industrial enterprise, the project of a railway through a most notable historic region, and passing along a route which had resounded to

131

the tread of armies thousands of years ago, was fraught with great possibilities of usefulness in opening up the nearer East to brisk trade with
Europe that would follow in the wake of the locomotive, and in infus-
ing the young Western spirit into the old East, carrying Western ideas,
Western modes of education, and Western science to the mother-lands
of civilization. . . . As the control of the historic highway stretching
from Constantinople to Baghdad has at all times involved the domination of the Near East, it has been necessary to sketch the history of Asia
Minor in its relation to the great civilizations of antiquity and to follow
that history through the period of Greek, Roman, Parthinian and Arabic control, past the efforts of the Crusaders to save the route for Christian Europe, to the final conquest of it by the Ottoman Turks.

. . . Until recently, the history of these lands has been looked upon
by the general public as the domain of the specializing historian, philol-
ogist and archaeologist. With the extension of the European war into
these eastern lands, they become a part—and an essential part—of the
general political situation.[1]

The expansion of railways across the Ottoman hinterland during the
late nineteenth century enhanced the access of Europeans with archaeological interests to remote sites. The English received the first railway concession in the Ottoman Empire in 1856 to build a line between İzmir and
Aydin. From that moment on, the acquisition of antiquities was wedded to
the digging activities necessary for railway construction. Soon after the
British began construction of the railbed in 1863, J. T. Wood began the
project that would develop into the excavation of Ephesus. Similarly,
the excavation of Bergama emerged from railroad construction. The discovery of the Mschatta gate in 1903 and its subsequent export depended
on the project of the Hijaz railway. As the rights to build railway lines
across Anatolia were sold to various European nations, new issues of territorial control came to be played out in disputes over the ownership of antiquities found during railway construction.

The 1884 antiquities law failed to specifically mention railways as potential sites for the discovery of antiquities. Nonetheless, as railways expanded across the empire, the Ministry of Education repeatedly issued directives against the taking of antiquities by European railway engineers.
When the İzmir-Kasaba line, built in 1863, expanded to Afyonkarahisar in
1893, the museum immediately took an interest in the antiquities likely to
emerge from the construction of the railbed and requested the attention of
the Ministry of Education:

> Given that the Anatolia railway line under construction from İzmir has
> been approved and begun, it has been reported that some antiquities are

appearing and are going to the foreigners. . . . It would be appropriate for them to be sent to [İstanbul].[2]

The Damascus-Hama railway in Syria caused similar suspicions on the part of the museum, leading to vehement denials of interest in antiquities by the Société de Chemin de Fer d'Anatolie.[3]

The 1898 visit of the German kaiser with the sultan engendered the ambitious Baghdad railway project, designed to "link this enterprise in most romantic fashion with the most famous landmarks of Asia Minor and of Mesopotamia."[4] As part of the same agreement, the sultan conceded the rights to antiquities to the Germans in the secret treaty mentioned in the previous chapter. In contrast to the Ministry of Education's efforts to preserve antiquities as metaphorical markers of territorial sovereignty, the sultan was willing to dispose of the material remains of ancient cultures in exchange for modern European technologies.

In the 1910s the completion of railway lines by the German-owned Imperial Ottoman Baghdad Railway Company to Baghdad via Konya incited similar concerns over the acquisition of antiquities that might be found during the construction work:

> Because work has begun on the portion of the Baghdad railway after
> the Ereğli station and because in this regard the appearance of antiqui-
> ties is strongly expected, to avoid the perdition of such works that
> might appear the appropriate instructions have been given to the neces-
> sary people to immediately inform the Imperial Museum.[5]

Through such preemptive efforts, the government did not simply lay claim to antiquities, it also symbolically reasserted its physical control over land engraved with foreign railways. Such an emphasis on antiquities acquisition underscored the disjunction in ownership between the land itself and the rails marking, partitioning, and accessing its surface.

In regions where the sovereignty of the Ottoman state was coming under dispute through insurrection, the contest over antiquities acquisition clearly reflected local political struggles. During the 1910 extension of the Hijaz railway, foreigners as well as locals were implicated in the illegal acquisition of antiquities.

> With the report that foreign officials and various travelers working
> with the Hijaz Railway have, with the assistance of some locals, ac-
> quired antiquities near Mada'in as-Salih the appropriate instructions
> were given to the governorship of Syria. . . . While there is no sign that
> antiquities in the aforementioned region are being taken, measures for
> their protection as well as an investigation have been ordered.[6]

Sites that had previously been difficult to access became, with the extension of the railway, territories whose ownership could be questioned. In a climate of fear of European domination, the contest over antiquities became a metaphor for the contest over land enacted through the new accessibility of sites, both contemporary and archaeological. While the ownership of the land was not yet under dispute, the contest over unearthed antiquities masked a struggle for the control of territories recently made more accessible by rail. The railways not only provided more efficient transportation to sites, they also provided a new means of collusion between the foreign, imperialistically minded railway investors and local groups interested in shifting their allegiance away from the Ottoman state. The acquisition of antiquities along the railway lines thus formed a convenient mode of alliance between foreigners and local tribes—an alliance clearly feared by the central government more than the symptomatic cooperation in antiquities smuggling.

During the early twentieth century, the Ottoman government began to see the collection of antiquities as an incipient form of colonial territorial aspiration on the part of European governments. Antiquities, which had gained value as cultural markers of a Helleno-Byzantine heritage, were now signs of contemporary rule. In such an environment, it became increasingly imperative for the Ottoman government to retain antiquities as signs of their territorial sovereignty. This concern was doubly important where railways were concerned, as they provided increased foreign access to Ottoman territories.

This access quickly surpassed professional interests and entered the realm of leisure travel. Much as railways allowed for expanded archaeological venues, they also allowed for travel beyond the port cities of Constantinople and İzmir. For example, in his 1877 memoirs of the excavation of Ephesus, Wood recalled anecdotes of incompetent guides brought from Smyrna or hired locally who often provided incorrect information about the sites and hurried tourists back to the train station long before their hour of departure.[7] His work suggests that the tourist trade, while extant in İzmir, was still in its infancy. Only a few years later, Murray and Baedeker included Ephesus and the Troad in their guidebooks as sites that any intrepid traveler could visit on day trips by train from İzmir.[8]

As trains cut across the Ottoman hinterland, tourists began to visit ancient sites, unconsciously challenging the proprietary rights of archaeologist and native alike. The advent of site tourism reduced the archaeologist's exclusive adventure-ridden right to the site just as it reduced any local claims based on historical possession. Through his physical presence at the site, the tourist came to share in its cultural ownership. As soon as tourists began to arrive, the local tourist industry began to enter into conflict with the established mechanisms of control over the site, already disputed by the Ottoman state, site archaeologists, and, in some cases, local citizens.

By 1905 the practice of site tourism had developed into one regulated by the government, especially at the two most popular sites, both accessible by train: Ephesus and Baalbek. Each site was furnished with facilities for the sale of guidebooks and photographs. Unlike before, when tourists had hired any willing volunteer to guide them through the ruins, new regulations monitored tour guides for the profit of the site.

> Every guide who wants to have free entry to the ruins will pay a yearly fee of 200 piastres. He will also be responsible for the damages that may be caused by the people who visit the ruins under his guidance (inscription, or drawing of names onto the walls, breakage, theft, etc.). He will be given, by examination about the site, a diploma that he will have to show.[9]

In addition to the fee paid by tour guides, tourists began to pay for the right to enter the site.[10] In exchange, they received a map of the site and a ticket (fig. 13).

Similarly, by 1873 European travelers who previously had been barred from the Haram as-Sharif in Jerusalem could pay a small fee to examine the Dome of the Rock firsthand.[11] Over the following decades, scientifically trained tour guides came to supplant local traditions of guiding pilgrims to holy sites. In 1892 a "local association" of the Palestine Exploration Fund was founded in Jerusalem to serve modern tourists' need for facts rather than legends. After opening a shop inside the Jaffa Gate where tourists could purchase the society's publications and attend lectures, it began to train local tour guides. Before long the municipal council of Jerusalem decided to standardize the training of tour guides, and by 1895 all tour guides were required to pass an examination based on the knowledge derived from explorations that had occurred under the auspices of the Palestine Exploration Fund.[12]

Thus the tourist came to possess many of the marks of symbolic ownership—knowledge, photographs, and maps—that had initially belonged exclusively to archaeologists and later to the Ottoman state through its organ, the Imperial Museum.

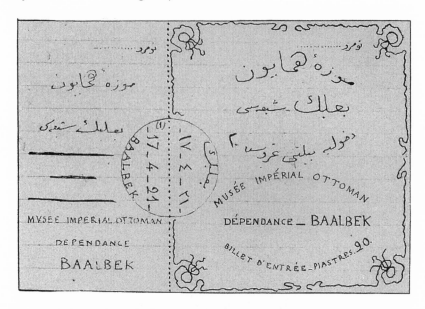

Fig. 13. Ticket to the Baalbek Site Museum, 1921 [IAMA]

VISUAL REPRODUCTION

While trains brought European tourists to archaeological sites, two- and three-dimensional reproductions could carry sites back to Europe. The technologies of reproduction—the making of plaster and paper casts and rubbings and the advent of photography and its subsequent adoption by archaeologists—constructed a mode of possession that partially dispensed with the imperative of physical ownership. Almost as much as the control of the actual archaeological artifact, control over its image became a mark both of possession and of authority over the objective and incontrovertible knowledge of that artifact.

The Imperial Museum was furnished with ateliers for the production of plaster casts. The three-dimensional plaster copy acted as a means of disseminating the "accurate" and objective knowledges inherent in the archaeological artifact without sacrificing the value inherent in the original. The inclusion of this type of reproduction in the 1884 law as an alternative for antiquities export marks it as a supplement for the actual archaeological artifacts under international contestation.

The differentiation between the plaster cast and the original in the Ottoman law marks a type of differential value between the original and the copy then under debate in the museums of Europe and America. The organization of the Imperial Museum focused on the breadth of the acquisitions, not on the concept of human progress that informed the collections of the West. In American museums, which also began to develop in the 1870s, the unavailability of original ancient sculptures led to the collection and display of plaster casts. Steeped in the nineteenth-century emphasis on aesthetic appreciation of great works from great cultures, museum curators often perceived little difference between the educational value of copies and that of originals. While ownership of an original signaled territorial mastery in the ongoing competition to excavate and export antiquities, the extensive display of plaster casts in museums throughout Europe and America was quite common and sufficed to demonstrate evolutionary aspects of the art historical canon. The type of learning that American museums were interested in promoting required authentic form rather than original statuary. The taxonomic organization of plaster-cast sculpture into models of progress served as a sign of art historical legitimacy for American museums emulating those of Europe. As Alan Wallach points out, some nineteenth-century American commentators believed that casts could provide an aesthetic experience equivalent or even superior to that afforded by originals. In a culture where education depended heavily on knowledge of the literary classics, the display of plaster casts in museums could make education and culture available to a broader audience who might not be able to afford extensive site travel.[13]

In contrast, it was the use of original sculptures in the Imperial Museum, not their organization or their complete illustration of the art historical canon, that lent the museum its cultural legitimacy. While both the United States and the Ottoman Empire attempted to use their museums to compete with existing European institutions, the United States was already implicitly part of the European cultural heritage. Its museum collections sought to prove their maturity, not their right to partake in Western Civilization.[14] In contrast, Ottoman museum collections were designed to create a niche for the empire in the European patrimony of the ancients. Thus the availability of original statuary, rather than the production of a comprehensive narrative of human progress, served the ideological needs of the museum with the greatest clarity. By placing emphasis on the possession of original works rather than on an art historical program, the new Ottoman law foreshadowed a development that would only come about in European and American museums after the turn of the century: the elimination of plaster casts from the collections. The education provided by European and American museums in the late nineteenth century had originally focused simultaneously on the power to acquire and on the dissemination of an encyclopedic, evolutionary model of culture. With the elimination of casts, it came to emphasize the financial, administrative, and territorial might required for the acquisition of originals—already the sole focus of the Ottoman collections, as is discussed in detail in the next chapter.

Plaster casts were but one of several modes of reproduction common to late-nineteenth-century archaeological practice. Not only could archaeologists produce technical drawings through the use of a camera lucida, they could also make rubbings and paper casts of archaeological finds. In his 1883 manual for the amateur archaeologist interested in exploring the lands of ancient Greece, Saloman Reinach, one of the first archaeologists affiliated with the Imperial Museum in Constantinople, made it clear that the primary duty of the itinerant archaeologist was the process of documentation.[15] He considered the prototypical archaeologist as sharing discursive similarities with entomologists and geologists. He suggested that the archaeologist would apply similar scientific methods as these practitioners to a different set of objects made available by the virgin landscapes of the Ottoman Empire. Thus they could render the territory visible in a different but parallel mode to that of the geologist and delineate taxonomy of objects much as an entomologist would apply the principles of positivist, Darwinian thought to the classification of insects.

Consistent with contemporary German practice, Reinach grounded his prototypical practice in philological interests and therefore instructed his traveler to copy every inscription that he encountered. However, since his travels through "potentially uncharted territories" were to be of use to the science of archaeology, the mere drawing of inscriptions by hand could not be sufficient to satisfy the objective reproducibility that was required. Only through appropriate technologies of reproduction could the many scripts strewn over the surface of the historically encoded Ottoman landscape be accurately deciphered, rendering them transparent to the positivist agenda of total knowledge. Reinach warned against copying only Latin and Greek texts and provided a wide variety of sample alphabets that might be encountered in the lands of Greece and Asia Minor. Thus the project of archaeology was to render the entire landscape of artifacts visible to the processes of international data collection. In this endeavor, objective methods of reproduction would enable the amateur archaeologist to enhance his credibility by reducing the element of human error inherent to the process of copying. Uncharted territories would be rendered legible by the archaeologist-explorer who rendered Asia Minor legible not through an understanding of its contemporary existence but through decoding the layers of its past.

The first mode of mechanical reproduction that Reinach suggests was *moulage,* a process whereby a wet piece of paper with a high rag content is molded to the surface of an inscription, creating a paper relief that could be transported from the site. While by modern standards this method seems excessively labor-intensive, Reinach pointed out that moulage was both more effective under various lighting conditions and less cumbersome than photography, which at that time required not only a camera but also reams of photosensitive paper that had to be kept in a light-sealed box until it could be developed.

However, as Reinach hastened to point out in his manual, the advent of photography brought entirely new possibilities to the documentary procedures of archaeology and in a sense rendered the need for artifacts more symbolic than it had ever been before.

PHOTOGRAPHY

Photography came to the Ottoman Empire in 1839, when news of its invention was published in the newspaper *Takvim-i Vakai* soon after its development by Louis Daguerre.[16] Throughout the world, the advent of photography revolutionized the range of visual experience available to any individual. Previously, people could experience the distant or the hidden only through verbal description or drawing, both of which were obviously mediated by the hand of the reporter or artist. In contrast, photography provided the opportunity for a mechanically objective, thus seemingly unmediated and thereby firsthand look at the world.

In the Ottoman Empire, photography began as a tool of Orientalist fascination and touristic voyeurism. It soon developed into a mode of self-representation controlled by the Ottoman state. Under Sultan Abdülhamid II photography moved from the realm of art into that of documentation and came to play a role in a growing ethos of order, organization, and ownership developing concurrently in the Imperial Museum.

The first photographers in the Ottoman Empire were interested in producing images of the East for an audience in Europe. In 1839 Frederic Goupil Fesquet was among the first to travel to the Middle East with the express purpose of making daguerrotypes of the Holy Land. During his return trip to Europe, he also took photographs of the port of Izmir, where the party of travelers stopped. Joseph Philbert Girault de Prangey visited the empire between 1842 and 1845 to take photographs of the Orient for his work, *Monuments Arabes d'Egypte, de Syrie, et d'Asie-Mineure dessinés et mesurés de 1842 à 1845*, published in 1846. Similarly, Maxime de Camp learned photography expressly to record his impressions of the Orient, which he published as *Souvenirs et paysages d'orient, Smyrne, Ephese, Magnesie, Constantinople, Scio* in 1848. All of these photographers had a fleeting relationship with the Orient. They visited it so as to supply Europeans with images of antique and exotic lands that had become legendary. For them, photography served as a supplement to the popular imagination.

Soon after the first wave of traveler-photographers passed through the empire, European citizens as well as members of the local European, Greek, and Armenian communities began to establish photographic studios in the primarily European sixth district of İstanbul, Pera. For many years, Muslims in the empire did not engage in photography, in part because of less active linguistic and cultural ties with Europe than was common in many of the minority communities and in part because of the close technical relationship between photography and professions often held by minorities, such as jewelry production. The iconoclastic tendencies of Islam may also have caused some Ottomans to refrain from participating in this profession. In 1840 James Robertson traveled to İstanbul to work on the improvement of Ottoman coinage. He soon decided to settle in Pera, where he set up a photographic studio to process numerous photographs of İstanbul. Between 1853 and 1855 he supplied Europe with photographs of the Crimean War. Like his European predecessors, Robertson produced photographs for a primarily European market. Unlike them, however, he maintained a long relationship with the Ottoman state, continuing to work with the Ottoman mint until 1876.

Unlike his predecessors, Basil Kargopolou, who opened a studio in 1850, addressed an audience of European tourists rather than send his images of the empire westward. On 6-by-9-centimeter cards, he produced images of the city and also studio portraits for which his customers could pose in a wide variety of Eastern costumes he kept on hand. Europeans had to come to the Orient to make these images of the city and of themselves into souvenirs. Unlike the owners of the previously published images of the Orient, these owners could use postcards as devices to remember and share what they themselves had seen. Personalized studio photographs could act in conjunction with city scenes to prove the presence of travelers in the Orient, where they had participated in the local ambience by wearing local dress—even if this participation was imaginary, as Europeans rarely changed their fashions while abroad, and upper-class Ottomans already wore fairly European styles of clothing. As official photographer for Sultan Abdülmecid II and Sultan Murat V, Kargopolou brought photography under the purview of the Ottoman state. Although he primarily worked on portrait and landscape photography for these rulers, his introduction of photography to the royal eye laid the groundwork for the profound change in the use of photographic images under Sultan Abdülhamid II.

Many other photographic studios soon joined those already in Pera. Most notable among these, the studio of Pascal Sébah, called El Chark, opened in 1857. His panoramic scenes and stereoscopes of scenes from Eastern life in photographs taken in Bursa, the Aegean coast, Athens, Egypt, and Libya not only catered to a local clientele but won him a reputation in Europe as well. After a long partnership with a Frenchman named A. Laroche and later with another named Bechard, he became partners with Policarpe Joaillier in 1884, and the name of the studio changed to Sébah and Joaillier in 1888.

El Chark was not alone in addressing the needs of both a European and an Ottoman clientele. In 1858 three Armenian brothers who later became known as the Abdullah Frères bought a photographic studio in a less affluent, less European section of İstanbul, Beyazit. In 1867 they sold this shop in favor of a more central location on the main street of Pera and subsequently became one of the most famous photographic establishments and galleries of the era. Sultan Abdülaziz proclaimed the Abdullah Frères the official court photographers and Outstanding Artists of the City, an epithet they continued to use until the closure of the shop in 1899, when it was sold to Sébah and Joaillier.

For the first few years after its introduction to the empire, photography served as a curiosity for the upper classes. Before long, however, the Ottoman government began to see photographs as tools for self-promotion outside of the empire. In 1867 they decorated the model Turkish coffeehouse and model Turkish villa of the Paris Universal Exposition with panoramic scenes of İstanbul made by the Abdullah Frères photographic studio. Similarly, they published a book of regional costumes with photographs taken by the Sébah studio in conjunction with the 1873 Vienna World Exposition.[17] For the first time, the photographs used in these expositions presented a controlled, firsthand view of the empire to the exhibition visitor. The photographs served as tools rather than artwork, as advertisements rather than souvenirs.

The cumbersome nature of photographic equipment made it a difficult tool for field archaeology. Yet photography's ability to document and carry sites to distant lands and thus to mark the experience of the practitioner made it an attractive tool not simply for archaeological exploration but also for marketing archaeological finds as modes of cultural expression. For example, when Schliemann used a portrait of his wife, who was Greek, to model the jewelry he found, he attempted to create a vision of her as Helen of Troy and thus promote his claim that he had discovered the treasure of Priam. His subsequent use of the photographs to sell his finds to Germany opened the doors to an international competition for the treasures, which has since grown to include Russia, Greece, and Turkey.[18]

By the end of the century, photography began to supplant other processes of reproduction. In his manual for the amateur archaeologist, Reinach may have given explicit instructions for multiple forms of reproduction, but the sole image in the text is an engraving of a camera in its travel bag, implicitly wedding the activities of the archaeologist to that of photographic documentation. While the philological archaeologist could make do without a camera, the archaeologist interested in antiquities or statues was well advised to collect antiquities via the photograph, since he could not do so in actuality because of increasingly restrictive laws. Reinach contrasts the act of documentation of works in the museums of Athens and İstanbul, already complete, with the lack of documentation of objects outside of the museums. These uncollected objects could become part of the scientific record of European archaeology—enter their intellectual purview—through the process of photographic collection, understood as a necessary task that had barely begun.

> No doubt, the important ruins that are indicated in the guides are known through careful engravings or perfectly exact heliogravures; but even in Athens and Constantinople, how many interesting works of art are still unedited or have only been reproduced in an insufficient manner! . . . The monuments dispersed outside the museums and large cities almost completely await an editor.[19]

Indeed, one of the main projects undertaken under the reign of Abdülhamid II (1876–1909) was the photographic documentation of the entire empire. Abdülhamid appointed numerous photographers in the empire to take pictures of a wide variety of subjects for him to examine and collect in albums. While many of the photographs were taken by commercial firms like Sébah and Joaillier and Abdullah Frères, the government also hired independent photographers, most notably Ali Riza Pasha and Bahriyeli Ali Sami, to organize the collections and to take photographs of more restricted sites.

Unlike those from earlier periods, these photographs were made with the express purpose of acting as documentary and administrative devices and were taken with this objective in mind. As William Allen points out, the photographs of Abdülhamid's collection fall into three broad categories: landscape vistas, historical monuments, and scenes that depict current educational, industrial, and military developments.[20] In addition, the original albums included vast ethnographic records of people and costumes in various parts of the empire, as well as extensive photographs of prisoners. Abdülhamid, who was very interested in physiognomy, used these photographs to make decisions. For example, he used the photographs of prisoners to choose those who would benefit from the amnesty of 1901, associated with the twenty-fifth anniversary of his coronation. His study of physiognomy, as well as his express interest in modern versions of traditional institutions, such as prisons, schools, and hospitals, affirmed his interest in systems of order, analysis, and public control already established in Europe.

In his memoirs, the chief secretary to the sultan recalls that Abdülhamid often said, "Every picture is an idea. A picture can inspire political and emotional meanings which cannot be conveyed by an article of a hundred pages."[21] Clearly, for Abdülhamid, it was not only each photograph that provided information and enjoyment, but the compilation of photographs that enhanced his ability to know and thereby control his vast empire. He used these images as documents through which he could acquire unprecedented vision of his empire. Although the posed pictures of people and the photographs of empty buildings are far more controlled than the snapshots and candid images to which we are accustomed today, the premise of Abdülhamid's photographic collection had a panoptic effect. Rarely leaving the palace grounds for fear of assassination, Abdülhamid used photographs both to affirm the success of his modernization projects and to make decisions. Conversely, those in the photographs and those in charge of the spaces and events they document knew that the eye of the sultan, as represented by the camera, was evaluating their work as well as their participation in the empirewide project of modernization. Like the spies rumored to infiltrate every corner of his realm, the camera served as the roving eye of the sultan.

Sultan Abdülhamid II was quite aware of the documentary and expository power of well-compiled photographic collections. In 1893 and 1894 he sent fifty-one photo albums to the U.S. Library of Congress and to the British Library. The former gift came in response to an American gift of books of governmental reports and tables that the sultan found very impressive. While very little documentation accompanied the albums sent to Washington, those sent to London were accompanied by a message. P. Currie, the British ambassador to the Porte, reported that the albums were "presented by The Sultan to Her Majesty's Government for the use of the British public in order that it should be generally known in England what progress has been made in literature and science in Turkey since his Majesty came to the throne, and to show how greatly he is interested in the advancement of learning and education in his Empire."[22]

Museums were among the new, European-style institutions documented in the Abdülhamid photographic collection. Like the pictures of other modern institutions, those of the museums do not show any people. Rather, they document the physical layouts of the museums, providing the sultan with a tour of the institution in absentia. This mode of documentation underscores the sultan's interest in the museum. The images focus on neither the objects in the collections nor the audiences who would see them. Rather, the images underscore the fact of the institution itself as a marker of progress.

While today photographic rights may seem uncontrollable, the paucity of cameras in the empire, especially outside of major cities, made their use subject to state attention. The antiquities laws and museum regulations recognized the processes of reproduction as supplements for the act of actual ownership. According to the 1884 law, the archaeologist lost the right to take actual antiquities but retained the right to copy them in plaster or to take their photographic image. While the right of physical ownership of the object marked the territoriality of the empire, the possession of knowledge remained primarily European.

Nonetheless, access to photographic reproductions of archaeological sites remained important. For example, in their attempt to control antiquities under threat from railway construction in Syria, the governor's office telegraphed the central administration that five French priests who had just returned to Damascus from the site of Mada'in al-Salih had taken photographs. Although perhaps not important in itself, their activities merited attention because the previous year they had colluded with members of the Fuqara tribe in the acquisition of antiquities. Photographs marked interest in archaeological sites, making their photographers into objects of interest for the government.[23] However, the photograph itself played merely a supplemental role to the original artifact and therefore did not pose a territorial threat.

Fig. 14. Archaeologists on site in Bergama, 1879 [German Archaeological Institute, İstanbul]

Photography not only created a mode of visual ownership for archaeological finds, it also documented the process through which artifacts were found. The portraits of archaeologists at sites in Anatolia reflect the imperialist ethos of the time. For example, in a portrait of archaeologists in front of their work station at Bergama (fig. 14), the seal of the kaiser on the unfinished wooden boards effectively plants a German flag on Ottoman territory. At the sites archaeologists were often photographed in groups, either without any native workmen or in clear separation from them, reflecting the boundaries between the intellectual European and the native laborer played out in the dispute over ownership, whereby the rightful owner became the one who studied and understood the object rather than the one who farmed it from his own land.

Two photographic publications produced by Osman Hamdi to document the archaeological activities of the Imperial Museum corrupt the act of European proprietorship through the very act of Ottoman participation. *Une*

Fig. 15. Osman Hamdi (standing amid the ruins) on site with workers at the Nemrut Dağ excavations, 1883 [Cezar]

necropole royale à Sidon, which publicized Osman Hamdi's excavations in Sidon, underscored the dissemination of the museum's new acquisitions in photographic form and their absence in European museums.[24] Because the first sarcophagus found at Sidon had been taken to the Louvre in 1855, the possession by the Imperial Museum of the sarcophagi found at the same site brought to light a failure in European acquisition. Through the publication of the sarcophagi's photographs, Europe could possess the images of the artifacts but remained distant from the actual finds.

Similarly, the preemptive excavation of the site of Nemrut Dağ in the face of German hopes to excavate there, as well as the subsequent publication of the finds, underscored a German failure.[25] The objects, too monumental to transport, were owned only through the photographs of their excavation.

The cooperation implied by the position of actors in the scenes of Ottoman excavation corrupts the genre of excavation photography using the same method that Osman Hamdi used in his paintings, where the Orientalist style was co-opted to portray active rather than passive Oriental characters. Here, the mutual participation of the elite intellectual and the local worker implied in the photographs suggests a shared ownership that contrasts with the split proprietorship suggested by photographs of European excavators and their work teams (fig. 15). While as a member of the European-educated Ottoman elite Osman Hamdi no doubt had far more in common with his European counterparts than with rural day laborers in Syria, his role as the director of a museum representing the empire may have informed the choice to include workers in excavation photographs to a far greater extent than in those taken under the auspices of European excavations. Here his posture, standing over the ruins in contrast to the squat often used by Turkish villagers, conveys his class status in a shared relationship with the ruins.

As they touched on various aspects of archaeological collection in the Ottoman Empire, the technologies carrying the world into the modern era depended on Ottoman attitudes toward European science in the empire. A leading Young Turk activist of the time, Ahmet Rıza, wrote that Muslims would be converted to modernity not through a conversion to Christianity but rather through a conversion to positivism. The emphasis on the scientific nature of archaeology, the humanism inherent in the study of antiquity, and the strategies of totalistic display possible in a museum environment made the Imperial Museum an ideal arena in which to effect such a conversion where it counted—among intellectuals who might visit the museum.

Through its legislation of antiquities, control over the technologies associated with archaeology, and its institution of a new museum, the Ottoman state began to situate itself symbolically in a universalist cultural arena both for Europeans and for the Ottoman elites. However, far from creating an easily acceptable cultural backdrop for the empire, the museum went against many of the formal precepts of the state in which it developed. The very program of having a museum constituted largely of Helleno-Byzantine objects, let alone the secularist and nationalist agendas promoted by the museum, suggests links between Osman Hamdi and opposition groups of the late nineteenth century, in particular the Young Turks and the Freemasons.

Hanioğlu summarizes the Young Turks' early ideology as "scientific, materialist, social Darwinist, elitist, and vehemently anti-religious."[26] The secularism—even atheism—implicit in the collection and display of pagan art made a bold statement linking clearly non-Islamic histories with Ottoman lands and national patrimony, especially in an era when Abdülhamid was eager to underscore the Islamic nature of the Ottoman state.

Likewise, the emphasis on archaeology as a scientific activity paralleled the Young Turks' emphasis on positivism as a scientific endeavor, along with their use of the term *funun* to place it in an Islamicly acceptable guise. For example, in 1891 an article in *Servet-i Funun* defined archaeology as "the name of an important science . . . [t]hat today is one of the most important.

The word 'archaeology' can be understood through the translation 'the science of antiquities,' such that by the word 'antiquities' we wish to indicate all types of memorabilia from the annals of antiquity and various ruins."[27] This article fails to explain how archaeology constituted a science, or which activities inherent to it—such as collection, identification, or organization—were perceived to adhere to a scientific process. It was important, however, that archaeology be seen as an objective, positivist discourse alongside other sciences, such as chemistry and natural history, which had led Europe to progress. The adamant inclusion of archaeology in the category of science, in conjunction with the equation of science with progress, suggested that participation in such an activity would aid the Ottoman emergence from intellectual stagnancy toward scientifically humanistic advancement.

Between 1876 and 1908 the Freemasons were among the most active opposition organizations in the empire and often worked in tandem with the Young Turks. They envisioned a "new Byzantine state" that would unite Turks and Greeks in the shadow of an enlightened Ottoman sultan.[28] Osman Hamdi's great interest in framing the Helleno-Byzantine patrimony within an Ottoman guise and taking possession of antiquities as national treasures suits such a program. Similarly, the racially elitist overtones implicit in the study of antiquities in Germany since its Winkelmannian origins would have easily made the collection of such antiquities in the Ottoman Empire appeal to intellectuals interested in social Darwinism—especially if they considered that the "superior" races depicted in Helleno-Byzantine statuary had lived on the same soil and breathed the same air as the subjects of the Ottoman Empire. As these ideologies slowly became the commonplaces of Ottoman intellectual thought, the interest in antiquities came to constitute an increasingly coherent ideological program.

6 Antiquities Collections in the Imperial Museum

During the reign of Abdülhamid II, objects that had been gaining value as markers of a common identity began to fall into a system of categories and a complex of institutions of display characteristic of nineteenth-century Europe. In contrast to Europe, which was eagerly collecting trophies from recent colonial conquests, the Ottoman Empire was trying to hold on to its territories by collecting representative trophies and uniting them in the hierarchical, orderly world of its museums.

In Europe the museum spaces that developed to display the fruits of the labors of collection reflected epistemologies and ideologies central to the ethos of late-nineteenth-century France, Britain, and Germany. The exhibits of large institutions such as the British Museum and the Louvre led the visitor through displays that illustrated the modern idea of human progress by constructing a unilinear path from the arts of the Egyptians and ancient Greeks to those of the Roman Empire, the Renaissance, and, finally, the modern states. Similarly, the organization of displays often reflected taxonomic principles made possible by Darwin's radical notions of evolution, which seemed to prove the assertion that art, like life, evolved along a unique teleological track of progress from the primitive to the civilized. The popularity of Darwin's work in intellectual circles had led to the adoption of such strategies among art historians such as Gottfried Semper and Adolf Furtwängler who drew from natural history models.[1] The ideological indoctrination implicit in museum spaces did not stop with the content of the collections or the ordering of displays, which laid out the primacy of certain objects over others and created a spatial narrative that would be read as the visitor meandered through the exhibits. As visitors walked up to the imposing architecture and ambled through the quiet, spacious galleries, they also learned to participate in modern rituals of state reflecting democratic, secular, and educational ideals. In the late nineteenth century, museums became inseparable from the nationalism, patriotism, and imperialism that pervaded European politics and culture.

Can the same be said for the museum spaces developed in the Ottoman Empire? As the Imperial Museum expanded to address new needs, how did ideological debates framed by contemporary political and cultural issues manipulate spaces for the purpose of display? The Ottomans may have learned to construct museums from European models, but the schema—the order of the world projected by those museums—reflected an Ottoman, not a European, reality. Ottoman museums were not for art. In Europe,

> [a]rt was the complementary (civilized) foil to its implicit and imaginary obverse, that enigma of the Enlightenment, the (uncivilized) fetish: that "safely displaced synechdoche of the Enlightenment's other." . . . It was a powerful instrument for legitimizing the belief that what you see in what you make is what in some deep, essential way you truly *are*. The form of your work is the *physiognomy* of your truth. At the same time, it provided a powerful instrument for making palpable the proposition that Europe was the brain of the earth's body, and that all outside the edifice of Europe was its prologue. Of course that external anterior, that Other, was the necessary support and defining instance of what constituted the presence, the modernity, of Europe.[2]

Ottoman museums had to answer a fundamental question: was the empire part of the brain or part of the body; part of the colonial world or part of the colonizing world; or was there a third place between the dominated and the dominating, or rather between those losing their domination and those gaining it in the former's stead? Ottoman museums housed objects that acted as a foil against the art of European civilization. The archaeologist Chris Scarre asserts:

> Greek and Roman remains were regarded as part of the cultural heritage of Western Civilization; but no European came forward to claim the cultural remains of the exotic territories as part of the Western heritage. On the contrary, the archaeology of the colonial world was invoked to demonstrate the superiority of the supposed mainstream of human cultural development, the tradition that had culminated in white European and North American society.[3]

The Ottoman Empire lay at a geographically ambivalent point in this colonial project: it was the site where Europeans did indeed come forward to claim the cultural remains of exotic territories precisely to disenfranchise the exotic inhabitants of those territories. Is it possible that the protonational Ottoman archaeological counternarrative—that ownership of the past pre-

Fig. 16. The Tiled Pavilion, late nineteenth century [German Archaeological Institute, İstanbul]

sented a Janus face of territorial legitimacy—presaged the counternarratives composed in the late-twentieth-century postcolonial quest for breaking through the binaries of power via ambivalences within hegemonic texts? Perhaps. But it could only do so through the production of the museum as a text not simply of objects but of identification, not of progress but of possession.

ANTIQUITIES IN THE TILED PAVILION

For the first time in the history of Ottoman museums, in the Tiled Pavilion Osman Hamdi used the spatial arrangement of objects, above and beyond the mere fact of their ownership, to make political statements. Unlike the Magazine of Antiquities, the Tiled Pavilion did not merely house the antiquities collection but displayed it according to an expository spatial plan. The organization that was chosen for the museum avoided European display strategies in order to address many of the issues that prompted its establishment and expansion during the late nineteenth century.

In front of the monumental staircase, two fragmentary stone lions placed on column capitals announced the entrance to the Tiled Pavilion (fig. 16).

Fig. 17. Left side of the portico of the Tiled Pavilion, late nineteenth century [German Archaeological Institute, İstanbul]

Taken at face value, the lions participated in a familiar trope for marking a grand entrance. The history of their acquisition, however, gives their placement a secondary meaning. These sculptures had been removed from Halicarnassus as a result of C. S. Newton's interest in them. Their placement at the entrance to the museum clearly suggested the process of dominion over antiquities that was signaled by the museum itself. By making reference to Newton's failure to acquire the lions, it underscored the struggle over antiquities under way in the Ottoman Empire and reminded the museum visitor of a thwarted attempt at antiquities acquisition. The placement of the lions visually reiterated the minister of education's emphasis on the protective measures embodied by the new antiquities laws and by the museum as mentioned in his inaugural speech.

The statue of Bes from Cyprus, located at the right end of the portico, was balanced on the left by a statue of Jupiter from Gaza (fig. 17). As a visual introduction to the entire museum space, these two statues served as a frame for the breadth of territory from which the empire could collect impressive antiquities. Nearby, funerary stelae and architectural fragments testify to the scattered nature of the collections, which had come to the museum through arbitrary processes of gathering rather than through organized archaeological expeditions. The monumentality of the Bes statue was one of the causal factors in moving the collection to a new larger location, and placed at the entrance, it served as a symbol of the archaeological glories within.

The importance of the Bes statue was highlighted by the juxtaposition of a diminutive Helleno-Byzantine sculpture next to it. In an article written for the journal *Medeniyet*, Déthier explained the importance of its discovery beside a rare newspaper illustration: "Its coarse form will displease those who seek the beautiful in art, but if one gives importance to the level of progress in art, that is, wonders about the history of mankind's skill at representation, one can see that few antiquities merit the importance of this statue afforded it by science."[4] In citing aesthetic considerations in the evaluation of archaeological artifacts, Déthier's words reveal his interest, as a European, in the art historical epistemological system of progress. However, he died before he could play a role in organizing the museum, which would consistently avoid positivist as well as aestheticist exhibitionary strategies.

Murray's 1893 travel guide provides an early glimpse into the museum's organization. In the vestibule and in the room to its right, Murray reported seeing Assyrian, Egyptian, Kufic, and Hittite remains. Thus on entering, the visitor passed the earliest collections of the museum. This organization suggested a chronological model for the collection by placing the works of early civilizations together and allowing them to act as an introduction to the Hellenistic masterpieces displayed in the main hall and its lateral vaults (*iwan*).

Hellenistic antiquities acquired a prominent role not only through their display in the center of the building but also through the message their exhibition expressed. Each of three sections in the main hall featured an object from a different location. To the right the head and torso of an Apollo figure from Trailles (near Aydin in southwestern Anatolia) and to the left a bas-relief from Salonica served as lateral focal points for the exhibit. In the center of the main hall, at the rear of the main *iwan*, stood a colossal statue from Crete depicting Hadrian trampling the allegorical figure of a child. Above the statue hung a stele from the Temple of Jerusalem, warning gentiles against transgressing the limits of their court. In conjunction, and placed centrally in the museum exhibit, these two works echoed and underscored the theme of antiquities conservation introduced by the lions of Halicarnassus in front of the museum. Like Hadrian, the Ottoman Empire stood victorious over invaders by laying claim to antiquities. Juxtaposed to the inscription above, this statue warned foreign (implicitly Christian) archaeologists against transgressing the limits of their excavation permits.

In the hall of bronzes, located in the room to the left of the main *iwan*, the theme of antiquities acquisition continued to inform the display. A case in the center of the room was devoted to objects found by Schliemann, and wall niches exhibited Assyrian and Babylonian cylinders and cones that had been given by the British Museum as reparation for illegally exported antiquities.[5] The room to the right contained antiquities from Cyprus, of particular interest because the island had recently come under British administration in 1878.[6] The display of objects from Cyprus asserted a memory of Ottoman possession over a former territory. As suggested in Münif Pasha's speech, the display of antiquities from Cyprus was probably spurred by the large-scale export of antiquities by Luici P. di Cesnola, American consul to Cyprus until 1879, when he returned to the United States to become director of the Chicago Art Institute.[7]

The museum exhibits were rearranged soon after Murray's visit. While the Greek and Roman antiquities remained in the main hall, the vestibule was rearranged to house Byzantine works, and the portico held a small collection of "Frankish monuments."[8] Himariote and Palmyrian works were collected in the chamber to the right of the central hall, replacing the finds from Cyprus.[9]

Just as Yemen lay peripherally to the Ottoman and the Roman Empires, the collections from Yemen were displayed peripherally to the main body of sculptures. Their collection, spurred by Yemen's violation of the antiquities law, served to assert Ottoman control over renegade territories. In 1885 the traveler Edward Glasser reported that Arabs were trafficking in antiquities with impunity because of the incomplete control of the Ottomans over these distant territories.[10] Thus, like the earlier displays in the same side room, their exhibit used the Ottoman ability to acquire objects from Yemen as a symbol of territorial sovereignty.

A photograph from the Abdülhamid albums shows the Greek and Roman antiquities as they were arranged in the main hall (fig. 18). The busts decoratively displayed on top of a centrally placed sarcophagus indicate that the curators were more interested in displaying the imperial collections than in using them to construct educational models of progress. The catalog refers to this as a "historic" arrangement, yet the display scarcely followed the standard European norms for evolutionary periodization. Was Osman Hamdi unaware of these conventions? Trained as an artist in Europe, he had visited the museums of both Paris and Vienna. Moreover, as a sympathizer of the Young

Fig. 18. Interior of the Tiled Pavilion, late nineteenth century [Abdülhamid Photographic Collection (APC)]

Turk party, which had been founded by medical students who avidly followed the debates concerning evolution, he would have been well aware of the implications of positivist display.[11] The museum's decision to eschew a positivist evolutionary organizational strategy raises the question, what was the value of this alternative organizational strategy over that of the European model?

In contrast to many chronological schema used to arrange Euro-American museum collections, that of the Imperial Museum led the visitor backward rather than forward through time. From the streets of late-nineteenth-century İstanbul, he stepped toward the era of Ottoman conquest, as embodied by the pavilion itself. On the portico, he met with Frankish works, remnants of European attempts to conquer the territories of Asia Minor and the Near East, particularly during the Crusades. From there, he moved to the vestibule, where he encountered Byzantine works. In the earlier arrangement, the time sequence had been broken at the entry to the museum, where the visitor entered the Bronze Age from the portico of the fifteenth-century building. After the post-1893 modifications, the transitional space linking the exterior of the building to the interior, Frankish and Byzantine works acted as a bridge between a recent past and a more distant one, much as Constantinople itself was often conceived as a cultural bridge between East and West. The other foot of this bridge lay in the Helleno-Byzantine past, squarely at the core of the museum display.

Thus the exhibit produced a historiography for the Ottoman Empire that looked West rather than East, neglecting the Islamic past in favor of a heritage shared with Europe.

While obviously the scale of the Imperial Museum in the Tiled Pavilion cannot be compared in size or scope to the Louvre Museum in Paris, the meanings invested in their respective organizational strategies shed light on the spatial program of the Ottoman institution. In the Louvre of the nineteenth century, classical and Renaissance art occupied the most monumental, centrally located spaces. Similar strategies were adopted in many American museums founded during the 1870s, where the great civilizations of Egypt, Greece, and Rome led to a centrally placed Renaissance.[12] In the Tiled Pavilion, classical civilization itself took center stage, and its display served as a marker of the Ottoman Renaissance: the Tanzimat. Peripheral spaces, such as the Himariote room and the Byzantine vestibule, led to a Hellenistic golden age—a shared patrimony for all European culture—housed within the distinctly Ottoman frame of the Tiled Pavilion. The museum would not collect beyond the ancient past as the act of collection itself signaled the present—not in continuity from the ancient past, but in rupture from the Islamic-Ottoman one.

The museum used an epistemology that had a strategic value in diametric opposition to the teleological result of European supremacy produced by the evolutionary narrative of European art history. Bruce Trigger asserts that "the notion that the material remains of the past could be a source of information about human history independently of written records had to await the replacement of cyclical and degenerationist views of human development by the widespread intellectual acceptance of evolutionary perspective."[13] Then why invert an evolutionary agenda in this early Ottoman museum? If one assumes a positivist epistemology as the sole impetus for the modern, one implicitly rejects the potentially superseding primacy of political motivation. Although the Ottomans were interested in positivism and theories of evolution, these were not the narratives spoken for them by archaeology. Rather, the museum exhibits recognized archaeology not as a mode of abstract history writing but as a colonial technology of political history engaged in writing the past for the present.

THE SARCOPHAGUS MUSEUM

Although foreign archaeologists often found ways to circumvent the restrictive stipulations of Ottoman antiquities laws, increased archaeological activity in the 1880s, the conservation brought about by the law, and the acquisitional and archaeological efforts of the Imperial Museum ensured that its collections quickly exceeded the space available in the Tiled Pavilion. Among the most important acquisitions was a group of sarcophagi discovered by a villager in 1887 near Sidon, in the province of Damascus. While digging the foundations for a building, a villager named Mehmet Efendi uncovered caves that turned out to be an ancient necropolis. On hearing of the site, Osman Hamdi immediately went to Sidon to excavate the sarcophagi. Twenty-six sarcophagi were recovered and sent to the museum in İstanbul.

The size of the new sarcophagus collection made it an ideal seed for the construction of a new museum building. The directive for its construction proudly asserts, "Because the solidity and weight of the antiquities recently found in Sidon makes their entrance into and their protection within the Imperial Museum impossible, [it has been decided that] there is a need for a new hall."[14] Osman Hamdi hired Alexandre Vallaury, who had been teaching architecture at the school of fine arts and who had designed the Yıldız Palace, to design a museum building for the sarcophagi. The construction of a single-level museum began in 1888. After repeated appeals for more money, the plan was expanded to include a second level in 1889, and the new building opened as the Sarcophagus Museum (Lahitler Müzesi) on June 13, 1891.[15] The upper story housed a library, a photography studio, and a studio for the production of plaster casts. Although provided for in the museum charter along with the antiquities collections, the natural history museum that Osman Hamdi intended for the upper story was never established, and the Islamic collection was not included in the museum displays for several years.

The symbolism of the neoclassical architecture chosen by Vallaury for the museum, along with its resonance with the collections within, suggest that the new museum stood as a sign of the Ottoman Empire's relationship to Europe and to its territories. The use of sculptures as punctuation between windows and columns on the building, the inset Ionian columns along the exterior, and the fanned cornice on the edge of the roof suggest that the plan was probably based on the temple design of one of the sarcophagi in the collection, the Sarcophagus of the Wailing Women (fig. 19).[16] Through its emphasis on Helleno-Byzantine sarcophagi, the museum adopted Europe's concentration on the Greco-Roman past as a seminal site for Western Civilization. By using a sarcophagus found in the empire as the model for the museum, however, the architectural style repositioned this heritage as part of the local, drew attention to the shared roots of Ottomans

Fig. 19. Sarcophagus Museum, 1891 [*Servet-i Funun* 54]

and Europeans, and visualized the inclusion of the Ottoman Empire in Western Civilization as an empirical, archaeologically proven fact. While appropriating Western idioms of culture and heritage, the new museum building repositioned the people of the Ottoman territories as the most direct native descendants of the people who had made these objects and thus as the rightful heirs to the Hellenistic legacy. The neoclassical architecture of the new building across from the arcaded, Turkic Tiled Pavilion strengthened the affinities between the two architectural styles, as if to imply integral cultural links between them. The architecture also positioned the new museum in the family of Euro-American museums, which nearly always used neoclassical forms and entrances that resembled Greek temples.[17]

Reports on the museum repeatedly made comparisons between the new museum and those of Europe, asserting that the new museum had entered the ranks of those in Paris, London, and Rome. For example, an article in the elite literary journal *Servet-i Funun* stated: "Thanks to our Sultan . . . Europeans can see how the Ottoman state has entered a period of progress. They write about the service of archaeology to the spirit of arts and progress in their press. They admit that for the examination of history and fine arts, just as London, Paris, and Rome have each been a center of the treasures of antiquities, İstanbul has also become the same way."[18] Articles in *Servet-i Funun* also repeatedly cited an article in the French-language journal *Gazette des Beaux Arts* that praised the new museum as entering the pantheon of Europe's great antiquities museums.[19] The well-known author Ahmet Midhat even praised the sculptures placed outside the building for making the environs of the museum resemble the public gardens of Europe.[20] Within and without, the new museum marked the march of progress by creating a little piece of Europe in the Ottoman capital. Its message was not, perhaps, that this past did not belong to Europe but that a Europe based on Greco-Roman antiquities had to include the Ottoman Empire out of which many of those antiquities emerged.

The museum visitor entered the Sarcophagus Museum through a monumental stairway leading past a columned portico and into a small vestibule, flanked on the inside by the two lions that had previously stood before the entry to the Tiled Pavilion, repeating the reference made earlier to Ottoman mechanisms of control over antiquities. The two symmetrical halls of the museum housed the various sarcophagi from the tombs at Sidon, along with various stelae that the museum had already collected.

The sarcophagi provided the museum's first large-scale and relatively complete archaeological collection from a single site. Their production at multiple times and places also could have allowed the museum to display them according to a developmental art historical model. As Osman Hamdi explained, the earliest of the sarcophagi, that of the Phoenician ruler Tabinath, was made in Egypt. Its style was replicated by wealthy Phoenicians, as demonstrated by a number of anthropoidal sarcophagi found in the tombs. A Greco-Roman sarcophagus style, in the form of a miniature Greek temple, eventually supplanted the Egyptian style, as exemplified by the so-called Sarcophagus of the Wailing Women and by the Grand Sarcophagus, which depicts the victory of Alexander the Great. The collection found in the necropolis even included a sarcophagus marking this transition, carved such that the exterior resembled a temple while the interior retained an anthropoidal form. The 1893 catalog of funerary monuments at the museum remarks that each of the sculptures surpasses its cousins in European museums as samples of the period it represents.

Nonetheless, although the 1893 catalog described the collection of sarcophagi in particular as providing "an uninterrupted series from primitive Ionian art to Byzantine art," the exhibit itself did not follow an evolutionary epistemology, which would have required the placement of the early, anthropomorphic sarcophagi and the architectural, "Alexander" sarcophagus at opposite ends of the museum space. Instead, the plan of the museum shows the sarcophagi in the collection arranged geographically according to the site of their manufacture (fig. 20). Thus the anthropoidal sarcophagi, made in Egypt and later in Phoenicia, were grouped together, as were the Alexander sarcophagus and three smaller sarcophagi made in Attica. This stylistic arrangement allowed for works from other excavations to be included among the main body of finds from Sidon, giving a geographic rather than an evolutionary structure to the exhibit.

A spate of journal and newspaper articles advertised the new museum building to the public even before it opened, emphasizing both the international effort that went into the making of the museum and collective ownership of the antiquities it held. Although the architect was French and the cases for the objects were ordered from England, the articles assert that the value of the museum was perceived as distinctly Ottoman. As one newspaper explained, "The archaeological works put [in the museum] are very valuable to our archaeology and art history, and worthy of examination."[21] The importance of archaeology was defined in terms of its relation to civilization and the progress it represented: "Today in finding the spirit of civilization in the fine arts, archaeology has the highest position with respect to its importance and service, even when compared with painting. Now how can it be excused that this important science that Europeans call the soul of civilization was absent from our country until a few years ago?"[22]

The museum thus came to embody physically the ambivalence of the Ottoman archaeological and museological project. In a discussion of stereotypes, Bhabha states, "[I]n the objectification of the scopic drive there is always the threatened return of the look; in the identification of the Imaginary relation there is always the alienating other (or mirror) which crucially returns its image to the subject; and in that form of substitution and fixation that is fetishism there is always the trace of loss, absence. To put it succinctly, the recognition and disavowal of 'difference' is always disturbed by the question of its re-presentation or construction."[23] The physical form of the Ottoman Imperial Museum reproduced the fetish of Hellenism as the Other of European imagination, attempting to steal back the historical gaze from the colonial European powers. Yet the notion of progress within the Ottoman Empire did not entail developing from that primitive moment to a modern civilized one. Instead, it required that the empire come to partake in that which was already civilized in a narrative that made such civilization already indigenous to it. That this museum lacked the power to produce a real threat to the Hellenistic fetish of Europe is beside the point; within the Ottoman Empire and for a circumscribed

Fig. 20. Sarcophagus display at the Imperial Museum, ca. 1911 [Edhem 1909]

elite, it re-presented the ancient past to produce a counternarrative to an increasingly hegemonic Occident.

THE IMPERIAL MUSEUM

Archaeological acquisitions continued to come into the museum, necessitating two new wings, opened in 1903 and in 1908, respectively. Documents indicate that the museum was overflowing with objects: "Since it has been understood that the many very valuable antiquities that appeared from the excavation of the Lakina shrine at Milas in Aydin will not fit in the existing antiquities museum building, [it is ordered that] a new building be constructed on the esplanade in front of the Tiled Pavilion for their situation and display."[24]

The newspaper *Ikdam* reported on the speeches made during the opening ceremony in November 1903. The ceremony began with prayers and the minister of education's invocation, which was replete with Arabic, reflecting the religiously conservative ethos of Abdülhamid's reign. In his speech, Osman Hamdi praised the sultan for having created a venue appropriate for showing the richness of the Ottoman Empire and the historical importance of its territories.[25] Although the museum collections suggested an ideology frequently in opposition to that of the sultan, the museum was always framed as a device for proving the worth and fraternity of the empire to Europe. European museums continued to provide the measure for the growing museum:

Fig. 21. Monumental staircase inside the Imperial Museum, ca. 1903 [APC]

> With the display of ancient fine arts decorating the various salons of
> the new wing of the Imperial Museum, a state of mutual equality with
> the museums of Europe has been gained, in light of both the classifi-
> cation and the presentation [of the collection] . . . and thus will open on
> the day of victory of the [sultan] as a sign of the prosperity and rejoic-
> ings of the state.[26]

The new wing contained Hittite and Byzantine works, as well as works
from Sidimara near Konya and a second-story room for architectural
pieces, including wall spaces for friezes from Magnesia and Lagina. A monumental staircase (fig. 21), flanked by lions from the Byzantine Boucouleon
palace in İstanbul (which had been part of the city gate at Çatladıkapı), led
to a third story that housed a collection of clay statues, the coin collection,
and the library.[27]

Construction of the third wing began in 1904. At the groundbreaking,
Osman Hamdi praised the sultan for allowing the museum to grow at a
pace never seen in the museums of Europe.[28] Again, the quantity of acquisitions on display exemplified progress and provided the primary impetus
for the new construction. With the opening of the third wing, all the sculptures in the Tiled Pavilion moved to the expanded museum, and site excavations continually provided new objects for display (fig. 22).

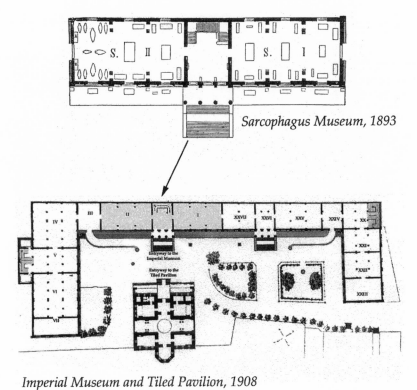

Sarcophagus Museum, 1893

Imperial Museum and Tiled Pavilion, 1908

Fig. 22. Ground plans of the Sarcophagus Museum and the Imperial Museum and Tiled Pavilion, 1893, 1908 [Sarcophagus Museum Catalog; Mendel 1912]

What type of organization informed the expanded museum? As before, the lion sculptures from Halicarnassus graced the entrance, and sarcophagi and funerary monuments continued to flank the vestibule. Gustave Mendel suggested that it might have been better to group the objects by region rather than by style.[29]

Yet each room seems to have depended on a different organizational strategy. For example, while some rooms, such as room XX, where the finds from excavations at Aphrodesias were displayed, were devoted entirely to a single excavation, others were arranged by type, such as the hall of architectural fragments (fig. 23). The ownership of the artifacts, rather than the stories that they could be made to tell through the process of exhibition, constructed the primary objective of the display. Indeed, the 1914 catalog explains the provenance of each object in great detail, stressing the intrigues often involved in acquisition. Likewise, the exhibits seem to have

Fig. 23. Imperial Museum, Hall xxi looking into Hall xxii [Edhem 1909]

emphasized the contemporary geography of archaeology more than linking the antiquities with a reconstructed classical past.

How did the spaces of the new museum instruct the visitors who entered? Unlike in the museums of Europe and America, visitors did not amble through carefully orchestrated halls designed to chart symbolic markers of civilizations onto a map of human progress. Plaster casts of famous works did not produce an evolutionary model of stylistic progress. Rather, the museum spaces instructed through the variety of their collections: the large number of sites within the empire contributed to rich and multifaceted collections of original works. The fact of their exhibition, not their organization, symbolized the ideals of progress which they embodied—a progress not of evolution but of participation in that which was symbolic of progress, Western Civilization. Like the Tiled Pavilion and the Sarcophagus Museum before it, the Imperial Museum continued to disregard taxonomy in favor of an expository, even geographic mode of organization.

Unlike in the Tiled Pavilion, however, where the architecture continually referred the viewer both to the Ottoman site and to the Helleno-Byzantine past, in the new museum the neutrally neoclassical architecture, coupled with the absence of text, constructed a universalist—and thus implicitly European—space. The museum visitor might just as well have been in Paris, London, or Rome. The museum provided an experience antithetical to the expectations of most visiting Europeans, who came East to experience its exoticism. Conversely, for the Ottoman visitor, this experience of entering Europe from the streets of İstanbul provided a means of imagining the Ottoman present into a European framework of civilizational roots. Instead of participating in European culture as an adoptive adjunct, Ottomans could claim a shared heritage and use the museum as a vehicle with which to stage that heritage. The spaces of the museum created a geographically neutral space for an individual accustomed to European aesthetics and institutions, and who expected the modern to coincide with the Western. Exhibits culled from Ottoman lands set into a framework conceived through European tastes and conventions constructed an amalgam of cultural display appropriate for the hopes of post-Tanzimat reformers.

If "in France, the museum . . . was born from the articulation of three general elements: republicanism, anticlericalism, and successful aggressive war,"[30] in the Ottoman Empire, the museum was born from the articulation of internationalism (participation in "world" culture, as defined by Europe), secularization (implicit in the emphasis on figural form and heathen artifacts), and the conservation of existing territories. Whereas in France and Britain items gathered from around the world and displayed in museums became symbols of international colonial dominion, in İstanbul items gathered from Ottoman soil implied that the cultural treasures of international fame were in fact local. To comprehend the radical implications of this strategy, one may envision, for example, the Venus de Milo and the Nike of Samothrace contextualized as part of Ottoman rather than European heritage. Would they still remain icons of Western classicism?

The rearticulation of antiquities as signs outside of their European signage makes literal Homi Bhabha's notion that "on the margins of metropolitan desire, the *founding objects* of the Western world become the erratic, eccentric, accidental *objets trouvés* of the colonial discourse."[31] These objects worked as anticolonial discourse because they took the foundations on which the discourse of the West was constructed and resituated them as foundations of a different but parallel discourse. In the early twentieth century, Ziya Gökalp wrote, "A civilization is the shared property of independent nations because the individual nations which are its possessors have brought it into existence by living a shared life. For this reason, every civilization is international. But there are special forms that a civilization takes in each nation which are referred to as culture."[32] Such a notion of civilization made it possible to take the same foundations and construct independent routes of cultural change; it thus stood in the face of a teleological narrative of progress in which all paths led to a Western future. The architecture of the new building of the museum reframed the postulates of neoclassicism along the same lines. As the Ottoman nation took a form of civilization different from that of Europe, it too could formulate a local vision of neoclassical modernity, parallel to and disparate from its European counterpart.

Archaeological objects from around the empire were not placed on display for the sake of antiquity but for the sake of modernity; they formed an essential part of retaining and constructing a modern Ottoman identity. In a time when nationalist uprisings threatened the unity of the empire, the museum attempted to promulgate the idea that the empire constituted a unitary state. Osman Hamdi expressed the symbolic relationship between the conservation of the sarcophagi of past civilizations and the conservation of Ottoman culture in his 1908 painting, *Keeper of the Mausoleum* (fig. 24). Here he depicts himself as an Ottoman dervish standing before two Ottoman sarcophagi. He transposes his role as the director of a museum based on sarcophagi to an Ottoman frame of reference. He reveals himself as someone with great respect for the Ottoman past, with an alter ego specifically charged with the maintenance of a tomb and thereby metaphorically of memory. Transposing this image back onto his job in the museum, he seems to imply that his preservation of Helleno-Byzantine sarcophagi in the museum in fact was an act of preservation of the Ottoman and that through his real-life activities he performed the imaginary spaces of his paintings. He represents the difference inherent in the Ottoman preservation of Hellenistic objects by revealing the Ottoman garb underlying his European suits and the Ottoman cultural legacy underlying the veneer of Helleno-Byzantine antiquities collected in the museum.

Osman Hamdi's *The Weapons Merchant* (fig. 25) of the same year suggests a dynamic role for the museum as an educational institution in the prenatal Turkish nation. In a stone basement, the merchant sits on a discarded Helleno-Byzantine capital, surrounded by various weapons and helmets with which he apparently plies his trade. As an older, bearded figure surrounded by objects that were actually in the museum, the merchant emerges as Osman Hamdi himself, leaning against a stone from the distant past in order to give an Ottoman sword to a youth, who is critically examining it. The capital acts as a base for the preparation of the youth for some unspecified battle. The juxtaposition of the weapons to the capital

Fig. 24. Osman Hamdi, *Keeper of the Mausoleum* (1908), oil on canvas, 122 × 92 cm, İstanbul Museum of Painting and Sculpture [Cezar]

Fig. 25. Osman Hamdi, *The Weapons Merchant* (1908), oil on canvas,
175 × 130 cm [Cezar]

implicates both in the education the youth is receiving. Only with the base of history, or only with Helleno-Byzantine foundations, or only with the base of Western Civilization, or only with the recognition of that civilization within the Ottoman can the youth contemplate the sword—a fight for self-preservation. The weapons and the merchant alike rely on the capital on which the older man rests. Unlike in *The Tortoise Trainer*, where Osman Hamdi depicts himself as an educator without any hope, here he expounds from a pulpit of antiquity to a student capable of fighting. This shift in Osman Hamdi's attitude may have reflected his support for the ongoing Young Turk Revolution, which he probably saw as opening a new era of hope for the modernization of the empire.

MUSEUM ENTERPRISES OUTSIDE OF İSTANBUL

The fight for antiquities represented a tripartite struggle between archaeological sites scattered across Ottoman territories and foreign archaeologists interested in enhancing European museum collections. At the fulcrum, the Imperial Museum in İstanbul acted as both a repository and a gateway for objects collected form the territories and reincarnated in museums. Just as the consolidation of antiquities from various regions of the empire in İstanbul served to represent its unity, the development of regional museums served as a second step toward the nationalization of the Ottoman museum venture.

Although the collection of antiquities was most concentrated in the capital, in the early twentieth century regional museums began to participate in the Ottoman consolidation of antiquities collection as a nationalistic venture. Museums at major archaeological digs, such as Bergama and Cos, allowed for the immediate inventory of antiquities as they emerged from the soil. While in theory such museums were intended to stem the tide of antiquities export, they also served as an intermediary space where finds could be apportioned among interested parties.

Local museums opened in Konya, Bursa, and Jerusalem—major cities that were central to archaeological activities. Spurred by the provision for regional museums in the 1906 antiquities law, as of 1908 plans were also under way for museums in Salonica, Sivas, and Izmir, none of which came to fruition during the Ottoman period.[33] The information about these regional museums is scattered at best, but the little that remains suggests a program for museums of antiquities resembling that in the capital to disseminate scientific archaeological knowledge to many regional centers within the empire, to create a space for the immediate inventory of antiquities, and to provide attractions for tourists.

The first regional museum was established in Bursa, where a public collection of Helleno-Byzantine and Byzantine antiquities, as well as a small Islamic section, was established in the courtyard of the new, modern, and exemplary İdadiye High School, where a small pavilion was built to house more valuable works in the collection. The museum opened ceremonially in 1904 on the anniversary of Abdülhamid's accession to the throne. Although under the central administration of the Imperial Museum, it was funded by the resources of the state (*vilayet*) under the leadership of Azmi Bey, who also directed the establishment of a similar museum in Konya. The museum followed display strategies similar to those used in the Imperial Museum, grouping objects by type, region, or period depending on the collection.

The small site museum at Bergama also seems to have followed a similar display strategy. A 1906 letter from Alexander Conze, then director of the Kaiserliches Archaeologisches Institut in Berlin, to the Ottoman Imperial Museum describes this museum in considerable detail. It was intended to house objects of lesser quality that were not considered worthy to enter the collections of the İstanbul museum. It both provided a space for site visitors to see the antiquities associated with the local excavation and lightened the heavy stream of acquisitions entering the İstanbul museum. To house the collections, the German archaeologists restored four rooms of the western section of the recently excavated minor market of Bergama. The first room housed marble fragments, the second housed primarily small ceramic objects, and the third was reserved for inscriptions; the fourth room was left empty for future finds. "The objects of the collection are an indispensable supplement to the architectural monuments that remain in place," Conze wrote. "The ensemble will always be an attraction for archaeologists and other scientific voyagers, as well as for amateurs. The objects would lose much of their scientific value if they were transported to another location and mixed with other objects."[34] His insistence on the localization of collections is ironic considering the large number of objects and huge architectural structures removed from the site to Berlin during the course of the excavations.

Like the site museum in Bergama, the project of the Jerusalem Museum received considerable support from Germany.[35] In 1914 Theodore Macridi suggested that the new museum replace a military depot on the western wall of the city fortress, called the Tower of David, "in the best location of the city, close to hotels and, above all, accessible to cars and chariots." He assured Halil (Edhem) that as soon as the tower was renovated, it would be visited by pilgrims to the city, and therefore it should be restored to its medieval-period appearance. Three nearby towers would be renovated to form the rooms of the new museum so that the architecture of the latter would not clash with the old structure and the "splendid antique monument would do honor to the city and the state." As in Bursa and Konya, although the museum would remain under the jurisdiction of the Imperial Museum, the municipality of Jerusalem was willing to the shoulder the burden of constructing the museum as it expected tourist revenues to enhance the city's budget in future years.[36]

Plans for the museum in Jerusalem, as well as those for Salonica, Sivas, and İzmir, were halted by the years of war that soon tore up the Ottoman Empire. As various European forces attempted to divide up the empire, the Imperial Museum attempted to keep an eye on the antiquities of the former empire, even in regions where the Ottoman government had lost any semblance of sovereignty.

With an elite lacking an education in the classics and weaned on a cultural trajectory different from the museologists of Europe, the adoption of Helleno-Byzantine antiquities as a cultural marker for the Ottoman Empire served not only as a sign of assimilation but also as a sign of resistance and a call for continued independence. The giant sarcophagus built to house antiquities mimicked the neoclassical garb of European museums even as it conscientiously identified itself as inherently Anatolian. From the mid-nineteenth century until the institution of the Turkish Republic, the act of collection took precedence over the museum experience. Displays designed to show wealth and ownership did not educate visitors about aesthetics or classicism so much as impress them with a new historical and cultural contextualization of the Ottoman Empire.

Jean Baudrillard suggests that "any given object can have two functions: it can be utilized, or it can be possessed."[37] Any possession escapes utility through the construction of metaphors, both around the object and around the act of possession. European museums used archaeological objects from Ottoman lands to construct a double metaphor: on the one hand, their ability to own these objects bespoke their contemporary economic, political, and potentially imperial prowess; on the other, it served as an aid in linking modern European nations with the illustrious classical past. Ottoman museums used the same objects to construct opposition to European hegemony, reproducing antiquities in a metonymic relationship not with the narrative construction of Western Civilization but with the assertion of possession over Ottoman territories.

7 Islamic Arts in Imperial Collections

In 1889 a directive issued by the Council of State (Şura-ye Devlet) set out the administrative program and the organizational practices of the Imperial Museum. The collections were to be organized as follows:

> The Imperial Museum is divided into six parts. The first is for Greek, Roman, and Byzantine antiquities. The second is for Assyrian, Caledonian, Egyptian, Phoenician, Hittite, and Himariote antiquities, as well as for works by Asian and African tribes. The third is for works of Islamic fine arts. The fourth is for ancient coins. The fifth is for examples of natural history. The sixth is for the collection, in a library, of books concerning the history and science of antiquities.[1]

These sections seem to have been proposed as equal divisions of the museum's exhibition complex, but their subsequent development followed diverse paths. The premier museums of the empire—first of military, then of archaeological antiquities—did little to promote the Islamic identity of the empire, even though the reassertion of the caliphate was a primary interest of Sultan Abdülhamid II. The sultan tried to retain a link with the western territories that had been lost to the Europeans by maintaining governance over Muslim minorities through his role as caliph. In the east, such assertions of caliphal power were equally important in the face of Arab nationalism, which emphatically called into question the Ottoman right to the caliphate and in doing so implicitly questioned the link between the Islamic and the Ottoman.[2] As Hasan Kayalı points out, "[B]y emphasizing his role as caliph, Abdülhamid generated support from Arabs, as well as from other Muslims within and outside the Ottoman Empire, at a time when the world of Islam was under Christian imperialist domination."[3] During the reign of Abdülhamid, the empire increasingly made use of Islamic symbolism to compete with the nationalist symbols emerging throughout the empire.[4]

Even as the empire promoted its political identity as leader of the Islamic world, it chose not to include works of art and culture pertaining to its Ottoman or Islamic identity in its museum until 1889. As the empire weakened during the early twentieth century, the identification of Islamic works of art became increasingly important to the production of a cohesive Ottoman national identity. Did this imply an increasing interest in religion, or in the politics of religious cohesion? Was this an "Islam" that designated religiosity or politics? The collection of Islamic arts in the late Ottoman Empire marks a moment of transition from the sectarian to the national, from the religious to the secular, and the imperial against the colonial.

The belated interest in Islamic antiquities at first seems ironic: the objects most readily accessible to Ottoman collectors—those in common use in mosques and elite households throughout the empire—were among the last to be collected. This contrasts sharply with the nineteenth-century development of museums in Europe, where galleries and museums assembled both religious and secular artworks to foster national spirit. The Louvre had been transformed into a museum as one of the first outward symbols of the new order brought about by the French Revolution. Gathering the insignia of church and crown for the public gaze, it declared the formulation of a new state (at least in theory) dedicated to public service. This vision of the state merged into a sequence of collections, from the ancient to the contemporary, through the media and styles associated with the various eras, formulating a coherent genealogy for the modern that coincided with a geographic progression from the East to the West.[5] In contrast, Ottoman museums exhibited autonomous collections, each of which displayed a single aspect of the new Ottoman identity but none of which promoted a model of cultural progress with its apogee in Ottoman modernity. Thus the museum did not even try to include collections of Ottoman art to parallel the painting and sculpture galleries of the Louvre or the British National Gallery. Indeed, for many years Ottoman museums avoided the suggestion of a present moment for the empire, displaying only multiple pasts from which it could garner various aspects of a modern identity. This disavowal of positivism not only produced an anticolonial strategy for the museum, it also coincided with an official distrust of positivism as heretical to Islamic norms.[6]

The collection of Islamic arts in the Imperial Museum was the first to exhibit a contemporary identity directly. Unlike Helleno-Byzantine antiquities or military spolia, Islamic antiquities were not only part of the Ottoman past, they were also part of the Ottoman present. The establishment of an Islamic arts section in the museum near the end of the nineteenth century reflects the growing interest in the immediate past of the Ottoman territories as well as the awareness of the nationalistic implications of this past. Certainly, the shift was not unique in İstanbul: in 1883 the Museum of Arab Art opened in Cairo, and Islamic archaeology emerged for the first time in 1885, with the excavation of Samarqand. However, it was not until 1893, with the Exposition d'Art Musulman in Paris that such arts became identified with religion rather than with region.[7]

Why is it that in a taxonomic system obsessed with geography and history as the primary identifiers of communal identity a religion suddenly emerged as a distinct category in European museums? The designation of new Islamic collections allowed for the display of a new category of objects without disturbing the time-space progression established by universal survey museums. The positivist organization of such European museums relied on a unique and hierarchical model for progress that would have been challenged by the presentation of multiple cultures, parallel in space and time, differing yet not competing in aesthetics and values. For an object to be displayed as Egyptian, Iranian, or Ottoman would have connoted its use in a locale with a secular history that could compete with the evolutionary model presented in the main body of the museum. Redefined as Islamic, the value of such an object came to be equated with an aesthetic practice assumed to span a wide range of histories, languages, cultures, and customs—indeed, perhaps to exist outside of time and even geography. In effect, by calling these objects Islamic, museums could render them external to time and place. In their quest to import Western models of progress, colonial powers often favored such a perception of their newly acquired territories. Much as "Orientalism assumed an unchanging Orient," the idea of Islamic collections assumed a temporally static aesthetic for the Islamic world and bounded a geographic region with a religious identifier.[8] It displayed the arts of "Islam . . . as a 'cultural synthesis' . . . that could be studied apart from the economics, sociology, and politics of the Islamic peoples."[9] Through this designation, "Islamic" came to denote an aesthetic value as much as a religious one. By identifying objects with religion rather than with region, such displays suggested several things—that non-Muslim peoples of the empire were apart from the shared cutural practices of the region; that all objects, even those designed for secular use, still somehow pertained to religion (perhaps because of the description of Islam as a way of life as well as a series of devotions); and that devotional objects should be moved from the metaphysical to the temporal realm for the sake of their protection and preservation in museums. "Islamic" essentialized an enormous set of cultural and artistic practices no less than the term "Christian" would in reference to all cultural and artistic works made in predominantly Christian lands.

In light of the Orientalist implications of the designation "Islamic," it is perhaps ironic that this new category served nationalist purposes when put into practice in the Ottoman Empire. It becomes less ironic in light of the constant slippage between European collections and their Ottoman counterparts, wherein Ottoman museums mimicked their European forebears only to subvert the assumptions of power implicit in them. Just as the archaeological collections redefined Helleno-Byzantine antiquities as part of the Ottoman (rather than the European) heritage, collections of Islamic antiquities reasserted the political affiliation of the Ottoman Empire and Islam. To promote Ottoman nationalism, the affinity between Muslim Ottoman citizens and Islam had to be harnessed as an identification with the Ottoman state. An emphasis on Islam as a national characteristic could mollify the many conservatives in the empire who worried that modernization would necessarily mean Westernization and, implicitly, Christianization. Moreover, by denying a national framework to the category of objects labeled "Islamic," the empire could avoid the problems of Arab nationalism plaguing its integrity in the real-life, political world outside of the museum. In the Ottoman context, Islamic collections provided a counterpoint to the growing association between Arabs and Islam. In effect, the neutralization of difference promoted by a category of art designated as "Islamic" supported the Ottoman cause as effectively as it did that of colonial European powers.

The Ottoman Imperial Museum established the Islamic Arts Division in 1889, but the collection grew very slowly. While Helleno-Byzantine antiquities were housed in the lavish new Imperial Museum, the Islamic antiquities moved from site to site, first in an upstairs hall of the museum and later in increasingly independent venues. Growing in the shadow of the antiquities collections, Islamic collections were never published in catalogs, nor were they extensively publicized in newspapers. The only early description of the collection comes from a short section of an extensive 1895 article about the museum by its assistant director, Halil (Edhem):

> [A]t one time during the Middle Ages when in Europe and in Asia no trace of civilization remained and knowledge and science had become nearly completely extinct, Islam and the Arabs appeared as a vehicle for the formation of a new civilization. The advancement of knowledge and

science and literature and art spread across the world and the Ottomans were the inheritors of this with their acquisition of the caliphate.

Since today old Arab works and old Ottoman works are among quite desirable and rare antiquities, these are also now being collected in the Imperial Museum and are being arranged for display in a special hall. In this section, the most striking item is in the corner: an ornate tile *mihrab* [prayer niche] from Karaman that is from the time of the Seljuk ruler Ala'al-din I. Stones with Kufic writing from the time of the Ahmed al-Malik of the Umayyad Caliphate; writing samples of famous calligraphers; book bindings, which are testimony to the fine handicraft of Ottoman artisans; Edirne-work cabinets; mother-of-pearl inlay book-stands; ringstones with Kufic writings; and quite breathtaking Persian carpets decorate this hall.[10]

In introducing the collection, Halil links its establishment with a re-minder that Europe's ascendancy depended on Arabo-Islamic science, a view often promoted by conservatives in the empire. As one parliamentar-ian explained in 1878, "We are a *millet* that originated from the Arab *mil-let*. . . . Just as we took civilization from the Greeks, Europe has taken it from us."[11] Thus Halil presents the desire to remember the Islamic past as more than a simple act of self-reflection or nationalist self-promotion. From the first display of Islamic arts, the presentation of artifacts still in use in the Ottoman present was also an act of resistance to European cul-tural hegemony. It balanced, or perhaps even completed, the Ottoman usurpation of the foundations of Europe represented by the archaeological antiquities on exhibit in the rest of the museum. Just as the wide-scale Ot-toman collection and display of Helleno-Byzantine antiquities exposed the ambivalent foundations of an exclusive pan-European Greek heritage, Halil suggests that the collection of Islamic arts underscored Europe's ac-tual dependence on the Islamic world for its subsequent greatness. In these paragraphs, Halil simultaneously exposes Europe's dependence on the Is-lamic world and the Islamic world's dependence on the Ottoman Empire in its role as protector of the caliphate. Thus he conflates the Islamic with the Ottoman, producing a national—not a religious—identifier.

Like its European counterparts, the Ottoman museum used religious objects as national identifiers only by divesting them of their religious sig-nificance. The symmetrical organization of the display (fig. 26) and the or-ganization of the collection by material precluded its assessment in any sort of religious framework, where disparate objects would be used to-gether in an architectural setting for the purpose of worship. In the mu-seum display, only the lanterns hanging from the ceiling and the carpets covering the floor retain their original spatial function. However, unlike in

Fig. 26. Islamic collections upstairs in the Imperial Museum, ca. 1903 [APC]

the mosque or tomb from which they came, the carpets were roped off from the very people who would have prayed on them in religious settings. Much as the museum's primary collections enforced secular notions through the display of pre-Islamic arts, the hall devoted to Islamic arts subverted the religious content of *mihrab* and Qur'an alike, transforming them into objects for the aesthetic rather than the spiritual gaze. Carol Duncan describes the museum as a space of secular ritual.[12] Indeed, while the architecture of the exterior promoted a humanist, quasi-religious veneration of the antiquities within, the Islamic arts upstairs invested objects with a new and secular ritual: impartial, categorical examination.

While the inclusion of Islamic arts acknowledged their cultural value in a way otherwise ignored by the Imperial Museum, the removal of objects from their religious contexts to the secular halls of a museum itself had revolutionary implications. In mosques, tombs, and dervish lodges, the objects collected by the museum had nonmaterial value associated with their function and sometimes also with their association with venerable figures from the past. Often such objects functioned as relics, or acquired local meanings from the legends and histories surrounding their use. In the museum, they exchanged such value for the secular equivalents of aesthetics and historical rarity and became secular signs of national eminence.

By redefining them as works of art to collect and display, the Islamic Arts Division of the Imperial Museum called into question the very identity of a devotional object.

The radical implications of Islamic collections in a museum setting were not far from the consciousness of the museum's administration. It was no surprise to Osman Hamdi that the new collections promoted a radical shift in Ottoman modes of education. Whereas once Ottomans learned about religion by reading the Qur'an, in the museum they would learn about the nation through the objects that once helped to transmit religious knowledge. In his 1890 work, *In the Green Mosque of Bursa* (fig. 27), Osman Hamdi uses a Mamluk candleholder and a lamp originally from the Gebze Çoban Mustafa Pasha Mosque and then in the museum collections and sets them in that quintessential early Ottoman mosque, completed in 1424.[13] Here Osman Hamdi depicts himself seated, receiving the wisdom of a teacher who reads aloud to him from the Qur'an, quite possibly one of those in the collection. Similarly, in the 1904 work, *The Fountain of Life* (fig. 28), he depicts himself reading the same Qur'an in front of a fountain in the Tiled Pavilion surrounded by objects from the museum's Islamic collection.[14] As the curator of these collections, Osman Hamdi subsumes the age-old role of religious scholar within the modern role of secular educator and suggests this relationship by depicting its inversion in his paintings. One might even wonder whether the fountain of life in the title refers to the physical site behind him or to the activity of erudition in which he—and the museum—engaged.

Such strategies came at a high cultural cost, as suggested in the subtle symbolic drama of his 1901 work, *Mihrab* (fig. 29). In this painting, a woman (as in *The Painter at Work,* modeled after his wife) sits on an inlaid Qur'an stand in front of the *mihrab.* She displaces many copies of the Qur'an, which lie disheveled at her feet. Although the incense at the foot of the *mihrab* continues to burn, the candle beside it stands extinguished. All of the objects in the picture—the Qur'an stand, the incense burner, the candleholder, and quite probably the Qur'ans as well—belonged to the growing collections of the Islamic section of the museum.[15] Although the removal of the *mihrab* and the Qur'an stand to the museum preserved them as objects of fine art, it simultaneously plundered their functions as aids to religious devotion. The museum saved devotional objects, but in doing so it secularized them.

Could any image be more shocking? As an allegorical representation of the museum, the painting implicates the Islamic collections of the museum in a secularist revolution that replaces religion with Western mores and a

Fig. 27. Osman Hamdi, *In the Green Mosque of Bursa* (1890), oil on canvas, 81 × 59 cm [Cezar]

Fig. 28. Osman Hamdi, *The Fountain of Life* (1904), oil on canvas [Cezar]

Fig. 29. Osman Hamdi, *Mihrab* (1901), oil on canvas, 210 × 108 cm,
Collection of Demirbank [Cezar]

disregard of religion in favor of art and the material world it favors. In the museum an aesthetic appreciation of Islamic arts displaces the worship of the Qur'an, just as this figure sits directly between the viewer and the *mihrab*, precluding prayer. She, along with all that she represents, displaces the Qur'an on its stand and becomes the object of devotion. In one guise, this figure, exposed in body and yet distant in her gaze, suggests the West: beautiful, alluring, distracting, and yet impassive and unattainable. Still, by placing a portrait of his own wife in front of the *mihrab*, Osman Hamdi made literal the classical metaphor between the beloved and the *qibla*, the direction of prayer toward Mecca for all Muslims, which is common in Persian poetry. Hafez writes, "Whoever comes to the *ka'beh* of your street/ Is like one praying before the *qibla* of your eyebrows."[16] Furthermore, during the late nineteenth century, feminization of the national spirit (akin to the notion of the French *patrie*) entered the Ottoman tradition. Thus the painting implicates the museum in an act of national devotion akin to that of the personal beloved and also marked a moment of transition in the symbolism ascribed to the female form. With this tour de force of layered metaphor spanning several traditions, Osman Hamdi highlights the pivotal role of the museum in constructing a revolutionary bridge from the traditional to the modern sphere.

How did such an ideological revolution play out in the material world? Despite the radical ramifications, the new, aesthetic value that emerged for Islamic artifacts subject to a secular gaze resulted not from existing secular ideals but from the very practical issue of theft. At the end of the nineteenth century, European travelers and collectors alike wanted Islamic artifacts for private and public collections. Local Ottoman citizens were often willing to sell the valuables of their local mosques to an increasingly lucrative market. As with Helleno-Byzantine antiquities, the collection of Islamic antiquities was precipitated by the European desire for collection as much as by ideological issues of cultural identification that followed to justify the museum's growing interests.

Scattered documentary reports of museum acquisitions provide clues about the changing modes of evaluation for Islamic artifacts. Before European collecting became an issue, acquisitions depended primarily on practical considerations in mosques. Among the first carpets included in the collections, those from the Sultan Ahmet Mosque and from the mosque of the Kamiller village in the province of İzmir were removed to the museum because, in addition to being old, they were deemed unhealthful for continued use.[17] In the documents concerning the transfer of these carpets from mosque to museum, two types of value accrue to the carpets. Because they

Fig. 30. Osman Hamdi, *Iranian Carpet Seller*, oil on canvas [Cezar]

performed a useful function in the mosques, their removal to the museum depended on their replacement. The mosques were not perceived to have lost something of extrafunctional value because of the historicity of the items: new carpets could act as substitutes with no additional provisions made for their antique or aesthetic value. Indeed, in practical terms, new carpets would have greater value because of their cleanliness. The antique value of the carpets came into play only through the museum's interest in them; outside of the museum, their historicity was perceived to have little value.

The value assigned to works of Islamic art shifted as reports of their theft by Europeans began to circulate. No longer left to perform their religiously prescribed functions in holy spaces, aesthetically prized historical carpets, Qur'ans, tiles, and metalwork began to develop a market among visiting Europeans who were eager to collect during their touristic forays into the Ottoman Empire. Osman Hamdi's 1905 painting, *Iranian Carpet Seller* (fig. 30), replete with the familiar cast of museum objects, depicts a contemporary problem: unlike Helleno-Byzantine antiquities, the commodification and export of which was at least partially legislated, valuable Islamic antiques were being sold to Europeans, both as souvenirs and for museum collections. It was not until 1906 that a revision of the antiquities law placed the same restrictions on Islamic and Ottoman artworks leaving the empire as on other antiquities. Like Helleno-Byzantine antiquities, Islamic antiquities gained legislative interest only after they began to be smuggled out of the country with impunity.

Despite Abdülhamid's emphasis on the Islamic identity of the Ottoman state, the Islamic collections of the Imperial Museum did not flourish fully until the end of his reign. There are several possible reasons for this. If the process of museum display reflects a process of producing an other in opposition to the self, then the religious emphasis of the government might have precluded the extensive secularization of Islamic arts through displays that inherently made religion into an objectifiable other. If, on the other hand, the museum reflects a changing definition of the identity of its audience, the increasingly public nature of the museum after the Young Turk Revolution may have encouraged the exhibitionary representation of Islamic Ottoman identity. In either case, the small scale of the Islamic Arts Division underscores the elusive objective of the Ottoman Museum project, to display a material basis for the projection of a pan-cultural narrative of national identity.

8 Military Collections in the Late Empire

In light of the auspicious beginnings of Ottoman museums in the dual collections at the Basilica of Hagia Irene, it would have been almost impossible to conceive of the construction of a modern Ottoman identity that did not make use of the prodigious military legacy of the empire in its construction of national heritage. Nonetheless, under Abdülhamid II, the weapons inside the former church were perceived as too dangerous to remain accessible to the public in any form. The museum closed and was heavily guarded.[1] The sovereign nonetheless retained an interest in the promotion of Ottoman identity through a military museum, and one was planned during the later years of his reign. Although this museum never came to fruition, Abdülhamid Album photographs of a model museum on the grounds of the Yıldız Palace suggest how the spatial organization of the museum, in concert with the texts interspersed in the display, was designed to bolster the image of a strong empire unified under its ruler. Far from reincarnating the old museum in a new location, the model museum led to a revised conception of the role that an Ottoman military museum could play, which led to the formulation of an increasingly glorious military museum even as the empire faltered.

THE MODEL MILITARY MUSEUM IN THE YILDIZ PALACE

When Abdülhamid II ordered a new military museum to be built near the Maçka arms depot, a commission composed of the German Gromkov Pasha, the German engineer Jachmund, and Ahmet Muhtar Pasha drew up plans. They called on local officials throughout the empire to send old arms to the new museum. Unlike before, in the new museum they intended to separate contemporary weapons from the outdated ones kept in the Military Store-house, as the Basilica of Hagia Irene was called once the museum was closed.[2]

The commission set up a private model museum on the second floor of the Acem Kasrı on the grounds of the Yıldız Palace, Abdülhamid II's residence. Set up as a private collection, the museum was seen only by the sultan and his assistants. However, plans were under way for a large new museum building. Had Abdülhamid not been deposed, a more extensive version of it would probably have been opened to the public in the Maçka district of Istanbul.[3] Thus this exhibit should not be considered merely a private museum but a model for the way in which the museum could promote the sovereign's ideology to its audience.

The exhibit featured weaponry arranged in rosettes behind display tables of artillery. Numerous banners and flags also decorated the rooms. Calligraphic panels punctuated the displays, rendering the agenda of the proposed museum readable. As a result of Abdülhamid's interest in emphasizing the religious role of the sultan and, in contrast to previous rulers of the nineteenth century, in accentuating religion as the primary justification for imperial power, the museum had a peculiarly religious cast—particularly in light of the modernist tradition that had been the hallmark of the Ottoman military since the eighteenth century.

In sharp contrast to the Christian connotations of the earlier museum site, the visitor entered the rooms of the model museum under a panel invoking the name of God with the traditional Muslim blessing, Bismillah ir-Rahman-i Rahim. Still, the focal point of the museum was arranged in the form of an altar, reminiscent of the configuration at the Magazine of Ancient Weapons (fig. 31). This new display seems to have included the helmet of Orhan Gazi, second sultan of the Ottoman dynasty, whose reign had emphasized expansion against the infidel. The symbolism of the helmet as the focal point of the museum highlights Abdülhamid's interest in the foundation myths of the Ottoman dynasty, shown also through new annual ceremonies at the tomb of Ertuğrul Gazi, Orhan's father.[4] The only mannequins placed in the museum wear early Ottoman armor and flank this altarlike exhibit, as if to stand guard over Orhan Gazi's helmet. Above, a panel inscribed "Long Live the Sultan!" (Padişahımız Çok Yaşa) linked the contemporary sultan, for whom the museum had been designed, with Orhan Gazi, forging a direct connection between the two. In the next room, the slogan "Prayers for the sultan are the cause of redemption" implied that loyalty to the sultan was a religious duty. Written in Arabic, the quotation suggested a saying of the Prophet (*hadith*), enhancing its authoritative value.

Fig. 31. Central display in the Model Military Museum at Yıldız Palace [APC]

Displays to each side of the altarlike focal point emphasized the role of the military in the Islamic cause. A panel to the right, also inscribed in Arabic, declared, "And know that paradise is under the protection of swords," while to the left, another Arabic panel asserted, "He said, 'Peace be unto him, swords are the keys to heaven.' " Below each panel, displays of historic swords illustrated the prowess of the Ottomans in battle against the infidel.[5] Elsewhere in the museum, another panel over a display of rifles assured that "There is no strength except in shooting," extending the imagery of power into the age of firearms.

Although this museum was never fully realized, the plan for its program illustrates that the Ottoman government was becoming quite skilled in framing the state's identity in the format of museological display. The previous military collection had developed into a space of ideological display over the course of its history and, because of the confusion of its collections, presented numerous messages of varying clarity. In contrast, the new museum projected a succinct agenda even in its prototype. As in the Imperial Museum, the shift from the word *mecmua* (collection) to the word *müze* (museum) may have indicated a conscious effort to turn a relatively passive institution of collection and wonder into an active institution in which exhibits promoted didactically ideals of historical pride and civic loyalty.

Whereas the previous museum had focused on the military as an institution and had only included the person of the sultan as the display's subject audience, Abdülhamid's new museum contextualized the contemporary sultan within the historical framework constructed by its displays. Through the juxtaposition of timeless aphorisms concerning loyalty to the dynasty with objects, the new museum ensured that the patriotism engendered by the glorification of history would correlate with loyalty to the contemporary sultan. The museum's manipulation of Abdülhamid's representational absence into a larger-than-life presence coincides well with his general occlusion from the public gaze. In doing so, it began to construct a national identity predicated on the existence of the eternal, almost mythic sultan.[6]

Like Abdülhamid's reign, the end of the model museum was sudden and swift. After his deposition, a commission formed in 1910 saw to the dispersal of items held in the Yıldız museum and the project of framing military antiquities had to be reconceived for a very different ideological program.

THE MILITARY MUSEUM AFTER THE YOUNG TURK REVOLUTION

During the last years of the empire, museums became programmatic parts of the effort to rally nationalist support for the Ottoman cause. After the Young Turk Revolution, museums actively entered the political arena. Hence museums became an expression of a national idea and eventually, during the national struggle, acquired mass support. The objects within, which were originally only symbols suggesting an as yet unarticulated and nondifferentiated post-Ottoman nationhood, became symbols for a country engaged in defining its locational, historical, and cultural identity.

While military objects had constituted an important part of the material representation of Ottoman identity in earlier collections, it was not until the last years of the empire that a military museum played a germinal role in the construction of a loyal Ottoman public. The new incarnation of the Military Museum differed from its predecessors in its gradual progression from a museum that created historical icons for adoration to one that created historical role models for emulation. It thus represented a shift in the mechanism of the relationship between the individual and the state from one of loyalty to one of nationalist participation.

After the institution of a parliamentary constitution in 1908, Ahmed Muhtar Pasha, who had been a member of the planning committee for the military museum under Abdülhamid II, instigated the reestablishment of the new museum at its previous location in the former Church of Hagia Irene. He received support from Mahmut Şevket Pasha, minister of war, who had become convinced of the importance of military museums and their effect on the culture of the populace after his tour of several new military museums in Berlin and Paris.[7] The new museum used many of the same objects that had previously been displayed in the Magazine of Ancient Weapons to emphasize dynastic power in a guise more appropriate for a parliamentary government. The new museum addressed a developing sense of Ottoman nationalism and used relatively modern methods to promote itself to the public and to attract visitors.

The decision to construct the new museum at the site of the former Magazine of Antique Weapons, on the grounds of the palace, underscores the role of the museum. Unlike the military museum proposed under Abdülhamid II, which used its location at the outskirts of the modern city to link the sultanate with progress, the traditional location focused attention on the history of the empire. The building itself served as a constant reminder of the Ottoman victory over the Byzantine Empire and thus brought to mind the apogee of Turkish-Islamic power over Greek-Christian forces.

In 1910 the museum was named the Museum of Military Weapons (Asliha-ye Askeriye Müzesi). It opened before all the displays were in place, suggesting a sense of urgency.[8] Unlike the earlier museums, the opening of the new museum was advertised to the public in newspapers and magazines, indicating that the government, aware of the propagandistic potential of a museum, was eager to spread its message among the people.

While occupying the site of the former Magazine of Antique Weapons, the new museum used a more cluttered display style reminiscent of trade fairs to present a space of fanfare.[9] In addition to the previous collections, the museum collected weaponry and armor from tombs and houses in the Bursa area. A military committee selected items they deemed suitable to be presented to "the public and foreign gaze" and representative of the glory of the early empire.[10] Also new to the museum program, paintings depicting the sultans contextualized the objects in a dynastic framework, and labels in Ottoman and in French elucidated the salient points of the exhibit. Unlike earlier military museums, which relied on the viewer's existing knowledge of history, the new military museum used these paintings and their labels to address itself to a public that needed to be taught the glorious history of the Ottoman state. Whereas at Yıldız, the labels consisted of quasi-religious slogans pledging allegiance to God and sultan, here they took the form of secular, nationalistic historical tracts. Still, like the Yıldız collection, this museum relied on text to contextualize its exhibits and to promote national loyalty.

In contrast to Edwin Grosvenor's photograph of the museum interior (see fig. 4), the photographs of the new museum show a very crowded space with weapons arranged in medallions and on tables, including a few glass display cases. Muskets and swords alike lay scattered on tables, like goods at a fair. Weapons and row upon row of cannons filled the rear galleries, and the great chain that had closed off the Golden Horn lay nearby. Banners and flags gave the space a patriotic and festive air; even the arrangement of the weapons made them far more decorative than menacing. Because no banners remained from earlier periods, new ones were designed by Sermed Muhtar and sewn by his mother.[11] Perhaps more than authenticity, the new museum expressed a more articulate form of exhibitionary staging than had graced the halls of earlier Ottoman museums.

Portraits displayed around the gallery constructed a historical context for the displays. The selection of rulers to be honored and the inscriptions that memorialized them in this public space provide important clues to how the initial program was designed to project an imperial image. Many of the portraits that hung from the banister between the first floor and the upper gallery were gifts from the new sultan, Mehmet Reşat (r. 1909–19), indicating that he played a role in ideologically framing the exhibits of the new museum.

The very use of portraiture underscored the modern, European cast of the museum. While Mahmud II had introduced imperial portraiture to the empire, the practice was not continued by his less religiously radical successors. The extensive use of portraits in the new military museum stood in particularly sharp contrast to Abdülhamid's absolute ban on the use of imperial portraiture during his reign and thus served as a sign of the new Young Turk order.[12]

To solve the absence of dynastic portraiture, the new Military Museum produced anachronistic oil-on-canvas portraits of all the sultans to illustrate the long-standing power of the family. Just as European museums used portraits to illustrate the long lineage of aristocracy, the military museum could use new portraits to illustrate the legacy of Ottoman might. The construction of this dynastic gallery used the specifically European medium of painting to represent the Ottoman state as European, like the Imperial Museum had used sculpture a generation earlier.

Fig. 32. Hasan Rıza, *Mehmet the Conquerer* (1913) [Çoruhlu]

The most elaborate portrait in the exhibit depicted Mehmet the Conqueror at the center of a medallion of swords and standards (fig. 32) similar to the rosette arrangement of weaponry throughout the exhibit. The accompanying label credited him with having brought the Middle Ages to an end with the conquest of İstanbul. The label shows an awareness of contemporary periodization in European history, as its author—probably Sermed Muhtar, son of Ahmet Muhtar and author of the museum's 1920 guidebook—conflates the end of the Middle Ages with the end of the

Byzantine Empire. Ironically, the label puts a positive twist on an event normally viewed negatively by European historians—the fall of Constantinople—and thus reframed a European style of periodization in an Ottoman guise.

Like the label for the portrait of Sultan Mehmet, those for the portraits of other early sultans emphasized the military skill with which they had expanded the empire.[13] The label for the portrait of Sultan Selim I eulogized him for the bravery and love of religion shown by his conquest of Egypt and the acquisition of the caliphate for the Ottoman dynasty. Similarly, the label for the portrait of Süleyman the Magnificent lauded him for his participation in numerous battles. More than his military prowess, however, the label emphasized his having glorified the name of the Ottoman family through these successful campaigns. With the inclusion of these three sultans, the museum made a courteous bow to the glory days of the empire, but through a wider array of later portraits, it chose to emphasize a more recent history in order to foster an image of progress.

The representations of more recent sultans emphasized their modernization practices and their close relations with Europe. The label for the sole portrait of Sultan Selim III credited him with having saved his state and nation through his "knowledge of science and justice and every sort of advancement and modern civilization." Similarly, the labels for two portraits of Sultan Abdülmecid emphasized the many reforms of the Tanzimat. Another label extolled the close ties he forged with Europe, exemplified by the alliance between the Ottomans, the British, the French, and the state of Piedmont.

The labels for the two portraits of Sultan Abdülaziz emphasized his reorganization of the army and the navy. They commended him for having commissioned the "famous" artist Chelebowski to portray important Ottoman victories in paintings that were, at the time, on display at the Military School (Mekteb-i Harbiye) and highlight his visit to the Paris exposition as an example of his participation in European civilization.[14] A painting of Sultan Mehmet Reşat himself (fig. 33) completed the presentation of recent sultans as the noble harbingers of progress.

Sultans Mahmut II and Abdülhamid II are notably absent from the display of later members of the dynasty. The reasons for the exclusion of Abdülhamid II are evident: Mehmet Reşat became sultan as a result of his deposition. While he had not actively participated in the coup d'état, it would not have been wise for him to associate himself with the deposed monarch by honoring his memory in the museum. The absence of Mahmut II, father of Abdülmecid and of Abdülaziz, is more puzzling. After all,

Fig. 33. Anonymous, *Sultan Mehmet Reşat* [Çoruhlu]

the government museum already owned the imperial portraits he had commissioned and displayed. Furthermore, like Selim III and Abdülaziz, both of whom were praised in the museum for their reforms of the military, Mahmut II had reformed the army, cunningly instituting a modern military corps and abolishing the Janissary orders. The modern army, for which the museum ostensibly rallied support, was largely a result of his efforts. And yet his name seems not to have been mentioned even once in the museum halls.

A clue for this absence can be found in the label accompanying the portrait of the museum director, Ahmet Muhtar. The label emphasizes Ahmet Muhtar's pure Turkish heritage, as well as his descent from a Janissary leader. The new museum represented the Janissaries as the main martial force of the empire, the repository of Ottoman military prowess. Swashbuckling and glamorous in the historical imagination but long since defunct, they no longer posed a threat to the ruler. Rather, an invocation of their memory as the loyal and brave defenders of the state could serve to encourage modern Ottoman citizens to fervently defend it as well. Unlike in the mid-nineteenth century, when they had only recently been abolished, in the early twentieth century the Janissaries could be safely resurrected. It would have been confusing to simultaneously praise their abolition and glorify their memory, so the museum chose to skip the portrait of Mahmut II, their archenemy.

No longer cadavers or effigies, in the new museum the Janissaries came to life, reinvented as a force with which to rally nationalist fervor. Men dressed as live mannequins, decked out in historical armor and costumes that were culled from the pages of Mahmut Şevket Pasha's 1902 work, *Osmanlı Teşkilat ve Kıyafet-i Askerisi* (Organization and Costume of the Ottoman Military).[15] The so-called historical units (*tarihi birlik*) posed for photographs in front of the second gate of the Topkapı Palace, the Middle Gate or Orta Kapı (fig. 34). Each of the approximately thirty men wore a different costume, making the depiction historically inaccurate. They carried arms, but their banners were more visible as they marched through the courtyard of the old palace and out past the first gate, the Imperial Gate or Bab-i Hümayun. A small band of musicians led the way, attracting attention to the group. For the first time in Ottoman museums, performance came to play an important role in engaging audiences.

The public was encouraged to participate in the museum through a campaign of newspaper advertisements. Some articles, including one by

Fig. 34. The Tarihi Birlik posing in front of the Orta Kapı [IMM]

the famous author Ahmet Midhat, simply encouraged Ottoman citizens to visit the new museum. Others encouraged them to participate by donating their families' military heirlooms. A 1909 article in *Tanın* lists some of the items already donated to the museum by the families of war veterans: an embroidered cap; an Ottoman sword; a Henri Martini rifle (used in the Crimean War); a book for the library; a pair of binoculars and a pair of blue-tinted glasses that had been used to spot the enemy in the Ottoman-Russian war; and photographs of some war veterans, including the first Armenian volunteer in the Ottoman Army.[16] Similarly, a short 1911 article and photograph in the magazine *Resimli Kitap* shows Ahmet Muhtar Pasha escorting the family of a veteran through the museum after having donated the clothing in which he had been killed.[17] No doubt, new recruits living in tents in the first courtyard of the Topkapı Palace visited the museum, as did families who came to visit their sons before they left for the front.[18] The museum thus became not only a site through which to honor the Ottoman dynasty and to glorify its military history, but also one where, through the processes of collection and display, the citizenry could imagine itself as a participant in that military tradition.

Entry into the museum space reinforced the experience of the visitor as a member of the military. The vestibule, still piled high with old arms and armor, led past the old chamber of the sultan and into the main hall. The chamber had been in use as a storage depot and had been restored by Ahmet Muhtar. According to its 1913 label, it contained two thrones of Sultan Selim III: his regular throne and the throne from which he watched the yearly parade of students graduating from the Mühendishane-i Berriye, the military and engineering academy he had founded. Represented in absentia by his throne, Sultan Selim III, identified as "one of our sovereigns who was loving of Turks and who did not shy from any sacrifice in innovations in the organization of the army," stood watch over a parade of visitors entering the museum. Like the graduates of the academy, they would leave the museum with an education—not in military engineering, but in nationalism.

As World War I progressed and foreign forces invaded the Ottoman Empire, the military museum came to play an important role in the war effort. It was remodeled in 1916 and featured new display strategies as well as activities designed to draw and engage large audiences. To an extent unprecedented in the empire, the new museum relied on performance and audience participation to draw people to the museum and provided extensive textual guides for its exhibits of both paintings and weapons. To a remarkable extent, the museum relied on modern programming techniques to draw visitors. A new sign outside advertised it as the Military Museum (Askeri Müze), and a medallion was painted in the main dome of the edifice to symbolize the museum (fig. 35). The medallion depicts numerous swords, spears, cannons, rifles, shovels, and trumpets and trombones emerging from a central drum. The centrality of the drum underscores the performative cast of the new museum.

In 1916 the Janissary mannequins returned from the Hippodrome to the gallery of the former Church of Hagia Irene.[19] Even in this mannequin form, the Janissaries were brought to life by a Qur'anic inscription hanging over the display, the only one apparent in this museum. From sura 8, aya 45, it reads, "O ye who believe! When you meet a force, be firm, and call God, in remembrance, and often, that ye may prosper." An important part of the performance of the Janissary band, known as a *mehter* band, is the quick repetition of the name of God, creating a battle cry with which to rally the fervor of Muslims and said to have inspired the Janissaries in their centuries of successful battle. Above the mannequins, a painting of the victorious 1664 battle of Yanikkale showed them heroically in action (fig. 36).

Unlike at the Hippodrome, where the Janissaries had signified the dead, the mannequins at the former church were framed by live Janissary per-

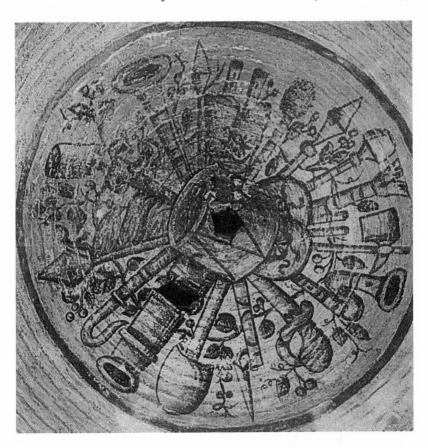

Fig. 35. Medallion representing the Military Museum, painted in the dome of the former Church of Hagia Irene [Ministry of Culture of the Republic of Turkey, brochure commemorating the 150th anniversary of Turkish Museums]

formances outside the museum halls. In contrast to the historical troop of 1913–16, the new live Janissary troupe of 1916 no longer had need of weapons. They dropped their arms in favor of musical instruments and played daily in front of the museum (fig. 37) and as accompaniment to movies shown at the new Military Museum cinema, made possible by the electricity just installed in the building. In the new *mehter* band, the auditory stimulus of military music replaced the visual stimulus of the former historical unit. As indicated on the medallion painted on the dome of the museum, the core of the museum's representative strategy became the drum, an auditory beacon to make hearts beat as one for the state.

Fig. 36. Military Museum, Janissary Gallery, ca. 1916–23 [IMM]

The band's costumes, quite different from the chain mail and armor chosen for the historical troop in the previous six years, were uniform and consisted of simple caftans and turbans—inauthentic as military gear but ap-
propriately historical if not historic for performance. A series of twenty-six
postcards sold at the museum commemorated the Janissaries for foreign
tourists. Like the banners sewn for the museum, the music of the military
band had been lost in the century since the abolition of the Janissaries.
Sermed Muhtar wrote new scores, which were published in periodical form
beginning in 1918. Contemporary *mehter* bands, particularly the one that
performs daily in front of the İstanbul Military Museum, still rely on the
staging and notation laid down at this time.[20] However, the band ceased to
perform from 1923, when the republic was instituted, until the 1950s, when
anti-Ottoman reforms were relaxed under the government of the Democratic Party.

Reinvented for the museum, the *mehter* band appeared to embody the
continuation of Ottoman military glory. Their performances became an invented tradition similar to those discussed by Hobsbawm, in which historical practices are redesigned under the guise of tradition for modern, often
political and nationalist purposes.[21] Originally, Janissary bands had used

Fig. 37. The *mehter* band performing outside of the Military Museum,
ca. 1916–20 [IMM]

music to inspire soldiers in battle. In contrast, the performances of the
mehter band were divorced from actual battle and served instead to inspire
national feeling among the general public as well as soldiers about to leave
for the front. In addition to its daily museum performances, the band traveled and roused national fervor at several venues, including benefits for veterans and refugees and hospitals where they entertained wounded soldiers.

The band also accompanied movies in a room adjacent to the entrance
to the museum. One might expect documentary, news, or propaganda
films to have been played at this venue. Indeed, the National Defense
League (Müdafaa-i Milliye Cemiyeti) donated a group of films to the museum in 1919.[22] But the theater showed many movies for the sole purpose
of entertainment. *Indian Revenge, Husband and Wife, The Alphabet of
Love, The Fiancés, and Disaster in St. Moritz*—all to the accompaniment of
the *mehter* band—seem to have been popular in 1923.[23] While moving
pictures entertained audiences, martial *mehter* music subliminally reminded them of the national cause.

Other entertainers, such as magicians and singers, also performed at the
museum (fig. 38). Visitors could pay one *kuruş* to see a panoramic view of

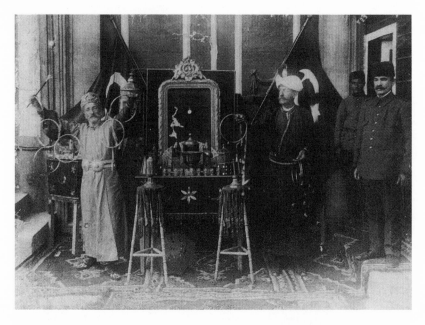

Fig. 38. Performers at the Military Museum, ca. 1916–23 [IMM]

İstanbul from the tower near the building, on the wall of Topkapı Palace. For another *kurush,* they could practice at the museum shooting range, or they could buy thumbtacks to decorate a historic wooden cannon set aside for that purpose. The cell initially built for Sultan Abdülmecid, where the thrones of Selim III had been displayed in 1910, became a room in which visitors could sign a guest book, marking their visits for posterity.[24] The museum became a space designed to attract visitors through any means necessary, so that it could perform on them sights and sounds that would produce loyalty and nationalist sentiment.

Through numerous photographs, as well as the labels of paintings, vitrines, and even dioramas that remain from this period, one can partially reconstruct the interior museum spaces as visitors must have experienced them. Visitors entered the spaces of a glorious history brought to life at the very entrance by a doorman in period dress (fig. 39), alive and in sharp contrast to the mannequin that had greeted Théophile Gautier. The weapons that had previously lain exposed on tables were now encased in glass cases and labeled. Paintings already owned by the museum were rearranged to illustrate the displays, and a plethora of new paintings depicting historical scenes, primarily battles, were added to the walls of the exhibits. The use of art to teach

Fig. 39. Group portrait of the Military Museum staff, ca. 1916–23 [IMM]

history was new to the empire and was precipitated by the need to educate a broader range of visitors who might not have already known or identified with Ottoman history. Like the Versailles museum, established in the 1830s as a "museum for the history of France," this museum effectively used paintings to combine history with contemporary politics.[25]

Fig. 40. Military Museum, view toward the apse, ca. 1916–23 [IMM]

As in the nineteenth century, the museum took advantage of the building's ecclesiastic architecture by using the apsidal focal point to express the central theme of the museum (figs. 40, 41). Now, however, a banner emblazoned with a *tuğra* (the symbolic signature of the sultan) shielded the mosaic cross on the semidome from view, obscuring the religious overtones of the architecture. The iconographic shift from cross to *tuğra* marks the incorporation of the former implicitly European-Christian scheme of display into a nationalistic ideology eager to divest itself of its foreign patrimony. Stathis Gourgouris suggests that the production of a national culture depends on the production of quasi-religious idols.[26] Indeed, the Military Museum produced a secular iconography of heroes the adulation of whom could promote a shared vision of national culture.

Below the banner emblazoned with a *tuğra*, the rows of helmets seen in Grosvenor's 1893 photograph of the apse remain. Instead of acting as a backdrop to dynastic relics, in the new display they form a backdrop for the portrait of Sultan Mehmet the Conqueror. In this painting, the sultan appears central to a medallion of arms, similar to that on the dome and to the arrangements of weapons on walls throughout the museum. In this display, as in the rest of the museum, the image replaced the relic as the signifier

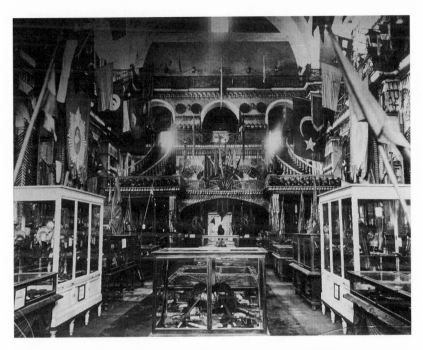

Fig. 41. Military Museum, view from the apse, ca. 1916–23 [IMM]

giving ideological meaning to the display of objects and to the museum as a whole. Throughout the museum, textual labels, often located on the paintings themselves, imparted precise information to direct the gaze of the viewer through the painted image to the objects, then past them into a carefully circumscribed model of history. In an Islamic culture that had eschewed the naturalistic representation of the human form, the production of historical figures as secular idols marked a sharp break with tradition.

While in the earlier incarnation of the new military museum, portraits alone had served to emphasize the importance of the Ottoman dynasty in imperial history, after the 1916 renovation historical genre paintings glorified entire Ottoman armies for modern soldiers to emulate. The apse was flanked with monumental paintings of the Battle of Varna, in which the Turks, led by Mehmet the Conqueror's father, Murat, defeated invading Crusaders in 1444. The image clearly referred to the strong patrimony of the Ottoman dynasty, which had repelled Europeans since time immemorial. Considering that the helmets in the apse had not been moved since 1893, it is quite possible that the Crusader armor displayed nearby as described by Grosvenor remained in the same location. In this case, the paintings contextualized the nearby artifacts from the Crusades. The paintings gained a second layer of meaning because they were among the paintings that Sultan Abdülaziz had commissioned from Chelebowski and because they previously had been located at the military school. Thus while the imagery of the paintings commemorated the early military history of the Ottomans, the conditions of their production testified to a more recent and progressive past. In their new location, the paintings exposed the public to a mode of visual education previously reserved for students at the military academy.

Throughout the museum, images of the Ottomans defeating Europeans reinforced the idea that, historically, military prowess had been in the hands of the Ottoman Empire, not European forces. The labels that remain in the İstanbul Military Museum Archive indicate that paintings displaying the naval battles of Preveze, Narta, and Trafalgar, the sieges of Belgrade and Vienna, the conquest of Belgrade, and the land battle fought at Maslak during the Crimean War were brought from the military school to the museum. Whereas these images had once formed a visual backdrop for students at the military academy, they now served to educate the museumgoing public. During a time of war, not only did soldiers need to be trained to think positively in their fight against the enemy, but civilians also had to be trained to believe that like their forebears, the Ottomans of 1916 could repel enemy forces threatening to lay hold of İstanbul and the entire empire.

In contrast to texts accompanying paintings in the museum since 1910, which focused on alliances and the growth of modern civilization, the labels for new paintings emphasized adversarial relationships and victory over the enemy. In most of these texts (and presumably images), the Ottomans are shown defeating French, British, and Russian enemies. The one exception, a painting depicting the Battle of Trafalgar, shows a battle between the French and the English, as if to remind viewers that while these countries were allies during the Great War, their history included deep rifts between them. The image may also have reminded the Ottoman viewer of one of Napoleon's major defeats after his conquest of Ottoman Egypt.

As the war progressed, displays of contemporary events that promoted the war effort continued to augment the collection. In 1917 two dioramas initially set up in the Red Crescent Hall (located at the Galatasaray School) moved to the Military Museum. One depicted the heroic defense of the Dardanelles during the world war; the other depicted the activities of the

Red Crescent in the Caucasus. These dioramas may have been located in the upstairs gallery, at one end of the Janissary display.

In 1921 three paintings of relatively minor characters in Ottoman history joined the museum collection. The extensive labels on these paintings explain how relatively unknown men had become national heroes. Lieutenant Colonel Hüssein Bey pressed on to victory in the Crimean War despite a crippling blow to his thumb. Hasan Efendi, who had made many sacrifices in the service of "our nation and people" would "remain in the memory of the nation a veteran worthy of remembrance." Sergeant İhsan Hidayet Efendi had been so heroic that he had become the subject of Namık Kemal's famous play, *Homeland or Silistre* (Vatan Yahut Silistre). He would be remembered for all time as a "member of the Ottoman nation, worthy to lie in the bosom of the nation for eternity." Through the inclusion of these nonroyal images, the museum created role models that almost any enlisted man could hope to emulate. People were no longer merely to be led by iconic members of the royal family. Instead, the museum produced exhibits through which they had the opportunity to become heroic members of the Ottoman nation, citizens (in)formed by the museum. Such images would have been inspirational to visitors who participated in the cause of expelling European powers.

The inclusion of Sergeant İhsan Hidayet Efendi in the museum was of particular importance in relation to its contemporary political cast. Namik Kemal's play concerned one of the last great battles of the empire, the successful forty-one-day siege of Silistria in 1854, which resulted in five times as many Russian as Ottoman casualties. The performance of the play incited such patriotism that its audience rioted and called for Sultan Abdülmecid's deposition in favor of his son, who became Sultan Murat V. In response, Namik Kemal was arrested immediately and exiled to Cyprus, where he remained until Murat V's accession three years later. Although it was his only play that he ever saw on stage, Namık Kemal came to believe fervently in the educational potential of the theater for the nationalist cause. Although the subject matter of the Crimean War had entered the annals of history, the intense patriotism of the play suited the increasing patriotism of the late Ottoman Empire. Symbolizing the public power of national fervor that had incited controversy a quarter of a century earlier, it was performed extensively at the time of the second constitutional revolution in 1908, when Abdülhamid II was deposed. Discovering that the soldier who had been the basis for the character Private Abdullah, İhsan Hidayet, was still alive, the director of the Military Museum, Ahmet Muhtar, invited the now elderly veteran, a villager from western Anatolia, to İstanbul as a state guest in 1912, during the Balkan Wars. Ahmet Muhtar asked him, "If they called you to war now, would you go to fight?" He answered, "I would go, my children." He then added a line from the play that had made the character based on him famous: "If I were to go, would it be the end of the world?"[27] What figure could be more suited for the image of the new museum, one that placed the average man at the center of the Ottoman historical narrative, replete with victories like the one at Silistria? What cultural sign could be more appropriate than that of a play dedicated to patriotism?

During the course of the war for liberation, the struggle evolved from world war outside of the empire to one that engaged multiple sides: invading European powers, eager to divide remaining Ottoman territories; the imperial government, trying to maintain itself at all costs; and a fledgling Turkish nationalist government, fighting against occupation and against puppet dynastic rule. In a situation of war, it is rare to have a single institution capable of addressing both a local audience and an audience of invaders. During the occupation of İstanbul, the Military Museum addressed itself to Ottomans as well as to foreigners, for whom the museum displays were labeled in French. But the histories presented to the Ottoman audience and to the foreign audience were quite different. Abbreviated labels in French promoted a far less nationalistic vision of Ottoman history while still reminding viewers of Ottoman victories, as well as former treaties with the allied powers. For example, the label for a painting depicting the Ottoman fleet in 1324/1909, which was added to the museum in 1917, explains the role of Mehmet Reşat in expanding the fleet and the elaborate ceremonies that accompanied it, whereas the French label simply names the ships. The achievements of sultans and the detailed heroics of veterans alike get short shrift in the French text, which gives enough information to let foreigners know what they are seeing but not enough to let them participate in the sense of pride generated through the longer labels. Also of note, despite the Ottoman-German alliance during the Great War, the museum displays curiously made no reference whatsoever to Germans.

The visitors to the Ottoman Military Museum have all died, but the comments that a few of them made in the guest book during the last years of the empire remain as testimony to the museum's nationalistic program. Two military students from the Kuleli Barracks wrote, "By touring the museum, I came to understand how heroic our soldiers of yore really were." Another entry expressed similar sentiments more poetically: "The preservation of the objects that testify to the nobility and the bravery of our children in arms in front of the eyes of the world is a holy duty." It was signed by Mehmet Ertugrul bin Sultan Mehmet Vahideddin Han'i Sadis, who was to be the last Ottoman sultan. In contrast, Jacque Brumonos, a captain in the French army, wrote that he had visited the museum four times, finding it better organized on each visit. As might be expected, he had a notably unemotional response to the objects within.[28]

By writing in this notebook, visitors to the museum became actors in the performance of nationalist expression that the museum was designed to foster. Visitors looked, touched, walked through, and listened to the past. When they were done, they had the opportunity to inscribe their involvement in that past in the guestbook and inscribe themselves in the history of the museum. The concern with the visitor—the many activities and entertainments designed to draw visitors to the museum; the procedures of labeling and illustration designed to control their gaze; and the encouragement of their participation in the construction of the museum collections—reflected a growing awareness of a new character on the Ottoman national scene: the citizen.

9 Islamic and Archaeological Antiquities after the Young Turk Revolution

By the end of the empire Ottoman museums had come full circle, with military collections regaining supremacy in the production of national identity. Nonetheless, despite all of the political confusion, economic turmoil, and prolonged military struggle of the last decade of Ottoman rule, the archaeological and Islamic museums in İstanbul did not simply manage to stay afloat, they became increasingly important voices for the emergent national struggle.

ISLAMIC ANTIQUITIES

While the Islamic identity of the Ottoman state had been central to Abdülhamid's political program, it was only during and after the constitutionalist Young Turk Revolution of 1908–10 that concern over Islamic antiquities began to enter public discourse with any frequency, in large part because of the Young Turks' interest in increased communication between the state and the populace. In 1910 newspapers began to report thefts of tiles and carpets from historical sites as far afield as Konya and its environs.[1] As a result of such reports the museum sent a long note to the Ministry of Education emphasizing the need to actively collect antiquities in the museum and requiring the participation of the Ministry of Pious Foundations in the preservation and maintenance of historical sites. As explained by the note,

> Since it is necessary to protect the objects of value, old and new, of the mosques in İstanbul and in outlying areas, the Ministry of Education is prepared to consider the proposition of guarding old objects in the Tiled Pavilion provided that the Ministry of Pious Foundations takes measures to preserve recent works; and in order to prevent the transfer of

even one of the stolen objects from the recent theft of [various lamps and vases from several mosques of Bursa and Eskisehir] to European museums, the Ministry of Education is charged with reporting the matter to the Office of Customs under the Ministry of Finance.[2]

It was not so much the inherent value of the objects that led to their collection but a distaste for the idea that Europeans would benefit from their theft by making them acquire aesthetic and exotic value in their museums. The ideology of the Young Turks began to transform the Islamic arts collection into an overt means of nationalist expression and of resistance against European cultural subsumation. In an environment pushing toward a Turkish identity independent of religion, objects that had originally had only religious value—or, beyond value, pricelessness—gained an aesthetic-historical value with which they could represent the country in the museum, which isolated them from their original religious roles. The danger of their loss lay not in their absence but in the degree of profit possible once they entered European collections.

The new market value of such objects required local officials to take new measures to protect old sites. In a note from the Police Commissariat of Beşiktaş to the İstanbul head of police, the local police chief complained of the potential dangers posed by tourists around the historical tomb of Barbaros Hayreddin Pasha:

> The standard of the tomb of Barbaros Hayreddin Pasha, in Beşiktaş, that dates from his first campaigns, is of great historical value, and it seems that Italian visitors have proposed to buy it for 6,000 liras. Many foreigners have recently been wandering around this tomb, and the balustrade around it is getting signs of wear. We are concerned that the guard may steal the standard because of its price. We request that, in accord with recent governmental decisions, this standard should be placed in the care of the Imperial Museum in order to not make way for the theft of a valuable historical object.[3]

Thefts made it necessary to assign value to objects of Islamic art that had previously never been considered in the light of commerce.

> Much as some experts have declared it impossible to estimate the value of seventy-two tile pieces from the time of the architect Sinan . . . stolen from the tomb of Sokollu Mehmet Pasha in Eyüb, it seems necessary to affix a price to them in order to serve as a basis for the legal process.[4]

To determine the value of these objects, the museum began to seek the services of antique dealers, who often were involved in the shady deals of transferring stolen goods to collectors.[5]

The new values assigned to Islamic artworks made it necessary for the museum to assume a more active acquisition policy. In 1910 the Ministry of Public Education decided to set up a commission under the leadership of the director of the Imperial Museum to determine the "appropriate methods and sturdy provisions" for the preservation of "Islamic and Ottoman arts" in the empire. For the first time, this statement provided a classificatory group for these objects that explicitly linked the sectarian term "Islamic" with the national term "Ottoman." The commission was assigned to divide the tasks of conservation and collection such that the Ministry of Pious Foundations would be responsible for the conservation of consecrated buildings, but the museum administration would be responsible for the preservation of mosaics, tiles, and other ornaments that could be removed from the surfaces of buildings.[6] Thus objects whose sole purpose had been to enhance the experience of worship through their inclusion in consecrated buildings were officially divested of this role. They were simultaneously reduced as aesthetic and historical works as they were raised as objects of market and museum value. After the French Revolution, one of the powerful symbols of the new order had been the removal of church regalia to the secular halls of the museum.[7] In the Ottoman Empire, the Young Turk Revolution was slowly setting the stage for the secularist revolution that was to come only a decade later: already, objects vested with religious significance were being recontextualized in a historical and national museum collection.

With plans for the construction of a new museum associated with the Ministry of Pious Foundations, in 1908 the Islamic collection moved from the upper corner of the archaeology museum building to the Tiled Pavilion (fig. 42).[8] This move was made possible by the opening of the third wing of the Imperial Museum in 1908, which provided enough display space to hold the antiquities that had remained in the Tiled Pavilion until that time. In giving the collection of Islamic and Ottoman art its own building, the spatial relationship between the collection of ancient antiquities and the collection of Islamic and Ottoman antiquities was significantly altered. Previously, the Islamic collections had settled into the recesses of the museum building as if an afterthought. Surrounded by the fifteenth-century architecture of the Tiled Pavilion, they confronted the legacy of the ancients held in the Imperial Museum with a very different cultural and historical aesthetic that represented a local, rather than an adoptive, history. Face-to-face on the outer precincts of the Topkapı Palace, the two buildings suggested a showdown of historical identities for the emerging Ottoman nation.

The growing interest in Islamic and Ottoman arts found expression not only in the preservation of consecrated sites and the objects associated

Fig. 42. Islamic antiquities in the Tiled Pavilion, ca. 1909 [Edhem 1909]

with them but also in a newfound interest in historical sites associated with the Ottoman family. Along the same lines, in June 1911 the commission for Ottoman history was sent to investigate a report concerning the house Osman had allegedly lived in in Bilecik. Although no documents could be found to corroborate the rumor that the house had belonged to Osman, officials sent a commission to Bilecik to investigate.[9] In 1911 the Ministry of the Interior issued a directive ordering the collection of standards, weapons, shields, and military clothing from the greater Bursa region, identifying their value as both national and artistic.[10]

In 1914 the Islamic collections of the Imperial Museum moved to the former charitable areas (*imaret*) of the Süleymaniye complex. The new Museum of Pious Foundations (Evkaf Müzesi) opened on April 14, a date chosen to coincide with the anniversary of the coronation of Sultan Mehmet Reşat. Objects culled from the historic mosques and tombs of the Ottoman Empire became resituated in a liminal space between the secularist display strategy of the museum and the directorship of the Ministry of Pious Foundations, interested more in their religious than their aesthetic value. With this return to a religious administrative framework, perhaps it is not so surprising that this museum established to protect Islamic antiquities soon lost many of its valuable carpets to thieves.[11]

Far from subsiding during the war years, the interest in Islamic antiquities became increasingly tied to nationalist projects and projections. In 1915 the Commission for Examination of Antiquities (Tedkik-i Asar-i Atika Encümeni) was charged with the investigation of works of "Turkish civilization, Islam, and knowledge of the nation" and with the publication of its findings.[12] In the same year the Commission for the Protection of Antiquities (Muhafaza-i Asar-i Atika Encümeni) was organized to supervise nationwide adherence to section 5 of the antiquities law, which listed all the mobile and immobile objects to which the law applied.[13]

Among their most important activities, the commission issued a report concerning the state of the Topkapı Palace in which, for the first time, Ottoman antiquities became extensively and explicitly identified with the preservation of a national heritage, and the preservation of objects became explicitly linked to the construction of national memory.[14] "Every nation," the commission declared, "makes the necessary provisions for the preservation of its fine arts and monuments and thus preserves the endless virtues of its ancestors as a lesson in civilization for its descendants." The Topkapı Palace was identified as having unique importance in that it was the only site where examples of nonpublic and nonreligious architecture had been preserved for several centuries. The commission viewed the preservation of buildings as equivalent to the preservation of four hundred years of Ottoman history that constituted "a national art history."[15] For the first time, Ottoman antiquities were designated solely in national rather than in religious or dynastic terms.

The government's continued interest in Ottoman antiquities during the war and increasing tendency to recast them as Ottoman and national rather than Islamic suggests that the value associated with these objects had acquired a thoroughly nationalist flavor. The official collection of Islamic artwork signified the rise of patriotic self-awareness in the face of imperial dissolution, reflected new reactions to emergent nationalisms in the former empire, and also foreshadowed secular notions of Islam that would develop fully under the Turkish Republic.

ARCHAEOLOGICAL ANTIQUITIES

As war divided the empire, scattered reports concerning antiquities suggest that museum objects continued to construct the cultural front lines of battle and that their value as expressions of territorial sovereignty increased in the context of war. For example, the museum tried to keep track of the antiquities exported from the Bergama museum during the Greek invasion of the west coast of Asia Minor.[16] Similarly, the Ottoman government maintained encoded reports concerning the excavations undertaken by Italian forces during their occupation of Bodrum.[17]

Although many of the European powers occupying the crumbling Ottoman Empire probably engaged in archaeological activities, the extensive correspondence between the Imperial Museum and the French throughout the war makes the story of French archaeological activities, and the Ottoman Museum's concern with them, the most accessible. French occupying forces were involved in archaeological activities in at least three regions: in Istanbul itself, in Gallipoli, and in Adana. Their activities in these three areas, as recorded by the correspondence between the museum director Halil (Edhem) and several administrators of the French Occupation Forces, provide a vivid example of the symbolic meanings invested in archaeological activities during the heat of battle and during the incertitude of occupation.

The correspondence between the French Occupation Forces of Ottoman territories and the museum begins in 1919, when Halil sent the Adana Museum a copy of the catalog of the Imperial Museum. He also requested a copy of the inventory of the collections of the Adana Museum. In thanking the French forces for their cooperation with the museum's efforts to maintain an inventory of antiquities in the empire, Halil agreed to facilitate the passage of certain antiquities from a mansion (*konak*) in Silifke to the Adana Museum. In response to this incentive and show of goodwill, Colonel R. Normand, the French governor of the city of Adana during the French occupation of Cilicia (known as the Administration des Territoires Ennemies Occupés, Zone Nord), sent the museum in İstanbul a copy of the provisional catalog. The list appended to the letter suggests a ragtag collection of fragments found by military personnel and by local civilians apparently supporting the French forces, including two Greeks, two Armenians, and a Muslim (either Turkish or Arab).[18] This exchange suggests that rather than continue to collect antiquities during the war, the Imperial Museum tried to control them by keeping an inventory rather than through acquisitions. Just as Europeans had sought to collect antiquities by means of modified technologies in response to Ottoman laws, the Ottoman government, rendered too ineffective to enforce its own laws, tried to maintain its ownership of the antiquities through the collection of information.

For the invading forces, the power to collect antiquities from occupied territories functioned as a sign of sovereignty even under the most adverse circumstances. In his account of the formation of the Adana Museum,

Colonel Normand explained, "As soon as [French] officers penetrated into this Occupied Enemy Territory, Northern Zone, it was logical, it was French to turn some of their first thoughts towards the cult of art."[19] He explained that the museum was set up to illustrate the evolution of various architectural fragments, such as columns, across the ages. Whereas in their museums the Ottomans had refrained from producing an evolutionary model of style, the French immediately instituted their own organizational patterns even in this small, object-poor museum. It thus became a microcosmic model of the greater French museum enterprise. The use of an evolutionary model even in this provincial museum underscores the very different epistemological choices made in İstanbul, where there were far more objects to support such a strategy had it been desired.

Although the Imperial Museum had been involved in collecting antiquities for many years, the French emphasized the humanitarian nature of their salvation of antiquities from the destructive properties of nature and, particularly, of people. For example, the French were horrified by the common use of ancient sarcophagi as horse troughs. So they collected them from outlying regions and brought them to the museum, where they drilled holes in them so that they could be used as outdoor planters. The French also expressed their humanitarian interests through their mission to educate the public, both Muslim and Christian, who increasingly learned to partake of the museum's mission of collection:

> As the reputation of the museum spreads advantageously every day and increasingly interests the public, all nationalities and all classes of people wish to cooperate in its enrichment. . . . [T]he work, initially begun in a purely archaeological spirit, acquires from day to day a political character, uniting diverse races and enemies in a common thought, making people of the most various conditions interested in a French idea.[20]

Thus the French presented the establishment of the Adana Museum as a humanitarian endeavor and a means of collectively imagining French colonial domination of the region as participatory and communal. Like the Ottoman government, which had encouraged regional governments to support a national effort to collect antiquities, the French tried to present local support of the museum as a barometer for the popularity of the French occupation. Their ability to use the museum as a political barometer depended on its cultural and supposedly apolitical character. Because on the surface the museum considered ancient history in supposedly neutral and scientific terms, it could covertly function as a political indicator of stability even in an area where domination would be quite temporary.

Not only did museum activities serve as a marker for the transfer of territorial sovereignty from the Ottoman Empire to France, it also caused the expulsion of non-French archaeologists from their excavations in Cilicia and thus emphasized the French victory over other occupying forces. Normand makes note of Hittite sites at Zincirli and Kargamıs deserted by the Germans and British respectively. The museum's acquisition of the finds of these sites thus served as a thinly veiled marker of military success even as Normand tried to present the museum as an institution that peacefully united various peoples under French dominion. In a similar vein, a rare Assyrian-Hittite basalt statue was quickly exported to the Louvre to serve as a trophy of the French occupation of Cilicia.[21]

Archaeological expressions of territoriality were not far from the minds of French forces even during the heat of battle. In April 1923 Halil wrote to General Charpy, commander of the French Occupation Forces in İstanbul:

> I have just learned that the French military authority of Gallipoli executed archaeological excavations at a location close to Sedd ul-Bahr.
>
> As my administration was never officially advised of the execution of these excavations, I request that you inform me concerning this matter. If it is the case that these excavations are still under way, I request that you order them suspended since the official regulations do not permit excavations without official authorization.[22]

Halil's letter suggests that although the museum had tried to remain informed about excavations throughout the war, it was only near the end of the foreign occupation of İstanbul that they began to regain some of the legal power necessary to demand participation in foreign archaeological activities. As General Charpy's reply makes clear, the French had taken advantage of the absence of Ottoman authority immediately at the time of occupation:

> In response to your letter of April 24, I have the honor of letting you know that it is in effect true that archaeological excavations were conducted by the French Occupational Forces at Sedd ul-Bahr, on the peninsula of Gallipoli.
>
> The first work was undertaken in 1915 by the troops fighting in this region. This work served as relaxation for them between battles and otherwise gave few results. The work was thus abandoned for several years and it was several months after my arrival in Constantinople that I saw that the excavations continued. Since the garrison of Sedd ul-Bahr was not very important and I could only make a weak effort, my plan was only to perpetuate the noble tradition established by those who preceded us. As the peninsula of Gallipoli was at this time under the Greek occupation, you understand why you were not officially advised of the execution of these excavations.

By downplaying the archaeological activities as unfruitful acts of relaxation, Charpy masked the French-Greek cooperation that the excavations most likely entailed. It seems unlikely that digging archaeological trenches could have served as relaxation for battle-weary soldiers. Rather, occupation forces were eager to use archaeological finds as a marker of the transfer of territorial control out of Ottoman hands and laws.

Similar excavations took place during the French occupation of İstanbul itself, where the Imperial Museum could not even keep a watchful eye over the nearby Makriköy (today's Bakirköy, just outside the city walls to the east of old İstanbul) or even the gardens of Gülhane, just down the hill from the museum. As in the case of the Adana Museum, French officials framed their involvement in archaeology in İstanbul as a public service. In a December 12, 1922, letter to Halil Bey, General Charpy wrote,

> [F]ar from having destroyed and sacked [the city] during its stay here, the French Occupational Corps made an effort to contribute to the beautification of your admirable city and not only responded to the charitable needs of your refugees, but also used the means which it had at its disposal for excavations, for the supplementation of the patrimony of art, which constitutes the fame of your capital.[23]

As the French occupation came to an end, many of the items excavated at Sedd ul-Bahr and at Gülhane and Makriköy entered the collections of the İstanbul Archaeology Museum. Of these, one case of antiquities was lost from Sedd ul-Bahr when it was dropped into the sea while being loaded onto the carrier *Agile*.[24] Did the crate really fall into the sea, or was its acquisition by the French forces a final expression of the archaeological freedom they, and other occupying forces, had taken advantage of during the war?

The politics of antiquities acquisition and collection changed dramatically during the war because of the waning territorial sovereignty of the Ottoman government. Nonetheless, the Imperial Museum's continued attempts to remain informed about ongoing archaeological activities in the empire, as well as the eagerness with which occupying forces continued to excavate even during battle, reaffirm the significance of antiquities not as artistic treasures but as markers of political ascendancy.

Conclusion

What can the study of Ottoman museums have to say for the twenty-first century? Although the "Islamic threat" has replaced the "Eastern Question" in Europe and the United States, many of the internal concerns—secularism, ethnicity, populism, and elite culture—as well as many of the country's international identifications—the only predominantly Islamic member of the North Atlantic Treaty Organization, vying for a slot in the European Economic Community—remain strangely similar. On the one hand, Turkey's self-identification as "Western" not only runs the risk of denying the experience and taste of the vast majority of its population, it also potentially suggests an adoption of the racist and belittling attitudes of the West toward the East, the first world to the third world, or the developed to the developing world—depending on which problematic terminology one chooses to adopt—toward its own people and traditions. On the other hand, accepting itself as Eastern runs the risk of also accepting all the disadvantages of the third world, the developing world, the previously colonized world. To label oneself as "developing" is to automatically mark oneself as following in somebody else's footsteps, somebody who has stepped first through the jungle and carved out a unique path of progress. In an age of European unification, such a label means denying itself the economic opportunities afforded by participating in Europe, as well as the hopes that have been vested in political and economic reforms and modernization for the past two centuries. A century after the institution of Ottoman museums, Turkey still struggles not only with the physical issues the museums addressed—antiquities smuggling, secularization, and militarism—but also with the metanarratives of identity that they ultimately represented. In an increasingly shrinking world cut between globalist and postcolonialist perspectives, Turkey partakes in both visions and as the corollary to this binary experience, remains a liminal outsider to each—just as it did at the beginning of the Turkish Republican project. The history constructed by Ottoman museums at the end of empire reveals the processes through which modern Turkey came to possess—and in turn became possessed by—its heritage. The museums thereby suggest how the many pieces of that heritage may fit together—neither as signs of backwardness nor as teleological strands of official historical narratives.

How, then, did Ottoman museums envision history? Like all museums, those of the Ottoman Empire chose particular sets of objects to collect and display. The mere selection of sets of objects and the shifts in their importance under the private and the public gaze reveal the ideological shifts in Ottoman identity during the latter years of empire. Unlike displays in the imperial treasury, those spaces designated as museums carefully classified objects according to type, provenance, and period. More than just a space of display, museums came to exemplify new systems of categorization that paralleled systems already established in Europe. Yet by eschewing the European museum's epistemological underpinnings, the Ottoman government adapted it to specifically local ideological needs.

Although the empire did not conceive of itself as having a clear national identity—in the sense of imagining a shared ethnicity, history, culture, and so forth among its citizens as a basis for self-rule—the ideology developing in Ottoman museums clearly included many of the underpinnings common to nationalist movements. In his study of small European national movements, Miroslav Hroch has suggested three phases of nationalism. In the first, he suggests that " 'a pre-national consciousness' develops unevenly among the social groupings and regions of a country . . . which was purely cultural, literary, and folkloric, and had no particular political or even national implications."[1] This type of protonational consciousness has some applicability to the collections of the Imperial Museum as they developed before 1906. Although the museum was designed to articulate Ottoman ownership of antiquities, it did not express any overt premise of national identity. It used symbols not to identify the unique properties of a nation but to produce affiliations with other nations and, through such affiliations, to differentiate Ottomanist culture from an existing world order that increasingly relied on European hegemony as much as on overt European colonial power.

Kayalı argues that "it is reasonable to assume that the Western-oriented segments of the Ottoman elite were drawn to the concept of the nation-state in the late nineteenth and early twentieth centuries, but not in any ethnic sense."[2] Indeed, the museums of the Abdülhamidian era proposed symbols of identity for the empire that relied not on Turkism but on collection as a symbol of national sovereignty and as a means of identifying with a European ideological system. As an expression of protonationalist sentiments, the museum did not seek to define symbols of identification unique to a Turkish or even an Ottoman nation. Rather, it used the ability to own and manipulate these symbols as itself symbolic of Ottoman territorial mastery. The symbols it chose—and those it decided not to choose—speak not simply of material interests in those objects but of a response to the epistemological subtexts that inform the act of collection. Much as exemplary institutions representing the late Ottoman ethos have served throughout this book to reveal developing ideologies of identity, those collections that never emerged conceal the resistance to hegemonic European models of the museum within the Ottoman museum project.

Despite the panoply of collections developed under the auspices of Ottoman museums, two types of collections common in the nineteenth century never entered their purview. While collections of contemporary painting were never even considered in the Ottoman museum project, the natural history collections delineated under the 1889 charter for the museum never came to fruition. While one could pass over these omissions as determined by the limited resources of the museum project, it seems more likely that the administrators who set up Ottoman museums were fully conscious not only of the types of museums extant in Europe but also of their modes of organization and operation. Their choice to only partially emulate European museums carried an ideological and even political importance. By avoiding European metanarratives of progress and evolution, the Ottoman museum infused the formal qualities of the European-style institution of the museum with narratives that subverted incipient European imperialism. In sharp contrast to the encyclopedic museum developed in Europe, the Ottoman museum eschewed the collection of anything remotely contemporary in its production, focusing instead on specific historical moments of its newly cataloged past. The key to this difference lies in the absence of natural history collections, which, while part of the original plan for the museum, never developed as an epistemological core for the museum. The absence of a natural history collection—the epistemological key to the European museum system of classification—underscores the essential differences between the practice of museology in Europe, where it was born and developed, and in the Ottoman Empire, where it mutated to serve very different epistemological, social, and political needs.

Among the typology of museums common in Europe, museums of natural history served not only to spread the impetus of the scientific revolution but also as an epistemological model for the classification of many varieties of collections. Over the course of its development since the sixteenth century, natural history had provided mirrors and models for the ways in which the ordering of the universe was understood and expressed. As Paula Findlen explains, "[F]rom their first inception in *wunderkammern* and princely collections, early museums charted Europe's attempt to manage the empirical explosion of materials that wider dissemination of ancient texts, increased travel, voyages of discovery, and more systematic forms of communication and exchange had produced."[3] In such museums, natural objects, objects of art, and ethnographic curios from around the world were often displayed in concert in order to exhibit the similitudes believed to order the patterns of the universe. The widespread network of Catholic missions around the world provided the framework that made such networks of collection and communication possible and also promoted the universalist ideals of knowledge aspired to by European collectors and, later, museums.[4] Just as it was "God's wish that Latin, the language of his church, should spread across the whole of the terrestrial globe,"[5] the globe could be collected, controlled through the revelation of its order, and thereby known and used for the "use and betterment of mankind"—a mankind based in Europe—as suggested by Francis Bacon.[6]

Absent from the humanist philosophical trends of the Renaissance and the scientific discourse of the Enlightenment that had led up to Europe's nineteenth-century models of natural history, the Ottoman Empire did not gradually develop institutions such as museums through which to order and express universalist projects. Perhaps more to the point, by the time museums entered the Ottoman panoply of institutions, the empire's imperial impetus toward universality had waned, leaving in its wake pockets of resistance to the potential incursion of Europe's imperialist zeal. In contrast to the great European museums that were mimicking the project of naturalists through the collection of artifacts from territories around the world, the Ottoman Empire used its museums to consolidate a national sense of self rather than to project an aura of international imperial potency.

The first actualized natural history museum in the Ottoman Empire was part of the same medical school from which the Young Turk movement emerged. According to its brief catalog of 1872, "the sciences of natural history have barely been considered in the Ottoman Empire."[7] Since "without collections or well-organized museums, the task of teaching natural history remains illusory," the ability to teach natural science—seen as an elementary part of a Western medical education since Galen's citation of natural history as the study of objects useful to medicine—was predicated on the availability of a natural history museum. Ostensibly, the purpose of such a museum would be to integrate Ottoman medical students into the active practice of Western styles of medicine. Perhaps more important, however, was the positivist political agenda espoused by the Young Turks that could be expressed most efficiently through the modes of ordering made possible by a natural history museum.

The collection (fig. 43) included forty-four stuffed mammals, eighty-two stuffed birds, five hundred skins of mammals and birds waiting to be stuffed, fifty-four fish specimens in spirits, thirty-eight reptiles, sixteen hundred seashells, ninety-four polyps, two hundred forty-six fossils, five hundred minerals and rocks, sixty-six wooden models of crystals, and eight physiological models. At the time its brief catalog was written, it had recently been expanded through a donation of forty-eight anatomical preparations and twenty-four microscopic preparations from a doctor in Vienna, and its curator, Dr. Col. Abdullah Bey, continued to augment the collections with rocks, plants, insects, silkworm cocoons, and fossils from Bursa and from the Bosporus region.

The catalog gives no indication of the museum's display strategies, but the list of items suggests that the collection was divided by phylum and included fossils, suggesting an evolutionist model of organization. The collection probably filled little more than a room and, with many gaps in its contents, could probably only serve to suggest an organizational strategy. As Abdullah Bey himself pointed out, "[A]ll of these objects are in a mediocre state and have little scientific value." If each item in the collection lacked value, one can only ask what the putative value of the museum as a whole could have been. More than teaching any object lesson from natural history, this small museum served to educate students about a style of science—natural history—that not only predicated the study of medicine but also promoted an orderly, universal, and progressive worldview as a natural ordering principle.

Unfortunately, no records remain of any subsequent changes made to this museum of natural history. Carabella Efendi's collection of whale bones along with antiquities in the 1870s suggests that the early developers of the antiquities museum may have had a natural history division in mind. Although the inclusion of a natural history collection in the Imperial Museum was stipulated from its formal conception in 1889, this vision was never actualized.

As soon as the Imperial Museum was built, in fact, its administration seems to have forgotten about the initial plans to include a natural history

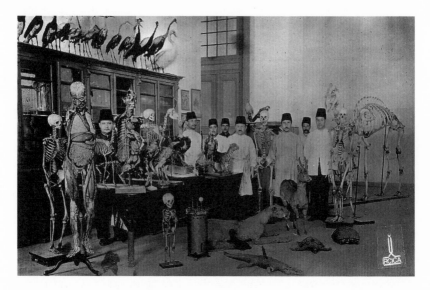

Fig. 43. Natural history collections at the Imperial School of Medicine [APC]

collection. In 1893 Najdi Efendi, a botanist living in Salonica, offered his services to the museum. "The establishment of a Museum of Natural History as a natural and indispensable complement to the Ottoman archaeological museum you have created makes itself evident," he wrote. Although he offered the ability to name all the plants of the Ottoman Empire and cited an extensive and valuable personal collection of a thousand photograms and cryptograms of Ottoman plants, he received a terse reply from the Imperial Museum. In 1899 the museum sent a similarly negative reply to the natural historian Ludwig von Tucher, who had proffered his services from Vienna. "As the formation of a museum of natural history is not under my jurisdiction," wrote Halil Bey, acting director to the museum, "and as the Imperial Museum of which I am the director is exclusively a museum of antiquities, I regret that it would be impossible to realize your proposals."[8]

What purpose was the proposed natural history section of the museum to fulfill, and why was it abandoned? Thus far this examination of museums in the Ottoman Empire has considered the aspects and moments of museological collections for which documentation remains. In the case of the natural history collection, there can be no documentation because there was no museum. This absence lies at the heart of the epistemological foundations for the Ottoman museological enterprise. In Europe natural history collections stood as the gateway to the taxonomic and progressive models followed in the display and organization of collections and marked the growing imperial domain of colonizing European nations. Their absence in the Ottoman Empire betokens a differing organizational objective and an oppositional political goal.

As Suzanne Marchand points out, the natural sciences played an important role in the articulation of formalist analysis that dictated the taxonomy and hierarchy of collections of antiquities. Gottfried Semper derived his evolutionist taxonomy for antiquities from George Cuvier's exhibit of animal skeletons at the Jardin des Plantes. He also cited Darwin's work as germinal to his conception of stylistic analysis.[9] While the Young Turks were quite taken with Darwinian thought and the museum directorship had close ties with the German museum establishment, it actively eschewed a formal stylistic organization for the galleries of the antiquities museum. Rather than use the exhibits to produce a model of progress for the emulation of the museum visitor, as suggested by the logic of collections organized according to formal stylistic analysis, the Imperial Museum chose to organize its collections through its pattern of acquisition. While small items may have been grouped together to suggest a formal stylistic evolution, large groups of finds—such as the sarcophagi of Sidon and the antiquities of Aphrodesias—merited halls of their own, irrespective of the "developmental" models that could otherwise have been proposed through the propitious dispersal of these collections.[10] In European museums pre-Helleno-Byzantine works served as a primitive foreground from which to herald the greatness of the ancients, and works of ancient art in turn served to set off the progress seen in art and civilization from the Renaissance to the present.[11] In contrast, in the Ottoman museum pre-Helleno-Byzantine works were shunted off to the far recesses, far from the entry-level center stage. Objects from later periods did not continue after the Helleno-Byzantine collections. The arrangement of collections in the Imperial Museum thus avoided an evolutionary, progressive vision of artistic production in order to emphasize its rich collection of Helleno-Byzantine works. In Europe such a focal point was merely a moment in the path of progress to the modern and progressively ideal present, in art as in society.

Like the natural history museum, the type of museum most common in European experience—the art museum—which had developed as the heir to the Renaissance cabinets of curiosities throughout Europe, was notably absent from the Ottoman interest in collection and display. While quite a few members of the Ottoman elite, as well as the students of the Arts Academy run by Osman Hamdi, produced European-style paintings and some Ottoman diplomats were known for their collections of contemporary European works, none of these were ever displayed in Ottoman museums.[12] Why? Mieke Bal argues that the spread of similar art objects into geographically scattered art museums mimics the process of uniformization of the imperialist project.[13] Had the Ottoman government chosen to include "art" in their collections, they would have adopted the aesthetic values of this art. Unlike colonial powers, who almost always used the museum as one of many institutions constructing a microcosmic replica of the European city beside the existent native one, the Ottomans were not interested in reproducing a little Europe of the East in İstanbul. The museums that they chose to build were based not on emulation but on contestation: their choice not to replicate the European museum project suggests that the Ottoman government acted as a semipermeable membrane in its adoption of European cultural examples. While some types of objects were suitable for collection and display, others did not fit the needs of the state.

The Imperial Museum was more interested in depicting the consolidation of Ottoman territories for the eyes of foreign visitors by adopting the Helleno-Byzantine legacy, glorifying military history and fostering a national and Islamic pride, than in promoting a progressive ideal to a disinterested local public to be educated through the museum. The inclusion of artifacts from many Ottoman territories marked the full expanse of the empire, even as it dwindled. The focus on the Helleno-Byzantine legacy focused attention on the Ottoman ownership of Asia Minor, increasingly called into question by the incursion of foreign railway operations and archaeological excavations. Much as European museums used their vast collections to collect symbols of their colonial territories in their capitals, the Ottoman Empire attempted to use archaeological acquisition to signify sovereignty over an empire that was, unlike contemporary European empires, slowly disintegrating. The European project of grand museums promoted an evolutionary vision of art that naturalized European hegemony over the world. In contrast, the Imperial Museum used the antiquities it collected to consolidate its territory and stand in the face of that universalist, progressive ideal. As such, a natural history collection with an evolutionist, progressive, positivist epistemology could only contradict the nationalist, consolidationist, oppositional stance that the collections of the Imperial Museum attempted to construct. Similarly, the military museum and the Islamic collections used objects as nodes of proud national identification rather than as tropes of progressive modernization.

The transfer of the museum from the context of western Europe to that of the Ottoman Empire caused an essential mutation in the museum, allowing the Ottoman institution to develop a trajectory independent from that of Europe. As museums became increasingly didactic toward the end of the empire, they became increasingly palpable symbols of the more democratic, more secular, and more independent order that would be born under the Turkish Republic. The periodic shifting in emphasis between the various types of museums only supports the notion of a shared underlying impetus to their establishment—to construct not simply a heritage of shared identification, but just as important an identity based on resistance. As Baudrillard points out with reference to class relations, "Imitation, copies, counterfeits, and the techniques to produce them . . . were all challenges to the aristocratic monopoly and control of signs. The problem of mimesis here is not one of aesthetics but of social power, the power to produce equivalences."[14] In the power hierarchy of colonial Europe and a vulnerable empire, the production of institutional copies such as the museum served to fold Ottoman identity into that of Europe, reducing the cultural distinctions between them, and thereby to narrow the differential of hegemony. The new museums were not replicas but simulacra—copies that lacked a referent in their land of origin, Europe.

As simulacra, these museums copied their European counterparts selectively, engaging in a mimicry common in the negotiation between the imperatives of colonial domination and the tactics of local resistance. As Bhabha suggests, "[T]he *menace* of mimicry is its *double* vision which in disclosing the ambivalence of colonial discourse also disrupts its authority."[15] The use of a European institution for anti-imperialist ends via the breakdown of its internal epistemological codes revealed the hierarchical and domineering project of the universalist and humanist European museum. The act of imitation knocked at the walls of humanism, which, like racism, employs the power of exclusion to define its ideal subject—the human, postulated as European or Western in its most progressively advanced form.[16] Standing at the geographic and political boundary of the several European discourses that constructed modernity, the West, and the links between them, the late Ottoman Empire used its museums to challenge this great divide of Othering while preserving and developing its right to speak its own histories and identities. Mimicry may be the highest form of flattery, but cultural camouflage can be the subtlest form of political resistance.

Notes

INTRODUCTION

1. Anthony D. Smith, *The Ethnic Origin of Nations* (London: Basil Black-well, 1986), 15.

2. Halil Berktay, "Tarih Çalışmaları," in *Cumhuriyet Dönemi Türkiye Ansiklopedisi* 9 (İstanbul: İletişim Yayınları, 1983): 2462–63. See also Uriel Heyd, *Foundations in Turkish Nationalism* (Leiden: Luzac, 1950).

3. Halil Berktay, *Cumhuriyet İdeolojisi ve Fuat Köprülü* (İstanbul: Kaynak Yayınları, 1983), 25.

4. Claude Cahen, *Pre-Ottoman Turkey* (London: Sidgwick & Jackson, 1968).

5. Berktay, *Cumhuriyet İdeolojisi*, 22, 64.

6. Unless otherwise indicated, the information for this highly summarized history of the empire comes from Stanford J. Shaw, *History of the Ottoman Empire and Modern Turkey*, vol. 1 (Cambridge: Cambridge University Press, 1976); and Stanford J. Shaw and Ezel K. Shaw, *History of the Ottoman Empire and Modern Turkey*, vol. 2 (Cambridge: Cambridge University Press, 1976).

7. İlber Ortaylı, *Gelenekten Geleceğe* (İstanbul: Hil Yayın, 1982), 42.

8. Ibid., 11.

9. Gülrü Necipoğlu, "The Life of an Imperial Monument: Hagia Sophia after Byzantium," in Robert Mark and Ahmet Ş. Çakmak, eds., *Hagia Sophia from the Age of Justinian to the Present* (Cambridge: Cambridge University Press, 1992), 196–98.

10. Halil İnalcık, *The Ottoman Empire, 1300–1600* (London: Weidenfeld and Nicolson, 1973), 41.

11. İlber Ortaylı, *İmparatorluğun en Uzun Yüzyılı* (İstanbul: Hil Yayın, 1983), 19.

12. Hasan Kayalı, *Arabs and Young Turks* (Berkeley: University of California Press, 1997), 3; Selim Deringil, *The Well-Protected Domains: Ideology and the Legitimation of Power in the Ottoman Empire, 1876–1909* (London: I. B. Taurus, 1998), 9.

13. A. L. Macfie, *The Eastern Question: 1774–1923* (London: Longman, 1989), 1.

14. Homi Bhabha, "Dissemination," in *The Location of Culture* (New York: Routledge, 1994), 139.

15. Bülent Tanör, "Anayasal Gelişmelere Toplu Bir Bakış," in *Tanzimattan Cumhuriyete Türkiye Ansiklopedisi*, vol. 1 (İstanbul: İletişim Yayınları, 1986), 10–16.

16. Şerif Mardin, "19. Yüzyılda Düşünce Akımları ve Osmanlı Devleti," in *Tanzimattan Cumhuriyete Türkiye Ansiklopedisi*, vol. 2 (İstanbul: İletişim Yayınları, 1986), 342–51.

17. Zeynep Çelik's *The Remaking of İstanbul: Portrait of an Ottoman City in the Nineteenth Century* (Seattle: University of Washington Press, 1986) provides an excellent example of how İstanbul acquired a fragmented pattern of development because of the many chefs working on the soup of the modern city.

18. Steven Caton, *Laurence of Arabia: A Film's Anthropology* (Berkeley: University of California Press, 1999), 10.

19. Ortaylı *İmparatorluğun en Uzun Yüzyılı*, 27–28.

20. Shaw and Shaw, *History*, 2:35. In 1840 the *Takvim-i Vaka-i* was joined by the first private newspaper in the empire, the *Ceride-i Havadis*, published in Ottoman under the auspices of an Englishman named William Churchill. Established in 1860 and 1862 respectively, the *Tercüman-i Ahval* and the *Tasvir-i Efkar* became the first private Turkish newspapers.

21. Selim Deringil, "The Ottoman Origins of Kemalist Nationalism: Namık Kemal to Mustafa Kemal," *European History Quarterly* 23:2 (April 1993): 167.

22. Berktay, *Cumhuriyet İdeolojisi*, 29.

23. Mardin, "19. Yüzyılda Düşünce Akımları ve Osmanlı Devleti," 348.

24. Berktay, *Cumhuriyet İdeolojisi*, 30.

25. Ilber Ortaylı, "Batılaşma Sorunu," in *Tanzimattan Cumhuriyete Türkiye Ansiklopedisi*, vol. 1 (İstanbul: İletişim Yayınları, 1986), 135.

26. Edouard Driault, *La question d'Orient* (Paris, 1898), 117, quoted in Linda Nochlin, "The Imaginary Orient," in *The Politics of Vision: Essays on Nineteenth-Century Art and Society* (New York: Harper and Row, 1989), 36.

27. Safvet Pasha served as minister of education from 1868 to 1871 and was appointed minister of foreign affairs in 1875.

28. Necdet Sakaoğlu, "Eğitim Tartışmaları," in *Tanzimattan Cumhuriyete Türkiye Ansiklopedisi*, vol. 2 (İstanbul: İletişim Yayınları, 1986), 480.

29. Berktay, *Cumhuriyet İdeolojisi*, 30.

30. Deringil, *The Well-Protected Domains*, 150–51.

31. Kayalı, *Arabs and Young Turks*, 25.

32. M. Şükrü Hanioğlu, *The Young Turks in Opposition* (New York: Oxford University Press, 1995), 3–4.

33. Ortaylı, *Imparatorluğun en Uzun Yüzyılı*, 32–33.

34. Kayalı, *Arabs and Young Turks*, 31.

35. Berktay, *Cumhuriyet İdeolojisi*, 36.

36. Ibid., 32–34; François Georgeon, *Aux origines du nationalisme Turc: Yusuf Akçura (1876–1935)* (Paris: Éditions ADPF, 1980).

37. Berktay, *Cumhuriyet İdeolojisi*, 48.

38. For an in-depth analysis of Ziya Gökalp's work, see Taha Parla, *The Social and Political Thought of Ziya Gökalp, 1876–1924* (Leiden: E. J. Brill, 1985).

39. Selim Deringil, "The Ottoman Origins of Kemalist Nationalism: Namık Kemal to Mustafa Kemal," *European History Quarterly* 23:2 (April 1993): 167.

40. Macfie, *The Eastern Question*, 123.

41. Shaw and Shaw, *History*, 2:273–366.

42. Paula Findlen, *Possessing Nature: Museums, Collecting, and Scientific Culture in Early Modern Italy* (Berkeley: University of California Press, 1994), 15.

43. Stathis Gourgouris, *Dream Nation: Enlightenment, Colonization, and the Institution of Modern Greece* (Stanford: Stanford University Press, 1996), 71.

44. Chantal Georgel, "The Museum as Metaphor," in Daniel J. Sherman and Irit Rogoff, eds., *Museum Culture* (Minneapolis: University of Minnesota Press, 1994), 116.

45. Tony Bennett, *The Birth of the Museum* (London: Routledge, 1994), 39.

46. Susan Pierce, *Interpreting Objects and Collections* (New York: Routledge, 1994), 6.

CHAPTER 1. MOVING TOWARD THE MUSEUM:
THE COLLECTION OF ANTIQUE SPOLIA

1. Beat Brenk, "Spolia from Constantine to Charlemagne: Aesthetics versus Ideology," *Dumbarton Oaks Papers* 411 (1987): 103.

2. Stephen Bann, "Shrines, Curiosities, and the Rhetoric of Display," in Lynne Cooke and Peter Wollen, eds., *Visual Display: Culture beyond Appearances* (New York: Dia Center for the Arts, 1995), 15–29.

3. Gülrü Necipoğlu, *Architecture, Ceremonial, and Power* (Cambridge, Mass.: MIT Press, 1991), 270.

4. E. D. Clarke, *Travels in Various Countries of Europe, Asia, and Africa* (London: T. Cadell and W. Davies, 1817), 3:11.

5. Sermed Muhtar, *Müze-i Askeriye-i Osmani, Rehber* (İstanbul: Necm-e İstikbal Matbaası, 1336/1920), 22.

6. İbrahim Hakkı Konyalı, *Türk Askeri Müzesi* (İstanbul: Ülkü Matbaası, 1964), 9.

7. Zeki Arıkan,"Tanzimat'tan Cumhuriyet'e Tarihçilik," in *Tanzimat'tan Cumhuriyete Türkiye Ansiklopedisi* 6 (İstanbul: İletişim Yayıncılık, 1985), 1584.

8. Tony Bennett, "The Exhibitionary Complex," in Reesa Greenberg, Bruce Ferguson, and Sandy Nairne, eds., *Thinking about Exhibitions* (New York: Routledge, 1996), 81–112.

9. Didier Maleuvre, *Museum Memories: History, Technology, Art* (Stanford: Stanford University Press, 1999), 14–16.

10. Quoted in Margaret S. Drower, "The Early Years," in T. G. H. James, ed., *Excavating in Egypt: The Egypt Exploration Society, 1882–1982* (London: British Museum Publications, 1982), 10.

11. Niel Asher Silberman, *Digging for God and Country: Exploration, Archaeology, and the Secret Struggle for the Holy Land, 1799–1917* (New York: Alfred A. Knopf, 1982), 72.

12. Donald Preziosi, ed., "Art as History: Introduction" and "The Art of Art History," in *The Art of Art History: A Critical Anthology* (Oxford: Oxford University Press, 1998), 21–30, 507–27.

13. Necipoğlu, "Life of an Imperial Monument," 204.

14. Gustave Mendel, *Musées Imperiaux Ottomans: Catalogue des sculptures greques, romaines, et byzantines,* vol. 1 (Constantinople, 1912–14; rpt. Rome: L'Erma di Bretschneider, 1966), 361.

15. Liz James, " 'Pray Not to Fall into Temptation and Be on Your Guard': Pagan Statues in Christian Constantinople," *Gesta* 35:1 (1996): 12–20.

16. Necipoğlu, "Life of an Imperial Monument," 199.

17. Mendel, *Musées Imperiaux Ottomans,* II, 393.

18. Richard Stoneman, *Land of Lost Gods: The Search for Classical Greece* (London: Hutchinson, 1987), 217–18. The British ambassador to the empire, Lord Stratford Canning, sent twelve of the seventeen relief panels to the British Museum in 1846. The rest remain in the collection of the İstanbul Archaeology Museum.

19. Mendel, *Musées Imperiaux Ottomans,* II, 393–406.

20. Semavi Eyice, "Arkeoloji ve Sanat Tarihi Hakkında," *Arkeoloji ve Sanat* I:1 (April–May 1978): 5–7.

21. Bruce Trigger, *A History of Archaeological Thought* (Cambridge: Cambridge University Press, 1989), 44.

22. A full discussion of such practices would require a separate study, but it might include the recognition of saints, common in Turkish folk Islam but foreign to traditional Islam. One practice of folk Islam involves tying pieces of fabric to a tree or bush growing in a location believed to be particularly auspicious. One such location is the acropolis of the city of Bergama (Pergamon), which today functions as a tourist site. It is difficult to ascertain whether the site retained its religious significance since antiquity or whether these practices have become associated with that site in more recent times.

23. M. Choiseul-Gouffier, *Voyage pittoresque de la Grèce* (Paris, 1780–1826).

24. Mendel, *Musées Imperiaux Ottomans,* I, 359.

25. IAMA, letter from Conze to Osman Hamdi, March 1, 1882; Mendel, *Musées Imperiaux Ottomans,* III, 573–78.

26. Mendel, *Musées Imperiaux Ottomans,* I, 471–96.

27. Stoneman, *Land of Lost Gods,* 46–47.

28. Jean Ebersolt, *Mission Archéologique de Constantinople* (Paris: Éditions Ernest Leroux, 1921), 25.

29. Stoneman, *Land of Lost Gods*, 175.

30. Richard Clogg, "The Byzantine Legacy in the Modern Greek World: The Megali Idea," in *Anatolica: Studies in the Greek East in the 18th and 19th Centuries* (Brookfield: Variorum, 1996), 257.

31. Michael Greenhalgh, *The Survival of Roman Antiquities in the Middle Ages* (London: Duckworth, 1989), 208.

CHAPTER 2. PARALLEL COLLECTIONS
OF WEAPONS AND ANTIQUITIES

1. Shaw and Shaw, *History*, 2:511.

2. Carter Vaughn Findley, *Ottoman Civil Officialdom: A Social History* (Princeton: Princeton University Press, 1989), 13–21.

3. Tahsin Öz, "Ahmet Fethi Paşa ve Müzeler," *Türk Tarih, Arkeoloji ve Etnografya Dergisi* 5 (1948): 1–6.

4. İstanbul Prime Minister's Archives (IBA) İrade-i Dahiliye 6662, 27 Zülkida 1262/November 16, 1846.

5. *Takvim-i Vakai* 292 (1261); Muhtar, *Müze-i Askeriye-i Osmani, Rehber*, 28.

6. Gustave Flaubert, *Oeuvres complètes: Voyages* (Paris: Société des Belles Lettres, 1948), 2:331.

7. Ibid., 331. Flaubert's use of the name "Mohammad" in reference to the sword may cause confusion with the sword of the Prophet, which had also once been kept in the former church. Other sources ascertain that this was the sword of Mehmet the Conqueror, not that of the Prophet, which was probably kept with the collection of holy relics kept in the Apartments of the Mantle of the Prophet (Hirkai Saadet Dairesi) in the Topkapı Palace.

8. Théophile Gautier, *Constantinople*, ed. Jacques Huré (İstanbul: Editions Isis, 1990), 256.

9. Selim Deringil, "The Invention of Tradition as Public Image in the Late Ottoman Empire, 1808 to 1908," *Comparative Studies in Society and History* 35:1 (January 1993): 7–8.

10. Gautier, *Constantinople*, 231.

11. Ahmet Midhat, "Askeri Müzesine Ziyaret," *Sabah* (May 2, 1910): 1.

12. Edwin A. Grosvenor, *Constantinople* (Boston: Little, Brown, 1900), 2:478–79.

13. Arıkan, "Tanzimat'tan Cumhuriyet'e Tarihçilik,"1584–87.

14. Öz, "Ahmet Fethi Paşa ve Müzeler," 7.

15. John Hewett, *The Tower: Its History, Armories, and Antiquities* (London: Master General and Board Ordinance at the Tower, 1845), xi. At this time military museums were still relatively rare. Among the most famous ones in Europe, the Austrian Army Museum opened to the public in 1891, and the Museum of the Army in Paris consolidated several collections in 1905. For more information, see J. Lee Westrate, *European Military Museums: A Survey*

of *Their Philosophy, Facilities, Programs, and Management* (Washington, D.C.: Smithsonian Institution Press, 1961).

16. Hewett, *The Tower*, 39–40.

17. Marina Warner, "Waxworks and Wonderlands," in Cooke and Wollen, *Visual Display*, 181.

18. Muhtar, *Müze-i Askeriye-i Osmani, Rehber*, 30.

19. Gautier, *Constantinople*, 276.

20. Ibid., 278.

21. Ibid., 282.

22. Edward Said, *Orientalism* (New York: Vintage Books, 1978), 96.

23. Albert Dumont, "Le Musée Sainte-Irene à Constantinople," *Revue Archaeologique* 18 (1868): 238–67.

24. IBA Y.MTV 76:36 (7.9.1310/March 25, 1893)

25. *Chicago Fair Illustrated/Şikago Sergisi* 2 (July 23, 1893), 24.

26. "Le Pavillion Ottomane," *L'Exposition de Paris de 1900* (Paris, 1901), 2:137–38.

27. See also Deringil, *Well-Protected Domains*, 154–64.

28. Trigger, *History of Archaeological Thought*, 149.

29. Ibid., 33.

30. Silberman, *Digging for God and Country*, 3–9.

31. Mogens Trolle Larsen, *The Conquest of Assyria: Excavations in an Antique Land, 1840–1860* (New York: Routledge, 1994), 157–65.

32. P. R. S. Moorey, *A Century of Biblical Archaeology* (Cambridge: Lutterworth Press, 1991), 2–4.

33. Committee of the Palestine Exploration Fund, *Our Work in Palestine* (New York: Scribner, Welford, & Armstron, 1873), 12–17.

34. Roland de Vaux, O.P. "On the Right and Wrong Uses of Archaeology," in James A. Sanders, ed., *Near Eastern Archaeology in the Twentieth Century* (New York: Doubleday, 1970), 67.

35. Zainab Bahrani, "Conjuring Mesopotamia," in Lynn Meskell, ed., *Archaeology under Fire: Nationalism, Politics and Heritage in the Eastern Mediterranean and Middle East* (London: Routledge, 1998), 165–66.

36. N. A. Silberman, "Promised Lands and Chosen Peoples: The Politics and Poetics of Archaeological Narrative," in Philip Kohl and Clare Fawcett, eds., *Nationalism, Politics, and the Practice of Archaeology* (Cambridge: Cambridge University Press, 1996), 255; Moorey, *A Century of Biblical Archaeology*, 18.

37. Ian Morris, "Introduction: Archaeologies of Greece," in *Classical Greece: Ancient Histories and Modern Archaeologies* (Cambridge: Cambridge University Press, 1994), 21.

38. Trigger, *History of Archaeological Thought*, 156–61.

39. Kostas Kotsakis, "The Past Is Ours: Images of Greek Macedonia," in Meskell, *Archaeology under Fire*, 51–52.

40. Frederick Hartt, *Art: A History of Painting, Sculpture, Architecture* (New York: Prentice-Hall, 1989), 624.

41. Trigger, *History of Archaeological Thought*, 38.

42. Frank Turner, *The Greek Heritage in Victorian Britain* (New Haven: Yale University Press, 1981), 1–2.

43. Suzanne Marchand, *Archaeology and Hellenism in Germany, 1750–1970* (Princeton: Princeton University Press, 1996), 7–10.

44. Ibid., xviii.

45. Ibid., 82.

46. Inderpal Grewal, *Home and Harem: Nation, Gender, Empire, and the Cultures of Travel* (Durham: Duke University Press, 1996), 108.

47. Daniel J. Sherman, *Worthy Monuments: Art Museums and the Politics of Culture in Nineteenth-Century France* (Cambridge, Mass.: Harvard University Press, 1989), 4.

48. Kotsakis, "The Past Is Ours," 52.

49. Gourgouris, *Dream Nation*, 139, 151.

50. Richard Jenkyns, *The Victorians and Ancient Greece* (Oxford: Blackwell, 1980), 13.

51. Morris, "Introduction: Archaeologies of Greece," 20.

52. Gourgouris, *Dream Nation*, 129.

53. Ibid., 52, 147.

54. Ibid., 72.

55. Michael Herzfeld, *Ours Once More: Folklore, Ideology, and the Making of Modern Greece* (Cambridge: Cambridge University Press, 1982), 50.

56. Morris, "Introduction: Archaeologies of Greece," 11.

57. Stephen Dyson, "Complacency and Crisis in Late-Twentieth-Century Classical Archaeology," in Phyllis Culham and Lowell Edmunds, eds., *Classics: A Discipline and Profession in Crisis?* (Lanham, Md.: University Press of America, 1989), 215; quoted in Morris, "Introduction: Archaeologies of Greece," 35.

58. Morris, "Introduction: Archaeologies of Greece," 25.

59. Pierre Vidal-Naquet, *Politics Ancient and Modern*, trans. Janet Lloyd (London: Polity Press, 1990), 186.

60. Lorenzo O'Rourke, *Renan's Letters from the Holy Land: The Correspondence of Ernest Renan with M. Berthelot while gathering material in Italy and the Orient for "The Life of Jesus"* (New York: Doubleday, Page, 1904), 208.

61. Vidal-Naquet, *Politics Ancient and Modern*, 189.

62. Namık Kemal, *Renan Müdafaainamesi* (Paris: Calman Lévy, 1883).

63. Frantz Fanon, *Black Skin, White Masks* (New York: Grove Press, 1967), 17.

64. Morris, "Introduction: Archaeologies of Greece," 23.

65. Michael Rowlands, "The Politics of Identity in Archaeology," in George Clement Bond and Angela Gilliam, eds., *Social Construction of the Past: Representation as Power* (London: Routledge, 1994), 133.

66. Hanioğlu, *Young Turks in Opposition*, 10.

67. Frederick Bohrer, "The Times and Spaces of History: Representation, Assyria, and the British Museum," in Sherman and Rogoff, *Museum Culture*, 198.

68. W. St. Clair, *That Greece Might Still Be Free: The Philhellenes in the Greek War of Independence* (Oxford: Oxford University Press, 1972), 58; quoted in Morris, "Introduction: Archaeologies of Greece," 24.

69. Stoneman, *Land of Lost Gods*, 172–73.

70. Christopher Hitchens, *The Elgin Marbles: Should They Be Returned to Greece?* (New York: Verso, 1997).

71. Stoneman, *Land of Lost Gods*, 185.

72. St. Clair, *That Greece Might Still Be Free*, 203–7; quoted in Morris, "Introduction: Archaeologies of Greece," 25.

73. Mendel, *Musées Imperiaux Ottomans*, 2:3.

74. IBA İrade-i Dahiliye 6662 (27 Zilkade 1262/November 16, 1846).

75. IBA İrade-i Hususiye 1311.M/8.

76. İlber Ortaylı, "Tanzimat'ta Vilayetlerde Eski Eser Taraması," in *Tanzimat'tan Cumhuriyet'e Türkiye Ansiklopedisi* 6 (İstanbul: İletişim Yayınları, 1985), 1599.

77. Semavi Eyice, "Arkeoloji Müzesi ve Kuruluşu," in *Tanzimat'tan Cumhuriyet'e Türkiye Ansiklopedisi* 6 (İstanbul: İletişim Yayınları, 1985), 1597.

78. Mendel, *Musées Imperiaux Ottomans*, 1:xi.

79. Stoneman, *Land of Lost Gods*, 216–26.

80. Mendel, *Musées Imperiaux Ottomans*, 2:117.

81. Ortaylı, "Tanzimat'ta Vilayetlerde Eski Eser Taraması," 1599.

82. Dumont, "Le Musée Sainte-Irene à Constantinople," 238.

83. Stoneman, *Land of Lost Gods*, 271–80.

84. Ella Shohat, "Gender and Culture of Empire," in Matthew Bernstein and Gaylyn Studlar, eds., *Visions of the East: The Orient in Film* (New Brunswick, N.J.: Rutgers University Press, 1997), 33–35.

85. *Servet-i Funun* 984 (1 Nisan 1326), 347.

86. Flaubert, *Oeuvres complètes*, 331–32.

87. Gautier, *Constantinople*, 256.

88. Dumont, "Le Musée Sainte-Irene à Constantinople," 237.

89. Déthier, *Bogaziçi ve İstanbul*, 42.

90. Gautier, *Constantinople*, 256.

91. Ebersolt, *Mission archéologique*, 21.

92. These sarcophagi were removed to the Ottoman Imperial Museum in 1916 (Ebersolt, *Mission archéologique*, 24).

93. Hanioğlu, *Young Turks in Opposition*, 13–15.

CHAPTER 3. THE RISE OF THE IMPERIAL MUSEUM

1. *L'Illustration* 1277 (August 17, 1867).

2. IBA Cevdet Maarif 221 1286/1869.

3. Letter to the Imperial Museum, cited by Halil Edhem in his preface to Mendel, *Musées Imperiaux Ottomans*, I, xiii.

4. Mustafa Cezar, *Sanatta Batıya Açılış ve Osman Hamdi* I (İstanbul: Erol Kerim Aksoy Kültür ve Eğitim, Spor, ve Saglık Vakfı Yayını, 1995), 232.

5. E. Goold, *Catalogue explicatif, historique, et scientifique d'un certain nombre d'objets contenus dans le Musée Imperial de Constaninople, fondé en 1869 sous le Grand Vezierat de Son Altesse A'Ali Pacha* (Constantinople: Imprimerie A. Zellich, 1871), 1.

6. Rezan Kocabaş, "Müzecilik hareketi ve ilk müze okulunun açılışı," *Belgelerle Türk Tarihi Dergisi* 21 (June 1969): 75.

7. Goold, *Catalogue explicatif*; Eyice, "Arkeoloji ve Sanat Tarihi Hakkında," 1598.

8. *Terakki* 200 (3 Cumadaevvel 1286/August 11, 1869); *Terakki* 363 (2 Rebiülevvel 1287/June 1, 1870).

9. Shaw and Shaw, *History*, 2:153.

10. P. A. Déthier and A. D. Mordtmann, *Epigraphik von Byzantion und Constantinopolis von den aeltesten Zeiten bis zum Jahre Christi 1453* (Vienna, 1864).

11. *Rehnüma: Müze-i Hümayun* (İstanbul: Mahmut Bey Matbaası, 1319/1902), ii, quoting the writ of the Grand Vizier to the Sultan (*arz teskeresi*) for the new law, from the Topkapı Palace Archives (Maruzat Arşivi).

12. Michel de Certeau, *The Practice of Everyday Life* (Berkeley: University of California Press, 1984), 35–38.

13. *Asar-e Atika Nizamnamesi* (İstanbul: Asır Matbaası, 1322/1874), 2.

14. Marchand, *Archaeology and Philhellenism in Germany*, 104.

15. John Carman, *Valuing Ancient Things: Archaeology and Law* (London: Leicester University Press, 1996), 45–55.

16. Tevfik Temelkuran, "Ülkemizde Götürülen Tarih ve San'at Hazineleri, İlk Eski Eserler Nizamnamesi," *Belgelerler Türk Tarihi Dergisi* 5:27 (December 1969): 72–73.

17. Ibid., 71–72, citing IBA Hariciye İrade 17050 (6 Sefer 1296/ January 30,1879).

18. *Şark* 388 (15 Safer 1292/ March 23, 1875).

19. Kocabaş, "Müzecilik hareketi ve ilk müze okulunun açılışı," 76–77, Cezar, *Sanatta Batıya Acılış ve Osman Hamdi*, I, 243–45; II, 515–16.

20. Kocabaş, "Müzecilik hareketi ve ilk müze okulunun açılışı," 78.

21. Tahsin Öz, "Topkapı Sarayı Müzesi Onarımları," *Güzel Sanatlar* 6 (January 1949): 68–71.

22. Cezar, *Sanatta Batıya Acılış ve Osman Hamdi*, I, 258.

23. Kenneth Hudson, *Museums of Influence* (London: Cambridge University Press, 1987), 22.

24. *Hakaik ül-vakai* 961 (23 Cumadaevvel 1290/July 18, 1873).

25. *Ruzname-ye Ceride-i Havadis* 2359 (13 Zülkida, 1290/ January 2, 1874); and *Başiret* 1123 (14 Zülkade 1290/January 3, 1874).

26. Çelik, *The Remaking of Istanbul*, 34.

27. *Vakit* 1735 (11 Ramazan 1297/August 17, 1880); also quoted in Cezar, *Sanatta Batıya Acılış ve Osman Hamdi*, I, 241–42.

28. Cezar, *Sanatta Batıya Acılış ve Osman Hamdi*, I, 253.

29. Ibid., 196–225.

30. Roger Benjamin, ed., *Orientalism: Delacroix to Klee* (Sydney: Thames and Hudson, 1997); Lynne Thornton, *The Orientalists: Painter-Travelers* (Paris: Poche Couleur, 1994).

31. Osman Hamdi, *Les costumes populaires de la Turquie en 1873*, Ouvrage Publié sous le patronage de la Commission Imperiale Ottomane par l'Exposition universelle de Vienne (Constantinople: Imprimerie du Levant Times & Shipping Gazette, 1873).

32. Paul Greenhalgh, *Ephemeral Vistas: The Expositions Universelles, Great Expositions, and World's Fairs, 1851–1939* (Manchester: Manchester University Press, 1988).

33. Mendel, *Musées Imperiaux Ottomans*, I, ix, quoting the *Catalogue des figurines greques de terre cuite*, iv.

34. Nochlin, "The Imaginary Orient," 45.

35. For a discussion of *The Women of Algiers*, see Zeynep Çelik, *Urban Forms and Colonial Confrontations: Algiers under French Rule* (Berkeley: University of California Press, 1997), 190–92.

36. Nochlin, "The Imaginary Orient," 45.

37. Laura Mulvey, "On *Duel in the Sun*: Afterthoughts on 'Visual Pleasure and Narrative Cinema,'" *Framework* 15–17 (Autumn 1981): 12–15.

38. Laura Mulvey, "Visual Pleasure and Narrative Cinema," *Screen* 16:3 (Autumn 1975): 16–18.

39. For an extensive survey of Orientalist paintings, see Benjamin, *Orientalism*.

40. Nochlin, "The Imaginary Orient," 37.

41. Trigger, *History of Archaeological Thought*, 15.

42. Marchand, *Archaeology and Philhellenism in Germany*, 84.

43. A. Khater, *Le régime juridique des fouilles et des antiquités en Égypte* (Cairo: Imprimerie de l'Institut Français d'Archeologie Orientale, 1960), 127–49.

44. Trigger, *History of Archaeological Thought*, 39. See also Donald M. Reid, "Nationalizing the Pharaonic Past: Egypt 1922–1952," in James Jankowski and Israel Bershoni, eds., *Rethinking Nationalism in the Arab Middle East* (New York: Columbia University Press, 1997), 127–49.

45. Frantz Fanon, *Black Skin, White Masks* (New York: Grove Press, 1967), 132.

CHAPTER 4. THE DIALECTIC OF LAW AND INFRINGEMENT

1. Marchand, *Archaeology and Philhellenism in Germany*, 93–95.

2. IAMA letter no. 4, 1882.

3. Marchand, *Archaeology and Philhellenism in Germany*, 193.

4. Cezar, *Sanatta Batı'ya Açılış ve Osman Hamdi*, I, 314; Osman Hamdi and Ozgan Effendi, *Le tumulus de Nemroud-Dagh* (Constantinople: Imprimerie F. Loeffler, 1883).

5. *Tercuman-i Şark* 111 (19 Şaban 1295/August 6, 1878), cited in Cezar, *Sanatta Batı'ya Açılış ve Osman Hamdi*, I, 298.

6. *Vatan* 1748 (24 Ramazan 1297/August 30, 1880), cited in Cezar, *Sanatta Batı'ya Açılış ve Osman Hamdi*, I, 310.

7. Marchand, *Archaeology and Philhellenism*, 201; Thomas W. Gaehtgens, "The Museum Island in Berlin," in Gwendolyn Wright, ed., *The Formation of National Collections of Art and Archaeology* (Washington, D.C.: National Gallery of Art), 67–71.

8. Cezar, *Sanatta Batı'ya Açılış ve Osman Hamdi*, I, 329.

9. IBA Meclis-i Mahsus İradeler 3401 (4 Rebiülevvel 1301/January 2, 1884).

10. Marchand, *Archaeology and Philhellenism in Germany*, 98.

11. Ibid., 80.

12. Stoneman, *Land of Lost Gods*, 136–49.

13. IBA Y.MTV 10:26:17.2.1300:5 (December 28, 1882).

14. Yehoshua Ben-Arieh, "The Geographical Exploration of the Holy Land," *Palestine Exploration Quarterly* (July–December 1972): 90.

15. IBA MV 1:56, 1302.Cumada al-ahir.17/April 3, 1885.

16. Silberman, *Digging for God and Country*, 193–94.

17. "Asar-i Atika," *Tercüman-i Hakikat* 3883, 25 Haziran, 1891.

18. "Asar-i Atika," *Servet-i Funun* 151 (20 Kanunsani 1309/ February 1, 1894), 336.

19. "Asar-i Atika," *Servet-i Funun* 106 (11 Mart 1308/March 23, 1892), 31.

20. "Asar-i Atika," *Servet-i Funun* 161 (31 Mart 1310/April 12, 1894), 70; "Asar-i Atika *Servet-i Funun* 168 (19 Mayis 1310/ May 31, 1894), 191; "Asar-i Atika," *Servet-i Funun* 202 (12 Kanunsani 1310/ January 24, 1895), 320.

21. "Asar-i Atika," *Servet-i Funun* (11 Subat 1308).

22. "Müze," *Servet-i Funun* 57 (2 Nisan 1308/April 14, 1892), 69, 74; "Vienna Müzesi," *Servet-i Funun* 103 (18 Subat 1308/March 3, 1893), 394, 397; image of Apollo Gallery in Louvre, *Servet-i Funun* 143 (23 Eylül 1309/October 5, 1893), 61.

23. "Asar-i Atika," *Servet-i Funun* 222 (1 Haziran 1311/ June 23, 1895), 213.

24. IBA İrade-i Hususiye 74:28.M.1314/ July 9, 1896; and Y. MTV 355:83, 14.2.1314/July 25, 1896.

25. Temelkuran, "1884 Eski Eserler Nizamnemesi," 74–76.

26. Marchand, *Archaeology and Philhellenism in Germany*, 102.

27. IBA MV 35:23, 1305.2.18/November 4, 1887.

28. IBA MV 36:57, 23 Sefer 1306/October 29, 1888.

29. IBA İrade-i dahiliye 75171, 3 Receb 1302 and 19 Receb 1302 (April 18 and May 4, 1885).

30. Kurt Geschwautler, "The History of the Vienna Ephesus Museum and Its Finds," in Gilbert Wiplinger and Gudrun Wlach, eds., *Ephesus: 100 Years of Austrian Research* (Vienna, Cologne, Weimar: Österreichisches Archäologisches Institut Verlag, 1996), 175.

31. IBA Y.A-HUS 379:53, 14.7.1315/December 8, 1897.

32. Marchand, *Archaeology and Philhellenism in Germany*, 197–203.

33. IAMA letter #34, June 27, 1898, from M. Masen to Osman Hamdi.

34. IBA Maarif İradeler 365:1997:1:15.N.1317/January 16, 1900.

35. IBA Hususi İradeler 1321.RA/90, 10 Rebi ul-ahir 1321/June 6, 1904.

36. Marchand, *Archaeology and Philhellenism in Germany*, 10.

37. IBA DH.HMS 9:4, 1321.5.26/August 19, 1903.

38. IBA BEO 187801, 13 Kanunsani 1320/January 26, 1905.

39. IBA BEO 182613 (1322/1905).

40. IAMA letter from D. S. Hogarth to Osman Hamdi, dated February 18, 1905.

41. IBA Maarif İradeler 705 (689)3, 27 Zulhicca 1322/February 6, 1905.

42. IBA BEO 188658 16 Zülhicca 1322 /February 20, 1905.

43. Marchand, *Archaeology and Philhellenism in Germany*, 210, 212; IBA BEO 190412, 25 Muharrem 1323/ March 31, 1905.

44. *Asar-e Atika Nizamnamesi* (Dar Saadet: Mahmud Bey Matbaası, 1327/1909), 2.

45. *Asar-e Atika Nizamnamesi* (1906), 3–4.

46. Marchand, *Archaeology and Philhellenism*, 180.

47. IBA BEO 217649, 15 Racab 1324/September 4, 1906; 220951, 1 Sevval 1324/November 17, 1906.

48. IBA BEO 220951 1 Sevval 1324/November 17, 1906.

49. IBA DH.MUI 88:46, 17 Cumada al-ahir 1328/June 24, 1910.

50. IBA DH.MUI 2574:124:20, 17 Şaban 1328 /August 22, 1910.

51. IBA DH.ID 28–1:28, 15 Racab 1329/July 11, 1911; DH.HMS 9:8 1329.7.16 /July 12, 1911.

52. Kotsakis, "The Past Is Ours," 51.

CHAPTER 5. TECHNOLOGIES OF COLLECTION

1. Morris Jastrow, *The War and the Bagdad Railway: The Story of Asia Minor and Its Relation to the Present Conflict* (Philadelphia: J. B. Lippincott, 1917), 82.

2. Cezar, *Sanatta Batı'ya Açılış ve Osman Hamdi*, 647, quoting Maarif Nezareti Belgeleri No. 5, June 21, 1305.

3. IAMA letter to Hamdi Bey addressed October 19, 1893.

4. Jastrow, *The War and the Bagdad Railway*, 7.

5. IBA DH.MUI 916:98–1:39:1328.CA.19/June 26, 1910.

6. IBA DH.MUI 88:46, 17 Cumada al-ahir 1328/June 24, 1910.

7. John Turtle Wood, *Modern Discoveries on the Site of Ancient Ephesus* (London: Religious Tract Society, 1877).

8. John Murray, *Handbook for Travelers in Constantinople, Brusa, and the Troad* (London: John Murray, 1893).

9. IAMA, letter from Macridi Bey to Hamdi Bey, dated 17 May 1321/May 30, 1905.

10. IBA DH.ID 3361:216:5:1333.M.17.

11. Committee of the Palestine Exploration Fund, *Our Work in Palestine* (New York: Scribner, Welford, & Armstrong, 1873), 36.

12. Silberman, *Digging for God and Country*, 159.

13. Alan Wallach, *Exhibiting Contradiction: Essays on the Art Museum in the United States* (Amherst: University of Massachusetts Press, 1998), 46–48. On the role of plaster casts in European collections, see also Martin Postle, "Naked Authority: Reproducing Antique Statuary in the English Academy, from Lely to Haydon," in Anthony Hughes and Ercih Ranfft, eds., *Sculpture and Its Reproductions* (London: Reaktion Books, 1997), 79–99.

14. Duncan, *Civilizing Rituals*, 60.

15. Saloman Reinach, *Conseils aux voyageurs archeologiques in Grece et dans l'Orient hellenique* (Paris: E. Leroux, 1886).

16. Engin Çizgen, *Photography in the Ottoman Empire, 1839–1919* (İstanbul: Haşet Kitapevi, 1987), 21. See also Louis Vaczec and Gail Buckland, *Travelers in Ancient Lands: A Portrait of the Middle East, 1839–1919* (Boston: New York Graphic Society, 1981).

17. Çizgen, *Photography in the Ottoman Empire*, 54–98.

18. Konstantin Akinsha and Grigori Kozlov, *Beautiful Loot* (New York: Random House, 1995), 6–11.

19. Reinach, *Conseils aux voyageurs archeologiques*, 72–73.

20. William Allen, "Analysis of Abdülhamid's Gift Albums," *Journal of Turkish Studies* 12 (1988): 33.

21. Çizgen, *Photography in the Ottoman Empire*, 22.

22. M. I. Waley, "The Albums in the British Library," *Journal of Turkish Studies* 12 (1988): 31, special edition "Imperial Self Portrait: The Ottoman Empire as Revealed in *The Sultan Abdülhamid II's Photographic Albums*," edited by Carney E. S. Gavin.

23. IBA DH.MUI 88:46.

24. Paris: Ernest le Roux, 1892.

25. Osman Hamdi and Ozgan Efendi, *Le tumulus de Nemroud-Dagh*.

26. Hanioğlu, *Young Turks in Opposition*, 10–13, 32.

27. "Asre Müferrit Abdülhamid Haniyede Terekkiyate Fenniye: Müzeye Hümayun—Avrupa Matbuatı," *Serveti Funun* 49 (Subat 1308).

28. Hanioğlu, *Young Turks in Opposition*, 33–41.

CHAPTER 6. ANTIQUITIES COLLECTIONS IN THE IMPERIAL MUSEUM

1. Marchand, *Archaeology and Philhellenism in Germany*, 105.

2. Preziosi, "Art as History," 516.

3. Chris Scarre, "The Western World View in Archaeological Atlases," in Peter Gathercole and David Lowenthal, eds., *The Politics of the Past* (London: Unwin Hyman, 1990), 13.

4. *Medeniyet* 6 (5 Şehval 1291), 47–48.

5. IAMA, letter from the British Ambassador to the museum, October 27, 1883; and Mendel, *Musées Imperiaux Ottomans*, II, 117.

6. Murray, *Handbook for Travelers*, 69–70.

7. Duncan, *Civilizing Rituals*, 59.

8. Osman Hamdi, "Introduction," *Catalogue des sculptures greques, romaines, byzantines et franques* (Constantinople: Mihran Imprimeur, 1893), vi.

9. Osman Hamdi, "Introduction," *Antiquités himarites et palmyréniennes: Catalogue sommaire* (Constantinople: Mihran Imprimeur, 1895). Late as this source is, it seems likely that the sculptures were on display in the museum soon after its opening because they were given to the museum by Ismail Pasha, governor of Yemen, in 1880.

10. IAMA, 1885 letter from Edward Glasser to the Imperial Museum.

11. Hanioğlu, *Young Turks in Opposition*, 182.

12. Duncan, *Civilizing Rituals*, 32–33.

13. Bruce Trigger, "Alternative Archaeologies: Nationalist, Colonialist, Imperialist," *Man* 19:3 (September 1984): 356–57.

14. IBA MV 23:34/ 1304.Za.27 = August 17, 1887.

15. Cezar, *Sanatta Batı'ya Açılış ve Osman Hamdi*, I, 261.

16. Remzi Oğuz Arık, *Türk Muzeciliğine Bir Bakış* (İstanbul: Milli Eğitim Basımevi, 1953), 3.

17. Duncan, *Civilizing Rituals*, 9–10.

18. *Servet-i Funun* 2:49 (6 Subat 1307), 266.

19. *Servet-i Funun* 49 (5 Subat 1308), 15; 54 (12 Mart 1308), 20.

20. "Yeni Müze," *Tercüman-i Hakikat* 3898 (7 Zilhicce 1308/ July 13, 1891), 2.

21. *Tercuman-i Hakikat* 3858 (18 Sevval 1308/May 27, 1891); 3872 (6 Zilkade 1308/ June 12, 1891).

22. *Servet-i Funun* 2:49 (6 Subat 1307), 266.

23. Homi Bhabha, "The Other Question—The Stereotype and Colonial Discourse," *Screen* 24:6 (November–December 1983): 33.

24. IBA Hususi İradeler 60:54:20.M.1317/May 30, 1899.

25. Cezar 268, quoting *İkdam* 3271 (26 Teşrinevvel 1319/November 8, 1903).

26. IBA Y.MTV 252:294 1321.S.12 = May 9, 1903.

27. Cezar, *Sanatta Batı'ya Açılış ve Osman Hamdi*, I, 268.

28. Ibid., 271.

29. Mendel, *Musées Imperiaux Ottomans*, III, ix.

30. Eilean Hooper-Greenhill, *Museums and the Shaping of Knowledge* (New York: Routledge, 1992), 173.

31. Homi Bhabha, "Of Mimicry and Man," in *The Location of Culture*, 92; emphasis in original.

32. Ziya Gökalp, *Türk Medeniyeti Tarihi*, quoted in Müjgan Cumbur, *Atatürk ve Milli Kültür* (Ankara: Kültür Bakanlığı Yayınları, 1981), 30.

33. Gustave Mendel, *Musées Imperiaux Ottomans: Catalogue des sculptures greques, romaines et byzantines du Musée de Brousse* (Athens: Impremerie P. D. Sakllarios,1908), v.

34. IAMA, #23, January 31, 1906.

35. IAMA, letter from Theodor Wiegand to Halil, June 14, 1910.

36. IAMA, letter #13 from Theodor Macridy to Halil, April 26, 1914.

37. Jean Baudrillard, "The System of Collecting," in John Elsner and Roger Cardinal, eds., *The Cultures of Collecting* (Cambridge, Mass.: Harvard University Press, 1994), 8.

CHAPTER 7. ISLAMIC ARTS IN IMPERIAL COLLECTIONS

Parts of this chapter have been published in "Islamic Arts in the Ottoman Imperial Museum," *Ars Orientalis* 30 (August 2000); "Osman Hamdi and the Subversion of Orientalist Vision," in Lucienne Thys-Şenocak and Çigdem Kafescioğlu, *Festschrift for Aptullah Kuran* (Istanbul: Yapı Kredi Yayınları, 2000).

1. Cezar, *Sanatta Batı'ya Açılış ve Osman Hamdi*, II, 547.

2. Selim Deringil, "Legitimacy Structures in the Ottoman State—The Reign of Abdülhamid II," *International Journal of Middle East Studies* 23:3 (August 1991): 345–59.

3. Kayalı *Arabs and Young Turks*, 35.

4. Şerif Mardin. *Religion and Social Change in Modern Turkey: The Case of Bediüzzaman Said Nursi* (New York: Pantheon, 1989), 129.

5. Carol Duncan, "Art Museums and the Ritual of Citizenship," in Ivan Karp and Stephen D. Lavine, eds., *Exhibiting Cultures: The Poetics and Politics of Museum Display* (Washington D.C.: Smithsonian Institution Press, 1991), 88.

6. Deringil, *Well-Protected Domains*, 45.

7. Stephen Vernoit, "Islamic Archaeology," *Muqarnas* 14 (1997): 3, 8.

8. Edward Said, *Orientalism* (New York: Vintage Books, 1978), 96.

9. Ibid., 105.

10. Halil (Edhem), "Müze-ye Hümayun," *Tercüman-i Hakikat/Servet-i Funun* 1313 (numero special et unique), 104.

11. Kayalı, *Arabs and Young Turks*, 36.

12. Duncan, "Art Museums and the Ritual of Citizenship," 7–12.

13. V. Bilgin Demirsar, *Osman Hamdi Tablolarında Gerçekle İlişkiler* (İstanbul: Kültür Bakanlığı Yayınları, 1989), 107–8.

14. Ibid., 131–33.

15. Ibid., 119.

16. Parviz Khanlari, *Devan-e Hafez* (Tehran 1359/1980), 98. Many thanks to Richard Davis for providing this insight and example. The *qibla* is the direction of prayer toward which all Muslims pray; the *ka'beh* is the stone and surrounding structure in Mecca that mark this direction.

17. IBA Y.A-HUS 281:90, 28:3.1311 (October 8, 1893); Y.A-HUS 327:19, 12.11.1311 (May 18, 1894); İrade-i Hususiye 1430, 1312.Za.26 (May 21, 1895).

CHAPTER 8. MILITARY COLLECTIONS IN THE
LATE EMPIRE

1. Konyalı, *Türk Askeri Müzesi*, 16–17; Grosvenor, *Constantinople*, 477.

2. IBA 249:69 (17 Cumada al-ahir 1321/1903) calls for the transport of old arms from Cidda to the imperial cannon factory. Y.MTV 258:32 (4 Muharrem 1322/1904) is a directive requiring the sorting of arms in the Harbiye Anbarı.

3. For a plan of the proposed museum, see Dianna Barillari and Ezio Godoli, *İstanbul 1900: Art Nouveau and Interiors* (New York: Rizzoli, 1996), 89.

4. Deringil, *Well-Protected Domains*, 31.

5. Shaw, *History of the Ottoman Empire*, 2:15; Asım Bıyık et al., *Askeri Müze/Military Museum* (İstanbul: Askeri Müze ve Kültür Sitesi Komutanlığı, 1993), 42.

6. Gourgouris, *Dream Nation*, 12.

7. Nejat Eralp, "1908–1923 Döneminde Türkiye Askeri Müzesinin Batılı Anlamda Kuruluşu ve Kültür Hayatındaki Yeri," *Onikinci Askeri Tarih Semineri* (Ankara, 1985): 289. Susan Brandt points out that many war museums were founded in Europe during the same years if not a little later. "The Memory Makers: Museums and Exhibitions of the First World War," *History and Memory* 6:1 (Spring–Summer 1994): 95–149.

8. Sermed Muhtar, *Müze-i Askeriye-i Osmani, Rehber*, 38.

9. Mehmed Sefa, *Delil al-Astane: Asimat il-khilafet il-azimi wa dar ussaadet İstanbul al Konstantaniye* (İstanbul: Matbaa al-adil, 1331 H./1913).

10. IBA DH.ID 28–1:18 (22 Ramazan, 1329/September 15, 1911).

11. Konyalı, *Türk Askeri Müzesi*, 29.

12. Deringil, *Well-Protected Domains*, 22.

13. All labels courtesy of the library of the İstanbul Askeri Müze/ İstanbul Military Museum.

14. The Polish-born Orientalist artist Stanislaus von Chelebowski (1835–84) lived at the court of Sultan Abdülaziz for twelve years, between 1864 and 1876. Thornton, *The Orientalists*, 48.

15. Reprinted Ankara: Kara Kuvvetleri Komutanlığı, 1983.

16. "Müze-i Askeri Müdüriyetinden," *Tanın* 5 (August 1909), 1.

17. *Resimli Kitap* 5:29 (April 1911): 403.

18. *Resimli Kitap* 3:18 (March 1328/1910): 484.

19. *Harb Tarihi Mecmuası* 2:19 (1335/1916), museum advertisement on back cover.

20. Many thanks to Colonel Sadık Tekeli of the İstanbul Military Museum for this insight.

21. Eric Hobsbawm and Terence Ranger, eds., *The Invention of Tradition* (Cambridge: Cambridge University Press, 1983), 1–12.

22. IBA MV 253:78 (1338.S.26/November 19, 1919).

23. *İkdam* (May 23, April 2, April 18, 1340/1923).
24. Sermed Muhtar, *Müze-i Askeriye-i Osmani, Rehber,* 37.
25. Hoffmann, "The German Art Museum," 7.
26. Gourgouris, *Dream Nation,* 27.
27. Namık Kemal, Şemsettin Kutlu, ed., *Vatan Yahut Silistre* (İstanbul: Remzi Kitabevi, 1982), 7–13; Seyit Kemal Karaalioğlu, *Namık Kemal: hayatı ve şiirleri* (İstanbul: İnkilap ve Aka Kitabevleri, 1984), 14–17.
28. Eralp, "1908–1923 Döneminde Türkiye Askeri Müzesi," 320–24.

CHAPTER 9. ISLAMIC AND ARCHAEOLOGICAL
ANTIQUITIES AFTER THE YOUNG TURK REVOLUTION

1. *Saadet* 432 (March 14, 1326/March 27, 1910); *Sabah* 7376 (March 22 1326/April 6, 1910).
2. IBA BEO 276305/ 29 Teşrinsani 1325/ December 12, 1909.
3. 1910 document, cited in Zarif Orgun and Serap Aykoç, "La Fondation du Musée Turque et le Musée des Arts Turcs et Islamiques," *Collection Turcica II, Traveaux et Recherches en Turquie 1982* (Strasbourg, 1984): 144–45.
4. 1909 document, cited in Orgun and Aykoç, "La Fondation du Musée Turque et le Musée des Arts Turcs et Islamiques," 130.
5. Archaeology museum document #37, July 21, 1325, cited in Nazan Ölçer, *Türk ve İslam Eserleri Müzesi: Kilimler* (İstanbul: Eren Yayıncılık, 1988), 38.
6. Orgun and Aykoç, "La Fondation du Musée Turque et le Musée des Arts Turcs et Islamiques," 140–41.
7. Hooper-Greenhill, *Museums and the Shaping of Knowledge,* 167.
8. Halil (Edhem), *Das Osmanische Antikenmuseum in Konstantinopel* (Liepzig, 1909).
9. IBA DH.ID 28–1:21/1329.Ca.4/ June 1, 1911.
10. IBA DH.ID 28–1:18/1329.R.22/ September 15, 1911.
11. Orgun and Aykoç, "La Fondation du Musée Turque et le Musée des Arts Turcs et Islamiques," 135.
12. IBA MV 239:22; 1333.Ca.5/ April 19, 1915.
13. IBA MV 212:115/ 1336.L.22/ July 30, 1918. This document declares the establishment of the commission three years after its report on the Topkapı Palace. In "Türkiye'de Müzecilik," *Cumhuriyet Dönemi Türkiye Ansiklopedisi* (1984): 1465, Sümer Atasoy cites 1917 as the year in which the commission was established. Such discrepancies suggest that the commission may have been disbanded and reestablished several times during the war years.
14. At this time the Topkapı Palace, home to the sultans until 1853, had for the most part fallen into grave disrepair. Some sections, such as the apartments of the Holy Mantle and the Baghdad pavilion, retained annual ceremonial functions. Certain parts of the harem continued to house former servants to the royal family. The grounds also included a small and short-lived ceramics

museum. However, the palace as a whole would not become a museum until after the establishment of the republic.

15. Sedad Hakkı Eldem, *Topkapı Sarayı* (Ankara: Kültür Bakanlığı, 1982), 100–101.

16. IBA DH-I.UM 20.22:14/10, 1338.S.12 = November 5, 1919; DH-I.UM 20/22:14/29, 1338.R.5 = May 23, 1920.

17. IBA DH.I-UM E/60:29, 1338.Za.8 /August 22, 1920.

18. IAMA, letters from Halil (Edhem) to Col. Normand, July 7, 1919; from Col. Normand to Halil, November 6, 1919, and December 14, 1919.

19. R. Normand et al., *Le Musée d'Adana* (Paris: Librarie Orientaliste Paul Geuthner, 1922), 1.

20. Ibid., 5.

21. Ibid., 8.

22. IAMA, letter of April 24, 1922.

23. IAMA, letter from Halil to Charpy, February 1, 1922; letter from Charpy to Halil, December 12, 1922.

24. IAMA, letter from ship commander Le Coq to the museum directorate, September 23, 1923, including an inventory of the items ceded by the French forces to the Turkish National Museums.

CONCLUSION

1. Hobsbawm, *Nations and Nationalisms since 1780*, 12.

2. Kayalı, *Arabs and Young Turks*, 9.

3. Paula Findlen, *Possessing Nature: Museums, Collecting, and Scientific Culture in Early Modern Italy* (Berkeley: University of California Press, 1994), 3.

4. Ibid., 34.

5. Michel Foucault, *The Order of Things: An Archaeology of the Human Sciences* (New York: Vintage Books, [1970] 1994), 37.

6. Findlen, *Possessing Nature*, 4.

7. Abdullah, *Le Musée d'Histoire naturelle de l'école impériale de médecine à Constantinople* (Constantinople: Imprimerie M. de Castro, 1872), 1. There were also some private zoological collections, such as that at the Saint Joseph Lycée. See Şennur Sentürk, *Nuh'un Gemisi Beyoğlunda/L'Arche de Noë à Beyoğlu* (İstanbul: Yapi Kredi Yayıncılık, 1998).

8. IAMA, #89, January 12, 1893; and #102, February 25, 1899.

9. Marchand, *Archaeology and Philhellenism in Germany*, 105–6.

10. The tradition of acquisition-based organization began with Goold's 1871 catalog, where only the plates reflected a formal stylistic ordering of objects. In his 1908 catalog, Mendel continued to use such a geographically based ordering system, where again the plates alone use a format of stylistic analysis. Mendel, *Musées Imperiaux Ottomans*, vii.

11. Duncan, *Civilizing Rituals*, 99.

12. Ingres's famous Bath, as well as Courbet's "pornographic" center of the universe, was originally in the collection of an Ottoman diplomat, but because of the prurient nature of his collection, he was not allowed to bring it back to the empire.

13. Mieke Bal, "The Discourse of the Museum," in Greenberg, Ferguson, and Nairne, *Thinking about Exhibitions,* 204–5.

14. Jean Baudrillard, *Simulacra and Simulations,* trans. Paul Foss, Paul Patton, and Phillip Beitchman (New York: Semiotext(e), 1983), 84–86.

15. Bhabha, "Of Mimicry and Man," 88. Emphasis in original.

16. Jean-Paul Sartre, *Critique of Dialectical Reason: I. Theory of Practical Ensembles,* trans. Alan Sheridan-Smith (London: New Left Books, 1976), 752. For a discussion on the relationship between colonialism and humanism, see also Robert Young, *White Mythologies: Writing History and the West* (London: Routledge, 1990), 119–26.

Bibliography

ABBREVIATIONS

APC   Abdülhamid Photograph Collection

IAMA   İstanbul Archaeology Museum Archives

IMM   İstanbul Military Museum library and photograph collection

MANUSCRIPT SOURCES

İstanbul Prime Minister's Archives/Basbakanlik Arşivi (İBA):

İrade-i Dahiliye 6662 (1262/1846)
Meclis-i Mahsus İradeler 3401 (1301/1884)
Y.MYV 76:36 (7.9.1310/1893); 249:69 (1321/1903); 258:32 (1322/1904);
    10:26 (1300/1882); 355:83 (1314/1896); 252:294 (1321/1903)
Y.A-HUS 379:53 (1315/1897); 281:90 (1311/1893); 327:19 (1311/1894)
BEO 280983, 281201, 281681, 287555, 285717 (1328/1910); 187801
    (1320/1905); 182613 (1322/1905); 188658 (1322/1905); 190412
    (1323/1905); 217649 (1324/1906); 220951 (1324/1906); 276305
    (1325/1909)
DH.ID 28–1:18 (1329/1911); 28–1:28 (1329/1911); 3361:216 (1333/1914);
    28–1:21 (1329/1911)
DH.MUI 88:46 (1328/1910); 2574:124 (1328/1910); 916:98–1 (1328/1910);
    DH.IUM E/60:29 (1338/1920)
DH.HMS 9:8 (1329/1911)
DH.MB.HPS.M 3347:44:27 (1339/1920)
DH-I.UM 20.22:14/10 (1338/1919); 20/22:14/29 (1338/1920)
MV 253:78 (1338/1919); 1:56 (1302/1885); 35:23 (1305/1887); 36:57
    (1306/1888); 23:34 (1304/1887); 239:22 (1333/1915); 212:115
    (1336/1918); 42:53 (1306/1889)
Cevdet Maarif 221 (1286/1869)

Maarif İradeler 365:199 (1317/1900); 705:689 (1322/1905)
Hususi İradeler 1321.RA/90 (1321/1904); 74:28.M.1314 (1896);
  60:54:20.M.1317 (1899); 1430 (1312/1895)
DH.HMS 9:4 (1321/1903)

PUBLISHED SOURCES

Note: Surnames were not part of Turkish practice until 1934. Therefore, all Ottoman sources are cited according to the given name of the author. For English-speaking readers, Arabic, Persian, and Turkish titles have been provided in English even when English does not appear in the original work.

Abdullah. *Le Musée d'Histoire naturelle de l'école impériale de médecine à Constantinople.* Constantinople: Imprimerie M. de Castro, 1872.
Abt, Jeffrey. "The Breasted-Rockefeller Egyptian Museum Project: Philanthropy, Cultural Imperialism, and National Resistance." *Art Journal* 19:4 (December 1996): 551–72.
Ahmet Midhat. "Askeri Müzesine Ziyaret" [Visit to the Military Museum]. *Sabah* (May 2, 1910): 1.
———. "Yeni Müze" [The New Museum]. *Tercuman-i Hakikat* 3898 (7 Zilhicce 1308/July 13, 1891), 2.
Akinsha, Konstantin, and Grigori Kozlov. *Beautiful Loot.* New York: Random House, 1995.
Ali Sami (Boyar). *Bahriye Müzesi Kataloğu* [Catalog of the Naval Museum]. İstanbul: Matbaa-ye Bahriye, 1917.
Allen, William. "Analysis of Abdülhamid's Gift Albums." *Journal of Turkish Studies* 12 (1988): 33–34.
Anderson, Benedict. *Imagined Communities.* London: Verso Press, 1991.
Arık, Remzi Oğuz. *L'Histoire et l'organization des musées turcs.* İstanbul: Milli Eğitim Basımevi, 1953.
———. *Türk Müzeciliğine Bir Bakış* [A Look at Turkish Museology]. İstanbul: Milli Egitim Basimevi, 1953.
Arıkan, Zeki. "Tanzimat'tan Cumhuriyet'e Tarihçilik" [Historiography from the Tanzimat to the Republic]. In *Tanzimat'tan Cumhuriyet'e Türkiye Ansiklopedisi,* 1583–94. İstanbul: İletişim Yayınları, 1985.
Asar-e Atika Nizamnamesi [The Antiquities Law]. İstanbul: Asır Matbaası, 1322/1874.
Asar-e Atika Nizamnamesi [The Antiquities Law]. Dar Saadet: Mahmud Bey Matbaası, 1327/1909.
"Asar-i Atika" [Antiquities]. *Servet-i Funun* (11 Subat 1308/February 23, 1892).
"Asar-i Atika" [Antiquities]. *Servet-i Funun* 106 (11 Mart 1308/March 23, 1892), 31.

"Asar-i Atika" [Antiquities]. *Servet-i Funun* 151 (20 Kanunsani 1309/February 1, 1894), 336.

"Asar-i Atika" [Antiquities]. *Servet-i Funun* 161 (31 Mart 1310/April 12, 1894), 70.

"Asar-i Atika" [Antiquities]. *Servet-i Funun* 168 (19 Mayis 1310/May 31, 1894), 191.

"Asar-i Atika" [Antiquities]. *Servet-i Funun* 202 (12 Kanunsani 1310/January 24, 1895), 320.

"Asar-i Atika" [Antiquities]. *Servet-i Funun* 222 (1 Haziran 1311/ June 23, 1895), 213.

"Asar-i Atika" [Antiquities]. *Servet-i Funun* 984 (1 Nisan 1326).

"Asar-i Atika" [Antiquities]. *Tercüman-i Hakikat* 3883 (25 Haziran 1891).

"Asre muferrit Abdülhamid haniyede terekkiyate fenniye: Müzeye Humayun—avrupa matbuati" [European Publications on the Imperial Museum]. *Servet-i Funun* 49 (Subat 1308/1891).

Atasoy, Sümer. "Türkiye'de Müzecilik" [Museology in Turkey]. *Cumhuriyet Dönemi Türkiye Ansiklopedisi* (1984): 1465.

Bahrani, Zainab. "Conjuring Mesopotamia." In Lynn Meskell, ed., *Archaeology under Fire: Nationalism, Politics and Heritage in the Eastern Mediterranean and Middle East*, 159–74. London: Routledge, 1998.

Bal, Mieke. "The Discourse of the Museum." In Reesa Greenberg, Bruce Ferguson, and Sandy Naire, eds., *Thinking about Exhibitions*, 201–20. New York: Routledge, 1996.

Bann, Stephen. "Shrines, Curiosities, and the Rhetoric of Display." In Lynne Cooke and Peter Wollen, eds., *Visual Display: Culture beyond Appearances*, 15–29. New York: Dia Center for the Arts, 1995.

Barillari, Dianna, and Ezio Godoli. *Istanbul 1900: Art Nouveau and Interiors*. New York: Rizzoli, 1996.

Başiret 1123 (14 Züyulkade 1290/January 3, 1874).

Baudrillard, Jean. *Simulacra and Simulations*. Trans. Paul Foss, Paul Patton, and Philip Beitchman. New York: Semiotext(e), 1983.

———. "The System of Collecting." In John Elsner and Roger Cardinal, eds., *The Cultures of Collecting*, 7–24. Cambridge, Mass.: Harvard University Press, 1994.

Ben-Arieh, Yehoshua. "The Geographical Exploration of the Holy Land." *Palestine Exploration Quarterly* (July–December 1972): 81–92.

Benjamin, Roger, ed. *Orientalism: Delacroix to Klee*. Sydney: Thames and Hudson, 1997.

Bennett, Tony. *The Birth of the Museum*. New York: Routledge, 1995.

———. "The Exhibitionary Complex." In Reesa Greenberg, Bruce Ferguson, and Sandy Nairne, *Thinking about Exhibitions*, 81–112. New York: Routledge, 1996.

———. "The Political Rationality of the Museum." *Continuum* 3:1 (1990): 35–55.

Berktay, Halil. *Cumhuriyet İdeolojisi ve Fuat Köprülü* [Republican Ideology and Fuat Köprülü]. İstanbul: Kaynak Yayınları, 1983.

———. "Tarih Çalışmaları" [Works on History]. *Cumhuriyet Dönemi Türkiye Ansiklopedisi* 9 (İstanbul: İletişim Yayınları, 1983): 2456–78.

Bhabha, Homi. "Double Visions." *Artforum* 30:5 (1992): 85–89.

———. *The Location of Culture.* New York: Routledge, 1994.

———. "The Other Question—The Stereotype and Colonial Discourse." *Screen* 24:6 (November–December 1983): 18–36.

Bıyık, Asım, et al. *Askeri Müze/Military Museum.* İstanbul: Askeri Müze ve Kültür Sitesi Komutanligi, 1993.

Bohrer, Frederick N. "The Times and Spaces of History: Representation, Assyria, and the British Museum." In Daniel J. Sherman and Irit Rogoff, eds., *Museum Culture,* 197–222. Minneapolis: University of Minnesota Press, 1994.

Brandt, Susan. "The Memory Makers: Museums and Exhibitions of the First World War." *History and Memory* 6:1 (Spring–Summer 1994): 95–149.

Brenk, Beat. "Spolia from Constantine to Charlemagne: Aesthetics versus Ideology." *Dumbarton Oaks Papers* 41 (1987): 103–9.

Cahen, Claude. *Pre-Ottoman Turkey.* London: Sidgwick & Jackson, 1968.

Carman, John. *Valuing Ancient Things: Archaeology and Law.* London: Leicester University Press, 1996.

Caton, Steven C. *Laurence of Arabia: A Film's Anthropology.* Berkeley: University of California Press, 1999.

Cezar, Mustafa. *Sanatta Batı'ya Açılış ve Osman Hamdi* I, II [Opening toward the West in Art and Osman Hamdi]. İstanbul: Erol Kerim Aksoy Kültür, Eğitim, Spor ve Sağlık Vakfı Yayını, 1995.

Çelik, Zeynep. *The Remaking of Istanbul.* Seattle: University of Washington Press, 1986.

———. *Urban Forms and Colonial Confrontations: Algiers under French Rule.* Berkeley: University of California Press, 1997.

Chaudonneret, Marie-Claude. "Historicism and 'Heritage' in the Louvre, 1820–40: From the Musée Charles X to the Galerie d'Apollon." *Art History* 14:4 (December 1991): 488–520.

Chicago Fair Illustrated/ Şikago Sergisi 2 (July 23, 1893).

Choisseul-Gouffier, Marie-Gabriel-Auguste-Florent, comte de. *Voyage pittoresque de la Grèce.* Paris, 1780–1826.

Çizgen, Engin. *Photography in the Ottoman Empire, 1839–1919.* İstanbul: Haşet Kitabevi, 1987.

Clarke, E. D. *Travels in Various Countries of Europe, Asia, and Africa* III. London: T. Cadell and W. Davies, 1817.

Clogg, Richard. "The Byzantine Legacy in the Modern Greek World: The Megali Idea." In *Anatolica: Studies in the Greek East in the 18th and 19th Centuries,* 253–81. Brookfield: Variorum, 1996.

Committee of the Palestine Exploration Fund. *Our Work in Palestine.* New York: Scribner, Welford, & Armstrong, 1873.

Cooke, Lynne, and Peter Wollen, eds. *Visual Display: Culture beyond Appearances*. New York: Dia Center for the Arts, 1995.

Çoruhlu, Tülin and Aysel Çötelioğlu. *Askeri Müze Resim Koleksiyonu* [The Painting Collection of the Military Museum]. İstanbul: Askeri Müze ve Kültürk Sitesi Komutanlığı, 1996.

Crimp, Douglas. *On the Museum's Ruins*. Cambridge, Mass.: MIT Press, 1993.

"Darsaadetde maçka silah deposu abniyeye hamidesi" [The Maçka Armory in Istanbul]. *Servet-i Funun* 188 (6 Tesrinevvel 1310/1894), cover.

Davison, Roderic. "Nationalism as an Ottoman Problem and the Ottoman Response." In William Haddad and William Ochsenwald, eds., *Nationalism in a Non-National State: The Dissolution of the Ottoman Empire*, 25–56. Columbus: Ohio State University Press, 1977.

de Certeau, Michel. *The Practice of Everyday Life*. Berkeley: University of California Press, 1984.

Demirsar, V. Bilgin. *Osman Hamdi Tablolarında Gerçekle İlişkiler* [Real Sources for Osman Hamdi's Paintings]. İstanbul: Kültür Bakanlığı Yayınları 1989.

Deringil, Selim. "The Invention of Tradition as Public Image in the Late Ottoman Empire, 1808 to 1908." *Comparative Studies in Society and History* 35:1 (January 1993): 3–29.

———. "Legitimacy Structures in the Ottoman State—The Reign of Abdülhamid II." *International Journal of Middle East Studies* 23:3 (August 1991): 345–59.

———. "The Ottoman Origins of Kemalist Nationalism: Namik Kemal to Mustafa Kemal." *European History Quarterly* 23:2 (April 1993): 165–92.

———. *The Well-Protected Domains: Ideology and the Legitimation of Power in the Ottoman Empire, 1876–1909*. London: I. B. Taurus, 1998.

Déthier, P. A. *Bogaziçi ve İstanbul* [Istanbul and the Bosporus]. Trans. Ümit Öztürk. İstanbul: Eren Yayıncılık, 1993.

Déthier, P. A., and A. D. Mordtmann. *Epigraphik von Byzantion und Constantinopolis von den aeltesten Zeiten bis zum Jahre Christi 1453*. Vienna, 1864.

de Vaux, Roland, O.P. "On the Right and Wrong Uses of Archaeology." In James A. Sanders, ed., *Near Eastern Archaeology in the Twentieth Century*, 64–80. New York: Doubleday, 1970.

Driault, Edouard. *La Question d'Orient*. Paris, 1898.

Drower, Margaret S. "The Early Years." In T. G. H. James, ed., *Excavating in Egypt: The Egypt Exploration Society, 1882–1982*, 9–36. London: British Museum Publications, 1982.

Dumont, Albert. "Le Musée Sainte-Irène á Constantinople." *Revue Archaeologique* 18 (1868): 237–63.

Duncan, Carol. *Civilizing Rituals: Inside Public Art Museums*. New York: Routledge, 1995.

Dyson, Stephen. "Complacency and Crisis in Late Twentieth Century Classical Archaeology." In Phyllis Culham and Lowell Edmunds, eds., *Classics: A*

Discipline and Profession in Crisis? 211–20. Lanham, Md.: University Press of America, 1989.

Ebersolt, Jean. *Mission Archéologique de Constantinople.* Paris: Éditions Ernest Leroux, 1921.

Elsner, John, and Roger Cardinal, eds. *The Cultures of Collecting.* Cambridge, Mass.: Harvard University Press, 1994.

Eralp, Nejat. "1908–1923 Döneminde Türkiye Askeri Müzesinin Batılı Anlamda Kuruluşu ve Kültür Hayatındaki Yeri" [The Formation of the Turkish Military Museum in a Western Sense and Its Place in Cultural Life in the Period 1908–1923]. *Onikinci Askeri Tarih Semineri* (Ankara, 1985): 285–324.

Eyice, Semavi. "Arkeoloji Müzesi ve Kuruluşu" [The Archaeology Museum and Its Foundation]. *Tanzimattan Cumhuriyete Türkiye Ansiklopedisi 6* (İstanbul: İletişim Yayınları, 1985): 1590.

———. "Arkeoloji ve Sanat Tarihi Hakkında" [On Archaeology and Art]. *Arkeoloji ve Sanat* 1:1 (April–May 1978): 5–7.

Fanon, Frantz. *Black Skin, White Masks.* New York: Grove Press, 1967.

Findlen, Paula. *Possessing Nature: Museums, Collecting, and Scientific Culture in Early Modern Italy.* Berkeley: University of California Press, 1994.

Findley, Carter Vaughn. *Ottoman Civil Officialdom: A Social History.* Princeton: Princeton University Press, 1989.

Flaubert, Gustave. *Oeuvres completes: Voyages* II. Paris: Société des Belles Lettres, 1948.

Foucault, Michel. *The Order of Things: An Archaeology of the Human Sciences.* New York: Vintage Books, [1970] 1994.

Gaehtgens, Thomas. "The Museum Island in Berlin." In Gwendolyn Wright, ed., *The Formation of National Collections of Art and Archaeology,* 53–78. Washington, D.C.: National Gallery of Art, 1996.

Gautier, Théophile. *Constantinople.* Ed. Jacques Huré. İstanbul: Éditions Isis, 1990.

Gavin, E. S. Carney, ed. "Imperial Self-Portrait: The Ottoman Empire as Revealed in the Sultan Abdülhamid II's Photographic Albums." *Journal of Turkish Studies* 12 (1988).

Georgel, Chantal. "The Museum as Metaphor." In Daniel J. Sherman and Irit Rogoff, eds., *Museum Culture,* 113–21. Minneapolis: University of Minnesota Press, 1994.

Georgeon, François. *Aux origines du nationalisme turc: Yusuf Akçura (1876–1935).* Paris: Éditions ADPF, 1980.

Goold, E. *Catalogue Explicatif, Historique, et Scientifique d'un certain nombre d'objets contenus dans le Musée Imperial de Constaninople, fondé en 1869 sous le Grand Vezirat de Son Altesse A'Ali Pacha.* Constantinople: Imprimerie A. Zellich, 1871.

Gourgouris, Stathis. *Dream Nation: Enlightenment, Colonization, and the Institution of Modern Greece.* Stanford: Stanford University Press, 1996.

Greenberg, Reesa, Bruce Ferguson, and Sandy Nairne, eds. *Thinking about Exhibitions.* New York: Routledge, 1996.

Greenblatt, Stephen. "Resonance and Wonder." In Ivan Karp and Stephen D. Lavine, eds., *Exhibiting Cultures: The Poetics and Politics of Museum Display*, 42–56. Washington, D.C.: Smithsonian Institution Press, 1990.

Greenhalgh, Michael. *The Survival of Roman Antiquities in the Middle Ages*. London: Duckworth, 1989.

Greenhalgh, Paul. *Ephemeral Vistas: The Expositions Universelles, Great Expositions, and World's Fairs, 1851–1939*. Manchester: Manchester University Press, 1988.

Gregory, Derek. "Scripting Egypt: Orientalism and the Cultures of Travel." In James Duncan, ed., *Writes of Passage*, 114–50. New York: Routledge, 1999.

Grewal, Inderpal. *Home and Harem: Nation, Gender, Empire, and the Cultures of Travel*. Durham: Duke University Press, 1996.

Grosvenor, Edwin A. *Constantinople II*. Boston: Little, Brown, 1900.

Gschwantler, Kurt. "The History of the Vienna Ephesus Museum and Its Finds." In Gilbert Wiplinger and Gudrun Wlach, eds., *Ephesus: 100 Years of Austrian Research*, 175–81. Vienna, Cologne, Weimer: Österreichisches Archäologisches Institut Verlag, 1996.

Haase, Claus-Peter, et al. *Oriental Splendor: Islamic Art from German Private Collections*. Hamburg: Museum für Kunst und Gewerbe, 1993.

Haddad, William W. "Nationalism in the Ottoman Empire." In William W. Haddad and William Ochsenwald, eds., *Nationalism in a Non-National State: The Dissolution of the Ottoman Empire*, 3–24. Columbus: Ohio State University Press, 1977.

Hakaik ül-vakai 961 (23 Cumadaevvel 1290/July 18, 1873).

Halil (Edhem). "Müzeler" [Museums]. *I Türk Tarih Kongresi* (1932): 532–66.

———. "Müzeye Hümayun" [The Imperial Museum]. *Tercüman-i Hakikat/Servet-i Funun* 1313 (numero special et unique): 104–7.

———. *Das Osmanische Antikenmuseum in Konstantinopel*. Liepzig, 1909.

Hanioğlu, Şükrü. *The Young Turks in Opposition*. Oxford: Oxford University Press, 1995.

Harb Tarihi Mecmuası 2:19 (1335/1916).

Hartt, Frederick. *Art: A History of Painting, Sculpture, Architecture*. New York: Prentice-Hall, 1989.

Herzfeld, Michael. *Ours Once More: Folklore, Ideology, and the Making of Modern Greece*. Cambridge: Cambridge University Press, 1982.

Hewett, John. *The Tower: Its History, Armories, and Antiquities*. London: Master General and Board of Ordinance at the Tower, 1845.

Heyd, Uriel. *Foundations in Turkish Nationalism*. Leiden: Luzac, 1950.

Hitchens, Christopher. *The Elgin Marbles: Should They Be Returned to Greece?* New York: Verso, 1997.

Hobsbawm, E. J. *Nations and Nationalism since 1780: Programme, Myth, Reality*. Cambridge: Cambridge University Press, 1990.

Hobsbawm, Eric, and Terence Ranger, eds. *The Invention of Tradition*. Cambridge: Cambridge University Press, 1983.

Hoffmann, Daniel. "The German Art Museum and the History of the Nation." In Daniel J. Sherman and Irit Rogoff, eds., *Museum Culture*, 3–21. Minneapolis: University of Minnesota Press, 1994.

Hooper-Greenhill, Eilean. *Museums and the Shaping of Knowledge*. New York: Routledge, 1992.

Hudson, Kenneth. *Museums of Influence*. London: Cambridge University Press, 1987.

İkdam (May 23, April 2, April 18, 1340/1923).

Impey, O. R., and A. G. MacGregor, eds. *The Origins of Museums: The Cabinet of Curiosities in Sixteenth- and Seventeenth-Century Europe*. Oxford: Oxford University Press, 1985.

İnalcık, Halil. *The Ottoman Empire, 1300–1600*. London: Weidenfeld and Nicolson, 1973.

James, Liz. " 'Pray Not to Fall into Temptation and Be on Your Guard': Pagan Statues in Christian Constantinople." *Gesta* 35:1 (1996): 12–20.

Jastrow, Morris. *The War and the Bagdad Railway: The Story of Asia Minor and Its Relation to the Present Conflict*. Philidelphia: J. B. Lippincott, 1917.

Jenkyns, Richard. *The Victorians and Ancient Greece*. Oxford: Basil Blackwell, 1980.

"Kadima-ye Yunanin Erkül ve Yahud Sibelt Kerest Nam Ma'bedleri Olduğu Kiyas Olunmuş Olan Harab İlahi Bakusun Kıbrısda Bulunan heykeli" [The Statue of the God Bes Found at the Sanctuary of Erkül or Sibelt in Cyprus]. *Medeniyet* 6 (5 Şehval 1291): 47–48.

Karaalioğlu, Seyit Kemal. *Namık Kemal: hayatı ve şiirleri* [The Life and Poetry of Namık Kemal]. İstanbul: Inkilap ve Aka Kitabevleri, 1984.

Karkar, Yaqub N. *Railway Development in the Ottoman Empire, 1856–1914*. New York: Vantage Press, 1972.

Karp, Ivan, and Stephen D. Lavine, eds. *Exhibiting Cultures: The Poetics and Politics of Museum Display*. Washington, D.C.: Smithsonian Institution Press, 1991.

Kayalı, Hasan. *Arabs and Young Turks: Ottomanism, Arabism, and Islamism in the Ottoman Empire, 1908–1918*. Berkeley: University of California Press, 1997.

Khanlari, Parviz. *Devan-e Hafez* [The Divan of Hafez]. Tehran: Intishar-i Tus, 1359/1980.

Khater, A. *Le régime juridique des fouilles et des antiquités en Égypte*. Cairo: Imprimerie de l'Institut Français d'Archaeologie Orientale, 1960.

Kocabaş, Rezan. "Müzecilik hareketi ve ilk müze okulunun açılışı" [The Museum Movement and the Opening of the First Museum School]. *Belgelerle Türk Tarihi Dergisi* 21 (June 1969): 74–78.

Konyalı, İbrahim Hakkı. *Türk Askeri Müzesi* [The Turkish Military Museum]. İstanbul: Ülkü Matbaası, 1964.

Kotstakis, Kostas. "The Past Is Ours: Images of Greek Macedonia." In Lynn Meskell, ed., *Archaeology under Fire: Nationalism, Politics, and Heritage in the Eastern Mediterranean and Middle East*, 44–67. New York: Pantheon, 1998.

Larsen, Mogens Trolle. *The Conquest of Assyria: Excavations in an Antique Land*. New York: Routledge, 1994.

L'Illustration 1277 (August 17, 1867).

"Louvredali Apollo Galenrisi" [Apollo Gallery in the Louvre]. *Servet-i Funun* 143 (23 Eylül 1309/October 5, 1893), 61.

Maarif 3:60 (7 Sefer 1310).

Macfie, A. L. *The Eastern Question: 1774–1923*. London: Longman, 1989.

"Maçka silahhanesi"; "Tüfenghaneye humayun esliha-ye nadire/Armes antiques: Musée de l'Artillerie de Constantinople." *Servet-i Funun* 55 (19 Mart 1308 /March 31, 1892), cover photo.

Mahmut Şevket Pasha. *Osman Teşkilat ve Kıyafet-i Askerisi* [Ottoman Military Organization and Costumes]. Ankara: Karakuvvetleri Komutanlığı, 1983. Reprint.

Maleuvre, Didier. *Museum Memories: History, Technology, Art*. Stanford: Stanford University Press, 1999.

Marchand, Suzanne. *Archaeology and Philhellenism in Germany, 1750–1970*. Princeton: Princeton University Press, 1996.

Mardin, Şerif. "19. Yüzyılda Düsünce Akımları ve Osmanlı Devleti" [The Ottoman State and Nineteenth-Century Schools of Thought]. *Tanzimat'tan Cumhuriyet'e Türkiye Ansiklopedisi* 2 (İstanbul: İletişim Yayınları, 1985): 342–51.

———. *Religion and Social Change in Modern Turkey: The Case of Bediüzzaman Said Nursi*. New York: Pantheon, 1989.

McClellan, Andrew. Nationalism and the Origins of the Museum in France." In Gwendolyn Wright, ed., *The Formation of National Collections of Art and Archaeology*, 29–40. Washington, D.C.: National Gallery of Art, 1996.

Mehmet Sefa. *Delil al-Astane: Asimat il-khilafet il-azimi wa dar us-saadet İstanbul al-Konstantaniyye* [Guidebook to Istanbul: Capital of the Caliphate and Gate of Felicity "Istanbul" Constantinople]. İstanbul: Matbaa al-adil, 1331/1913.

Mendel, Gustave. *Musées Imperiaux Ottomans: Catalogue des sculptures greques, romaines et byzantines du Musée de Brousse*. Athens: Imprimerie P. D. Sakllarios, 1908.

———. *Musées Imperiaux Ottomans: Catalogue des sculptures greques, romaines et byzantines*. 3 vols. Constantinople, 1912–14. Rpt. Rome: L'Erma di Bretschneider, 1966.

Meskell, Lynn, ed. *Archaeology under Fire: Nationalism, Politics and Heritage in the Eastern Mediterranean and Middle East*. London: Routledge, 1998.

Ministry of Culture of the Republic of Turkey. Brochure commemorating the 150th anniversary of Turkish museums.

Moorey, P. R. S. *A Century of Biblical Archaeology*. Cambridge: Lutterworth Press, 1991.

Mordtmann, A .D. *Belagerung und Eroberung Constantinopels durch die Türken im Jahre 1453*. Stuttgart: Cotta, 1858.

Morris, Ian. "Introduction: Archaeologies of Greece." In *Classical Greece: Ancient Histories and Modern Archaeologies*, 8–50. Cambridge: Cambridge University Press, 1994.

Mulvey, Laura. "On *Duel in the Sun:* Afterthoughts on 'Visual Pleasure and Narrative Cinema.' " *Framework* 15–17 (Summer 1981): 12–15.

———. "Visual Pleasure and Narrative Cinema." *Screen* 16:3 (Autumn 1975): 6–18.

Murray, John. *Handbook for Travelers in Constantinople, Brusa, and the Troad*. London: John Murray, 1893.

"Müze." *Servet-i Funun* 57 (2 Nisan 1308/April 14, 1892), 69, 74.

"Müze-i Askeri müdüriyetinden" [From the Administration of the Military Museum]. *Tanin* 5 (August 1909): 1.

Namık Kemal and M. Fuad Köprülü, eds. *Renan Müdafaanamesi* [Epistle of Defense against Renan]. Ankara: Milli Kültür Yayınları, [1910] 1962.

Namık Kemal and Semsettin Kutlu, eds. *Vatan Yahut Silistre* [Homeland or Silistria]. İstanbul: Remzi Kitapevi, 1982.

Necipoğlu, Gülrü. *Architecture, Ceremonial, and Power*. Cambridge, Mass.: MIT Press, 1991.

———. "The Life of an Imperial Monument: Hagia Sophia after Byzantium." In Robert Mark and Ahmet Ş. Çakmak, eds., *Hagia Sophia from the Age of Justinian to the Present*, 195–225. Cambridge: Cambridge University Press, 1992.

Nochlin, Linda. "The Imaginary Orient." In *The Politics of Vision: Essays on Nineteenth-Century Art and Society*, 33–59. New York: Harper and Row, 1989.

Normand, R., et al. *Le Musée d'Adana*. Paris: Librarie Orientaliste Paul Geuthner, 1922.

Ogan, Aziz. *Türk Müzeciliğin 100. Yıldönümü* [A Historical Survey of the Museum of Antiquities at İstanbul]. İstanbul: Türkiye Turing ve Otomobil Kurumu, 1947.

Ölçer, Nazan. *Türk ve İslam Eserleri Müzesi: Kilimler* [Museum of Turkish and Islamic Arts: Kilims]. İstanbul: Eren Yayıncılık, 1988.

Orgun, Zarif, and Serap Aykoç. "La fondation du Musée Turque et le Musée des Arts Turcs et Islamiques." In *Collection Turcica II, Traveaux et Recherches en Turquie 1982*. Strasbourg, 1984.

O'Rourke, Lorenzo. *Renan's Letters from the Holy Land: The Correspondence of Ernest Renan with M. Berthelot while gathering material in Italy and the Orient for "The Life of Jesus."* New York: Doubleday, Page, 1904.

Ortaylı, İlber. "Batılaşma Sorunu" [The Problem of Westernization]. *Tanzimat'tan Cumhuriyet'e Türkiye Ansiklopedisi* 1 (İstanbul: İletişim Yayınları, 1985): 134–38.

———. *Gelenekten Geleceğe* [From Tradition to Tomorrow]. İstanbul: Hil Yayın, 1982.

————. *Imparatorlugun en Uzun Yüzyılı* [The Empire's Longest Century]. İstanbul: Hil Yayın, 1983.

————. "Tanzimat'ta Vilayetlerde Eski Eser Taraması" [The Search for Antiquities in the Provinces during the Tanzimat]. *Tanzimat'tan Cumhuriyet'e Türkiye Ansiklopedisi* 6 (İstanbul: İletişim Yayınları, 1985): 1599.

Osman Hamdi. "Introduction." In *Antiquités himyarites et palmyréniennes: Catalogue sommaire.* Constantinople: Mihran Imprimeur, 1895.

————. "Introduction." In *Catalogue des sculptures greques, romaines, byzantines et franques.* Constantinople: Mihran Imprimeur, 1893.

————. *Les costumes populaires de la Turquie en 1873.* Ouvrage Publie sous le patronage de la Commission Imperiale Ottomane par l'Exposition universelle de Vienne. Constantinople: Imprimerie du Levant Times & Shipping Gazette, 1873.

————. *Une necropole royale a Sidon.* Paris: Ernest le Roux, 1892.

Osman Hamdi and Ozgan Efendi. *Le tumulus de Nemroud-Dagh.* Constantinople: Imprimerie F. Loeffler, 1883.

Öz, Tahsin. "Ahmet Fethi Paşa ve Müzeler" [Ahmet Fethi Pasha and Museums]. *Türk Tarih, Arkeolgya ve Etnografya Dergisi* (1948): 1–6.

————. "Topkapı Sarayı Müzesi Onarımları" [Topkapı Palace Museum Repairs]. *Güzel Sanatlar* 6 (January 1949): 1–20.

Parla, Taha. *The Social and Political Thought of Ziya Gökalp, 1876–1924.* Leiden: E. J. Brill, 1985.

"Le Pavillion Ottomane." In *L'Exposition de Paris de 1900* II (Paris, 1901), 137–38.

Pierce, Susan. *Interpreting Objects and Collections.* New York: Routledge, 1994.

Postle, Martin. "Naked Authority: Reproducing Antique Statuary in the English Academy, from Lely to Haydon." In Anthony Hughes and Ercih Ranfft, eds., *Sculpture and Its Reproductions,* 79–99. London: Reaktion Books, 1997.

Preziosi, Donald. "In the Temple of Entelechy: The Museum as Evidentiary Artifact." In Gwendolyn Wright, ed., *The Formation of National Collections of Art and Archaeology,* 165–72. Washington, D.C.: National Gallery of Art, 1996.

Preziosi, Donald, ed. "Art as History: Introduction" and "The Art of Art History."In *The Art of Art History: A Critical Anthology,* 9–30, 507–25. Oxford: Oxford University Press, 1998.

Quatert, Donald. "Clothing Laws, State, and Society in the Ottoman Empire, 1720–1829." *International Journal of Middle Eastern Studies* 29:3 (August 1997): 403–25.

Rehnuma: Müze-i Hümayun. İstanbul: Mahmut Bey Matbaası, 1319/1902.

Reid, Donald M. "Nationalizing the Pharaonic Past: Egypt 1922–1952." In James Jankowski and Israel Bershoni, eds., *Rethinking Nationalism in the Arab Middle East,* 127–49. New York: Columbia University Press, 1997.

Reinach, Saloman. *Conseils aux voyageurs archeologiques à Grece et dans l'Orient hellenique.* Paris: E. Leroux, 1886.

Rowlands, Michael. "The Politics of Identity in Archaeology." In George Clement Bond and Angela Gilliam, eds., *Social Construction of the Past: Representation as Power,* 129–44. London: Routledge, 1994.

Ruzname-ye Ceride-ye Havadis 2359 (13 Zülkida, 1290/January 2, 1874).

Saadet 432 (March 14, 1326/March 27, 1910).

Sabah 7376 (March 22, 1326/April 6, 1910).

Said, Edward. *Orientalism.* New York: Pantheon Books, 1978.

St. Clair, W. *That Greece Might Still Be Free: The Philhellenes in the Greek War of Independence.* Oxford: Oxford University Press, 1972.

Sakaoğlu, Necdet. "Eğitim Tartışmaları" [Discussions on Education]. *Tanzimat'tan Cumhuriyet'e Türkiye Ansiklopedisi* 6 (İstanbul: İletişim Yayınları, 1985): 478–84.

Şapolyo, Enver Behnan. *Müzeler Tarihi* [History of Museums]. İstanbul: Remzi Kitabevi, 1936.

Şark 388 (15 Safer 1292/March 23, 1875).

Sartre, Jean-Paul. *Critique of Dialectical Reason: I. Theory of Practical Ensembles.* Trans. Alan Sheridan-Smith. London: New Left Books, 1976.

Scarre, Chris. "The Western World View in Archaeological Atlases." In Peter Gathercole and David Lowenthal, eds., *The Politics of the Past,* 11–17. London: Unwin Hyman, 1990.

Schwartz, Hillel. *The Culture of the Copy: Striking Likenesses, Unreasonable Facsimiles.* New York: Zone Books, 1996.

Sedad Hakki Eldem. *Topkapı Sarayı* [Topkapı Palace]. Ankara: Kültür Bakanlığı, 1982.

Şentürk, Şennur. *Nu'hun Gemisi Beyoğlunda/L'Arche de Noë à Beyoğlu.* İstanbul: Yapi Kredi Yayıncılık, 1998.

Sermed Muhtar. *Müze-i Askeriye-i Osmani, Rehber* [Ottoman Military Museum Guide]. İstanbul: Necm-e İstikbal Matbaası, 1336/1920.

Servet-i Funun 2:49 (6 Subat 1307), 266.

Servet-i Funun 49 (5 Subat 1308), 15.

Servet-i Funun 54 (12 Mart 1308), 20.

Shaw, Stanford J. *History of the Ottoman Empire and Modern Turkey* I. London: Cambridge University Press, 1976.

Shaw, Stanford J., and Ezel K. Shaw. *History of the Ottoman Empire and Modern Turkey* II. London: Cambridge University Press, 1977.

Sherman, Daniel J. *Worthy Monuments: Art Museums and the Politics of Culture in Nineteenth-Century France.* Cambridge, Mass.: Harvard University Press, 1989.

Sherman, Daniel J., and Irit Rogoff, eds. *Museum Culture.* Minneapolis: University of Minnesota Press, 1994.

Shohat, Ella. "Gender and Culture of Empire." In Matthew Bernstein and Gaylyn Studlar, eds., *Visions of the East: The Orient in Film,* 19–66. New Brunswick, N.J.: Rutgers University Press, 1997.

Silberman, Niel Asher. *Digging for God and Country: Exploration, Archaeology, and the Secret Struggle for the Holy Land, 1799–1917.* New York: Alfred A. Knopf, 1982.

———. "Promised Lands and Chosen Peoples: The Politics and Poetics of Archaeological Narrative." In Philip Kohl and Clare Fawcett, eds., *Nationalism, Politics, and the Practice of Archaeology,* 249–62. Cambridge: Cambridge University Press, 1996.

Smith, Anthony D. *The Ethnic Origin of Nations.* London: Basil Blackwell, 1986.

Stoneman, Richard. *Land of Lost Gods: The Search for Classical Greece.* London: Hutchinson, 1987.

Tanör, Bülent. "Anayasal Gelişmelere Toplu Bir Bakış" [An Overview of Constitutional Developments]. *Tanzimat'tan Cumhuriyet'e Türkiye Ansiklopedisi* 1 (İstanbul: İletişim Yayınları, 1985): 10–16.

Temelkuran, Tevfik. "1884 Eski Eserler Nizamnamesi ve Türkiyeden Dış Ülkelere Götürülen Eski Eserler" [The 1884 Antiquities Law and Antiquities Taken to Other Countries]. *Belgelerle Türk Tarihi Dergisi* 65 (Subat 1973).

———. "Ülkemizden Götürülen Tarih ve San'at Hazineleri, İlk Eski Eserler Nizamnamesi" [Treasures of Art and History Taken from Our Country and the First Antiquities Legislation]. *Belgelerle Türk Tarihi Dergisi* 5:27 (December 1969): 70–76.

Terakki 200 (3 Cumadaevvel 1286/August 11, 1869).

Terakki 363 (2 Rebiülevvel 1287/June 1, 1870).

Tercüman-i Hakikat 3858 (18 Sevval 1308/May 27, 1891).

Tercüman-i Hakikat 3872 (6 Zilkade 1308/June 12, 1891).

Thornton, Lynne. *The Orientalists: Painter-Travelers.* France: Poche Couleur, 1994.

Trigger, Bruce. "Alternative Archaeologies: Nationalist, Colonialist, Imperialist." *Man* 19:3 (September 1984): 355–70.

———. *A History of Archaeological Thought.* Cambridge: Cambridge University Press, 1989.

"Tüfenghane-ye Hümayunda Eski Zirhlar" [Old Shields in the Imperial Armory]. *Servet-i Funun* 64 (21 Mayıs 1308/1893), 180.

Turner, Frank. *The Greek Heritage in Victorian Britain.* New Haven: Yale University Press, 1981.

Vaczec, Louis, and Gail Buckland. *Travelers in Ancient Lands: A Portrait of the Middle East, 1839–1919.* Boston: New York Graphic Society, 1981.

Vakit 1735 (11 Ramazan 1297/August 17, 1880).

Vernoit, Stephen. "The Rise of Islamic Archaeology." *Muquarnas* 14 (1997): 1–10.

Vernoit, Stephen, ed. *Discovering Islamic Art: Scholars, Collectors and Collections, 1850–1950.* London: I. B. Taurus, 2000.

Vidal-Naquet, Pierre. *Politics Ancient and Modern.* Trans. Janet Lloyd. London: Polity Press, 1990.

"Vienna Müzesi." *Servet-i Funun* 103 (18 Subat 1308/March 3, 1893), 394, 397.

Waley, M. I. "The Albums in the British Library." *Journal of Turkish Studies* 12 (1988): 31–32.

Wallach, Alan. *Exhibiting Contradiction: Essays on the Art Museum in the United States.* Amherst: University of Massachusetts Press, 1998.

Warner, Marina. "Waxworks and Wonderlands." In Lynne Cooke and Peter Wollen, eds., *Visual Display: Culture beyond Appearances,* 178–201. Seattle: Dia Center for the Arts, 1995.

Westrate, J. Lee. *European Military Museums: A Survey of Their Philosophy, Facilities, Programs, and Management.* Washington, D.C.: Smithsonian Institution Press, 1961.

Wood, John Turtle. *Discoveries at Ephesus:Including the Site and Remains of the Great Temple of Diana.* London: Longmans, Green, 1877.

Young, Robert. *White Mythologies: Writing History and the West.* London: Routledge, 1990.

Index

Note: Turkish proper names did not include surnames until 1934. Thus all Turkish names are listed by first name, with a surname in parentheses for those who lived long enough to take one. For example, Halil (Eldem) is listed under H.

Text: 10/13 Aldus
Display: Aldus
Compositor: Impressions Book and Journal Services, Inc.
Printer and binder: Edwards Brothers, Inc.